New SAT Reading Prep

2016 개정 SAT 핵심 대비 문제, 해설, 공략집

New SAT Reading Prep

2016 개정 SAT 핵심 대비 문제, 해설, 공략집

copyright © Kay Kwan Woong, 2015-2016

CONTENTS

Preface	6
New SAT Tips	9
Test 1	43
Test 2	61
Test 3	79
Test 4	97
Test 5	117
Test 6	135
Strategy	155
Test 1 Keys & Explanations	159
Test 2 Keys & Explanations	181
Test 3 Keys & Explanations	205
Test 4 Keys & Explanations	227
Test 5 Keys & Explanations	251
Test 6 Keys & Explanations	275

PREFACE

New SAT Reading Prep을 펴내면서

2016년 3월에 SAT가 개편되면서, ETS가 새로 출판된 official guide에 재미있는 설명을 실었다. Reading의 종류를 3가지로 나누겠다는 것인데, 다음과 같다.

1. Synthesis

2. Information and Ideas

3. Rhetoric

Synthesis란 우리말로 직역하면 합성이라는 의미인데, 지문 이외에도 도표나 그래프 등이 같이 출제된다고 해서 붙여진 이름이다. Information and Ideas는 객관적인 정보, 즉 사실에 해당하는 information을 이용하여 주관적 정보, 즉 주장에 해당하는 ideas를 도출하는 과정을 보여 준다고 만들어진 명칭이며, rhetoric은 의견을 전달하는 과정에서 표현이 어렵다(수사적이다)고 해서 생긴 이름이다. 즉 이 세 종류의 차이는 얼마나 주관적인 정보 즉 주장이 포함되어 있는가, 그리고 직접적이고 이해하기 쉬운 표현(direct and straightforward)을 사용하느냐 아니면 간접적이고 추상적인 표현(indirect and abstract; that is rhetoric)을 사용하느냐의 차이이다.

대략 12년간 SAT 수업을 한 경험으로 볼 때 대부분의 학생들이 가장 힘들어하는 내용은 사실이 아니고 주장이며, 직접적인 표현이 아니고 간접적인 표현이다. 그래서 지난 12년의 SAT 수업을 바탕으로 학생들이 어려워하고 성적이 잘 오르지 않는 부분에 집중해서 이 SAT Prep Book을 만들었다.

즉, 이 책은 단순한 SAT 준비서가 아니다. 이 책은 Official Guide 보다 더 Rhetoric에 집중하고 있는, 학생들의 약점을 파고드는, 매우 다루기 힘든 준비서이다. 결과적으로 각 회별 점수를 보면 실제 SAT 보다 어렵다는 것을 쉽게 알 수 있을 것이다. 그 이유는 상대적으로 쉬운 Synthesis나 Information and Ideas가 거의 없기 때문이다.

가르치는 입장에서도 문제의 초점과 실제 문제와의 관련성을 금세 이해하도록 해설을 수록했다. 출제 의도와 논리적 초점, 실제 문제와의 상관도를 분명히 알려주므로 언어에 근거한 논리적 분석력을 키우는 데 큰 도움이 될 것이다.

실제 시험의 형식을 따라 구성하기는 했으나, Rhetoric에 집중한 알짜배기 문제들로 이루어져 있으므로 굳이 문제 수를 실제와 완전히 동일하게 맞추지는 않았다. 또한 new SAT Official Guide에는 지문에 대한 설명이 있으나 이 책에서는 넣지 않았다. 따로 요약된 내용 없이 지문만 보고 글의 흐름이나 주제를 파악하는 훈련을 강화하기 위해서이니 이해를 바란다.

어려운 책이지만, 이 책이 보여 주는 논리적 분석력을 이해하고 받아들여 부디 원하는 점수를 받기 바란다.

저자 계관웅

NEW SAT TIPS

2016년 새로워진 NEW SAT, 어떻게 준비할까

1 2016년 NEW SAT의 형식적 변화
2 OLD SAT에서 NEW SAT로: 변화의 분석
3 분석을 토대로 한 NEW SAT 대비
4 Reading 능력을 배양하는 실전 훈련의 예

1

2016년 NEW SAT의 형식적 변화

다음은 2016년 바뀐 새 SAT의 주요 변화를 요약한 것이다.

NEW SAT from 2016

(A) MAIN CHANGES

1. Optional Essay: The analysis of a given passage(Evidence, Reasoning, and Style to build an argument)
2. No Guessing Penalty
3. Easier Vocabulary with More Relevance to Schoolwork
4. Focused Math Questions: Linear Questions, Complex Equations or Functions, Ratios, Percentage and Proportional Reasoning
5. Source Documents included on Every Test: broad range such science and social studies: selecting the quotation to support the answer
6. Founding Documents included on Every Test: such as the Declaration of Independence or the Bill of Rights

(B) ETS' Claim

1. More relevance to high school curricula
2. Social justice to quell the possibility of the rich to do much better on SAT

(C) The Real Reasons for the Changes

1. Competition with ACT
2. Preventing the interference from test prep schools

(D) Consequence

1. Probably the lessoning of philosophical and literary approaches
2. Resembling more of GRE
3. No way to predict the level of difficulty because it can be controlled in many different ways

(A) 주요 변화
1. 에세이는 선택 사항이며, 철저한 분석(증거 제시, 합리적 분석, 적절한 작문 스타일을 이용한 주장)에 근거한 글을 요구함
2. 추측에 대한 감점이 폐지됨. 지금까지는 답을 표기하지 않으면 0점, 틀리면 -0.25점
3. 고등학교 교육과 좀 더 연계성 있는 쉬운 단어로 출제
4. 수학 문제 출제 영역이 좁아짐
5. 매 시험 출제하는 지문의 원문 출제 및 사회연구나 과학 등의 다양해진 주제 출제
6. 매 시험에 반드시 역사적으로 중요한 지문 출제

(B) ETS가 주장하는 변화의 이유
1. 고등학교 교육과 연계성을 높임
2. 부유한 미국인이 더 높은 성적을 받을 가능성을 최소화

(C) 실제 이유
1. ACT와의 경쟁에서 밀리고 있음
2. 학원이나 개인지도 등을 통해 고득점을 받을 가능성을 최대한 낮출 목적

(D) 결과
1. 지금까지의 SAT의 특징인 철학적이고 문학적인 지문은 상당히 줄어듦
2. GRE와 유사해질 가능성이 매우 커짐
3. 단어가 쉬워지고 철학적·문학적 성향이 줄어든다고 하더라도 분석적인 면을 얼마나 강조하느냐에 따라 난이도를 조절할 수 있으므로 전반적으로 쉬워진다는 일부의 예측은 전혀 근거 없음

(E) 대책
논리적·분석적이라는 SAT의 특성으로 볼 때, 이 발표만으로 SAT 대비가 크게 달라질 것은 없음

2

OLD SAT에서 NEW SAT로: 변화의 분석

    2015년 나는 네이버 헌팅글리쉬 카페를 통해 SAT에 아무리 형식적인 변화가 심하게 일어나도 영어라는 언어의 특성상, 그리고 미국 대학들이 원하는 학생상(像)이 변하지 않는 한 본질적인 변화가 있기는 힘들 것이라고 예측했는데, 그 생각은 들어맞았다. 단, 형식적 변화를 제대로 이해해야만 내용상의 변화도 이해하기 쉽고, 내용상의 변화를 이해해야만 왜 본질적인 변화는 없었는지를 깨달을 수 있으므로, 우선 전반적인 형식적 변화를 먼저 설명하겠다.

(1) 모든 영역에서 일어난 형식적인 변화
- 감점제 폐지
- 철학적 내용 대폭 감소
- 고등학교에서 다루거나 다룰 것만 같은 내용 등장

(2) Critical Reading의 형식적 변화
- Sentence Completion의 폐지
- 특정 문제의 답을 알려주는 내용을 찾으라는 문제 등장

(예) 18번 : 다음 중 17번 문제의 답을 알려주는 내용을 담고 있는 지문의 위치는?

(3) Grammar의 형식적 변화
- Error Detection, Sentence Improvement, Paragraph Improvement의 통합
- 개개의 문제에 따로 문제 설명이 있으면 내용과 관련된 문제(Old Sentence Improvement, Old Paragraph Improvement), 없으면 순수한 Grammar 문제(Old Error Detection, Old Sentence Improvement)

(4) Essay의 형식적 변화
- 수험자의 주관적 판단이나 생각을 묻는 문제에서 주어진 글에 대한 비평문을 작성하는 문제로 변화
- 채점 기준을 세 가지로 명확히 밝힘

    여기까지가 겉으로 드러난 형식적 변화이다. 이 형식적 변화 때문에 마치 2016년 SAT가 쉬 워진 것처럼 보일 수 있지만 절대로 그렇지 않다! 이제부터 그 이유를 꼼꼼히 따져서 설명하겠다. 2015년까지의 문제 유형을 이용해 2016년 문제에 무리 없이 대비하는 방법도 분석한다.

(1) CRITICAL READING의 변화 분석

Sentence Completion이 폐지되었으므로 Critical Reading이 쉬워진다는 말을 하는 사람들이 있다. 과연 그럴까?

우선 Sentence Completion이 폐지되었으므로 단어가 전반적으로 쉬워진 것은 사실이다. 그러나 이 '전반적'이라는 말을 조심해야 한다. 왜냐하면 Sentence Completion에 출제되는 단어들은 대부분 Reading 지문에도 사용되기 때문이다. 다음은 『The Official SAT Study Guide(2nd Ed)』 390쪽의 Sentence Completion에 사용된 단어 중 일부이다. 이중 어떤 단어가 일반적인 대학 교양서적에 흔히 사용되는지 살펴보자. 당연히 너무 쉬운 단어는 사용하지 않는다.

- folly
- intricate
- ostentatious
- convoluted
- capricious
- loquacious
- decorous
- mitigated
- visceral
- ossified
- politicized
- venerable

위의 단어는 대부분 대학 교양과정에 흔히 사용되는 단어들이다. 즉, 2016년 SAT Critical Reading의 지문에도 사용될 것이라는 의미이다. visceral 정도가 너무 어려운 단어에 속한다. 실제 지문에는 쉬운 동의어(deep, instinctive, unReasoning, earthy)가 훨씬 자주 사용 되겠지만, visceral도 가끔 나오기는 한다.

다음에는 너무 쉬워서 위에 들지 않은 단어들을 살펴보자.

- foresight
- despair
- artistry
- bygone
- candid
- bombastic
- dispassionate
- deliberate
- instinctive
- versatility
- infighting

jingoism

legislation

    물론 Sentence Completion에는 Reading보다 어려운 단어들이 한 문장에 집중적으로 몰려 있으므로, 단어 실력이 현저하게 떨어지는 학생은 Sentence Completion이 더 어렵게 느껴질 수 있다. Reading에는 어려운 단어가 있더라도 다른 많은 쉬운 단어와 함께 쓰였으므로 문맥상의 추측이 Sentence Completion보다는 상대적으로 훨씬 쉬울 수 있다. 그러나 이런 차이는 문맥을 제대로 읽는 학생에게나 가능한 일이다. 만일 문맥을 읽기가 어렵다면, 어려운 단어가 Reading에 훨씬 덜 쓰이기는 하지만, Sentence Completion보다 Reading이 훨씬 어려울 것이다. 그러므로 Sentence Completion이 없어져서 상대적으로 Critical Reading이 쉬워지려면 문맥을 읽는 데 전혀 문제가 없어야 한다.

    그런데 여기 한 가지 문제가 남아 있다. Sentence Completion을 없애고 대신 Reading 지문의 단어가 더 어려워진다면, 2015년 문제까지는 문맥을 잘 읽던 학생이 2016년부터 상대적으로 힘들 수도 있다는 것이 그것이다. 현재 2016년 SAT 문제를 보면 앞으로 Reading 지문에 이전보다 어려운 단어가 더 많이 쓰일 것이라는 증거는 없지만, 정확한 경향을 파악하기에는 자료가 적으므로 아직 더 두고 볼 일이다.

    결론적으로, Sentence Completion이 폐지되어 Critical Reading이 훨씬 더 쉬워질 거라는 것은 착각에 불과하다. 실제로 현재 Critical Reading이 500~700점 정도인 학생을 열 명 정도 모아 테스트한 결과, 학생들 모두 2016년 SAT Critical Reading에서 적게 또는 심하게 점수가 떨어지는 현상을 보였다. 왜 도리어 점수가 떨어졌는지 구체적으로 살펴보자.

    우선 Sentence Completion의 폐지와 더불어 눈에 띄는 변화는 다음과 같다.

- 어떤 문제의 답이 되는 근거가 되는 내용이 지문의 어느 위치에 있는지 묻는 문제 출현
- 철학적 내용과 문학적 표현이 중심이 되는 지문의 감소(2015년까지는 출제 지문이 100퍼센트 철학적이고 문학적이었음)
- 저자의 주관적 견해가 없는 지문 출현(2015년까지는 출제 지문에 100퍼센트 저자의 주관적인 견해가 분명히 나타나 있었음)
- 고등학교 교재에 나타날 만한 내용의 지문 출현(2015년까지는 거의 전혀 없었음)

위의 변화를 잘못 해석하면 다음과 같다.

- 어차피 문제를 제대로 풀었다면 이런 문제는 당연히 맞을 테니, 맞으라고 낸 문제나 마찬가지 아닌가?
- 철학적이고 문학적인 내용 때문에 SAT가 어려웠던 것이므로, 이젠 당연히 쉬워진 것 아닌가?
- 주관적 견해가 없다는 것은 객관적 사실만 나타난다는 의미이므로 TOEFL 같은 시험이 돼버린 것 아닌가? 그렇다면 비평의 특징을 잃었으므로 당연히 저자의 의견이나 저자가 비판하는 의견을 분석하는 문제를 낼 수 없으니 쉬워진 것 아닌가?
- 고등학교 교재에 나올 만한 내용이라면 무조건 쉽지 않겠는가? 이미 익숙한 내용일 테니까.

    그런데 이런 잘못된 이해를 바로 SAT 출제사인 ETS가 노리는 것으로 보인다. ACT와 비교해서 너무 어렵다는, 고등학교 교육과 너무 동떨어진 것 같다는 비난을 피하려고 표면적으로나마 쉬워진 것처럼 보이게 하려는

듯하다. 어차피 대부분의 한국인들은 문제를 하나씩 제대로 분석하지 않을 것이고, 미국인들은 SAT 문제를 분석하지 않을 것이기 때문이다. 아주 드문 특이한 경우를 제외하고 미국인은 우리처럼 SAT 문제를 분석하고 전략을 세우고 대비하지 않는다.

그러나 문제를 하나씩 자세히 분석해 보면 결코 2015년까지의 문제보다 쉽다고 할 수 없다. 왜냐하면 다음과 같은 숨은 특징도 출현했기 때문이다.

(1) 우선 문제를 푸는 데 필요한 지문의 정확한 위치(line number)를 알려주는 문제가 줄었다

이는 매우 중요한 변화다. 주제와 직결된 문제라면 위치를 알려주지 않아도 크게 달라질 것이 없지만, detail(구체적인 내용)을 묻는 문제라면 대략 어떤 내용이 어느 위치에 있는지는 알아야 한다. 정확한 위치는 모르더라도 몇 번째 문단에 있는지, 또는 어떤 내용의 전이나 혹은 후에 나오는지 정도는 파악하고 있어야 정확한 위치를 찾기 쉬워진다. 만일 그렇지 않으면 이런 문제가 나올 때마다 지문 전체를 읽어야 하는 터무니없는 일이 벌어진다.

(2) 소설이 더 어려워졌다

2015년까지의 소설보다 더 어려워졌는데, 그 이유는 훨씬 더 문학적 특성이 강해졌기 때문이다. 이 문학적 특성(metaphor, sarcasm 등)이 어려운 단어들과 교묘히 결합하여 뻔한 내용이라도 이해하기가 어려워졌다. 원어민에게 훨씬 더 유리하다.

(3) 훨씬 더 분석력(Analytical Skills)을 요구한다

철학적이고 문학적인 접근은 전반적으로 많이 줄어든 대신 지문을 이해하고 문제를 풀기 위해서는 더 깊이 있는 분석이 필요해졌다. 그러므로 2015년까지의 문제와 비교하여 더 쉬울지 어려울지는 수험자의 분석 능력에 달렸다고 볼 수 있다. 2016년부터는 전반적으로 남학생이 유리하다고 볼 수도 있다. 일반적으로 남학생은 철학적이고 문학적인 내용과 표현에 여학생보다 약하고, 분석에는 상대적으로 강하기 때문이다. 물론 일반적으로 그렇다는 얘기다.

그렇다면 대책은 무엇인가?

(1) 문제를 풀기 위해 필요한 지문의 정확한 위치(line number)를 알려주는 문제가 줄어든 것에 대한 대책

계속 강조하지만 line number를 알려주지 않아도 문제가 주제와 직결된 경우에는 그리 어렵지 않다. 물론 주제를 제대로 파악하고 있다는 전제로 하는 말이다. 그런데 line number를 알려주지 않은 문제가 주제와 직접적인 관계가 없는 소위 detail 문제이면 얘기는 달라진다. 이런 경우, 지문에서 이 detail이 어디에 있는지 모르면 지문을 다시 모두 읽어야 하는 어이없는 일이 발생하게 되고, 시간이 모자라서 문제를 제대로 풀지 못하리라는 것은 뻔한 일이다.

대책은 지문의 전체적인 흐름을 신속하게 읽어내는 능력을 배양하는 것이다. 소위 글의 Organization(조직, 구성)에 대한 감각을 빠르게 터득하는 훈련을 하는 것이다. 대부분의 학습자가 많이 읽으면 이런 능력이 배양된다고 생각할 것이다. 그러나 많이 읽기만 해서는 절대 해결되지 않는다. 많이 읽기만 해서 해결된다면 왜 우리 주위에 어려운 글의 흐름을 빠른 속도로 판단하는 사람의 수가 이리도 적겠는가? 한국인이야 글을 많이 읽지 않아서 그렇다 치고, 왜 영미인들도 마찬가지일까? 지난 40년간 미국 고등학생의 SAT Critical Reading 평균 성적이 540점(67.5퍼센트)밖에 되지 않는다. 반면에 국내 최고의 특목고는 평균 성적이 700점 정도다. 이 점은 한국인이 글을 많이 읽지 않아서 이런 일이 발생하는 것은 아닐지도 모른다는 좋은 증거 중 하나이다. 그렇다면 이유는 무엇일까?

　한국인이든 미국인이든 글을 제대로 읽지 않는 경우가 많기 때문이다. 많은 사람들이 생각 없이 읽기만 하기 때문이다. 많이 읽는 것은 어떤 경우에도 좋은 습관이지만, 많이 읽으면서 분석적으로 생각하는 것만큼 효과적이지는 않다. 제대로 읽으려면 다음이 습관화되어야 한다.

- 예측(Prediction)

영미인이 쓴 제대로 된 글은 그 첫 문장에 반드시 앞으로 전개될 내용에 대한 힌트가 있으며, 그 힌트를 볼 수 있어야 한다. 간단한 예를 들어 보자.

It has been claimed that history repeats itself. (역사는 반복된다고 주장되어 왔다.)

주장에 이렇게 시제(has been)가 사용되면 거의 항상 지금까지(has been)와 지금(now)을 비교해서 지금까지는 ……했으나 지금은 그렇지 않다고 주장하려는 것이다. 이렇게 미리 알려주고 있는 힌트를 글의 도입부에서 읽어내는 학습자는 당연히 전체 흐름을 빨리 파악할 수 있다.

- 관계(Connection)

모든 문단과 문단, 문장과 문장, 단어와 단어, 개념과 개념 사이에는 관계가 있으며, 주어진 글에서 어떤 두 개념 사이의 관계가 분명하지 않으면 글의 초점을 이해하지 못한 것이라는 사실을 명심해야 한다. 다음이 가장 많이 사용되는 관계다.

　　일반화(Generalization)
　　구체화(Specification)
　　예시(Exemplification)
　　원인과 결과(Cause and Effect)
　　비교와 대조(Comparison and Contrast)
　　반박(Refutation)
　　예외(Exception)

이런 관계를 읽어내는 것은 글의 흐름뿐만 아니라 어떤 특정한 정보가 어느 위치에 있는지를 빠르게 유추하게 도와준다. 즉, detail 문제를 풀어야 할 때 그 detail은 기억나지 않더라도, 글의 흐름상(문단과 문단의 관계, 개념과 개념의 관계), 어느 위치(몇 번째 문단, 혹은 어떤 내용의 전이나 후)에 있는지를 효과적으로 알게 된다. 이런 능력이 훈련되지 않으면 모든 detail을 다 기억하든지, 아니면 매번 지문을 다시 읽어야 한다.

- 비교와 대조(Comparison and Contrast)

위의 관계의 예로 이미 나와 있는 것을 다시 강조하려는 것이 아니다. 위에서 비교와 대조는 문단과 문단, 개념과 개념의 관계를 이해하여, 글의 흐름을 빨리 판단하고 나아가서는 특정 내용의 지문 내의 위치를 효과적으로 예측하기 위한 것이지만, 글의 내용과 관계없이 9학년 이상의 독자를 위해 쓰인 모든 영미인의 글에서는 빠짐없이 비교와 대조가 나타난다. 이 점에서 비교와 대조는 일반화(Generalization) 등의 개념보다 훨씬 더 중요하다.

즉, 글을 읽으면서 어떤 개념이나 현상 등이 비교, 대조되고 있는지 보이지 않는다면 무조건 글을 잘못 이해한 것이니 빨리 처음으로 돌아가서 예측(Prediction)을 다시 해보고, 첫 두 문단의 관계(Connection)를 다시 이해하려고 노력해야 한다.

- 잘못된 추론(Wrong Inference)

가장 어려운 부분이다. Wrong Inference에는 두 가지가 있다.

문학적 표현(주로 비유(metaphor))이 지문에 어렵게 사용되어 내용상 혼동이 생기는 바람에 잘못된 이해(추론)를 하는 것이 첫 번째 경우이고, 지문의 내용을 바탕으로 문제에 교묘한 잘못된 추론이 이용되는 것이 두 번째다.

지문에 어려운 문학적 표현이 사용되지는 않았다면, 아무리 문제에서 논리적인 '말장난'으로 잘못된 추론을 일으키려고 해도 훈련으로 극복할 수 있다. 그러나 문학적 소양이 약해서 지문에 나타난 문학적 표현 때문에 혼동하는 경우는 문제를 많이 다루는 연습으로는 쉽게 해결되지 않는다. 읽는 양이 많아져야 하고, 특히 순수문학에 익숙해져야 한다. 순수문학에 사용되는 비유/은유적인 표현들을 인용하지는 못하더라도 별로 어렵지 않게 이해하는 수준은 되어야 한다.

단, 한 가지 긍정적인 면은 어떤 글이든지 이런 애매한 문학적인 표현이 사용된 내용은 주제와 직결돼 있을 것이므로 그 표현이 정확히 무슨 의미인지 모르더라도 주제를 알고 있으면 대충의 내용은 짐작할 수 있다는 것이다.

SAT에 출제되는 detail 문제의 대략 70퍼센트 이상이 주제와 직결돼 있다는 것은 매우 흥미로운 일이다.

(2) 더 어려워진 소설에 대한 대책

더 어려워진 소설에 대한 대책은 무엇일까? 물론 평소 많이 읽고 분석하고 토론하고 비평문을 쓰고 교정을 받았으면 된다. 그러나 그러지 못했으면 어떻게 해야 할까? 지금부터 소설을 읽을 때마다 다음과 같이 해야 한다.

- 각각의 소설에 쓰인 문학적 기술(literary skills: metaphor, simile, contradiction, irony, paradox 등)이 주제를 전달하는 데 왜 효과적인지, 또는 왜 그렇지 못한지를 이해하는 훈련을 해야 한다.
- 1인칭, 2인칭, 3인칭으로 쓰인 등장인물들의 소설 속 기능과 주제가 어떻게 연관되어 있는지를 이해하고 왜 각각 다른 인칭으로 사용되었는지를 이해하고 토론하는 훈련을 해야 한다.
- 어떤 사건이나 표현, 또는 등장인물의 말(대화나 생각)이 글의 흐름을 바꾸거나 변화를 암시하는 경우가 대부분이다. 그것을 찾아내고 왜 그것이 그런 기능을 했는지를 이해하는 훈련을 해야 한다.
- 모든 소설에는 갈등(Conflict)이 있게 마련이다. 갈등이 없는 소설은 소설이 아니다. 그 갈등을 찾아내고 그 갈등이 주제와 어떤 관계에 있으며, 주제를 전달하는 데 어떤 기능을 하는지 이해하고 설명할 수 있어야 한다.
- 모든 소설에는 비교와 대조(Comparison and Contrast)가 있다. 이 비교와 대조를 찾아내 주제와 어떤 관계에 있으며, 주제를 전달하는 데 어떤 기능을 하는지 이해하고 설명할 수 있어야 한다.

(3) 깊이 있는 분석력(Analytical Skills)을 요구하는 것에 대한 대책

우선 분석력이라는 말을 이해해야 한다. 영어에서 분석력이란 크게 두 가지를 의미한다. 비교와 대조(Comparison and Contrast), 원인과 결과(Cause and Effect)가 그것이다. 분석적인 글을 자세한 글과 혼동해서는 절대로 안 된다. 글이 자세하다고 해서 분석적인 것은 아니기 때문이다. 분석적이지만 단순하고 짧을 수도 있다. 9학년 이상이 읽어야 하는 글들은 대부분 분석적이다. 즉, 비교와 대조나 원인과 결과가 존재한다. 이 요인들을 찾아내 저자가 이 요인들을 어떻게 자신의 주장과 연결하거나, 주장에 이용했는지를 밝히는 연습을 충분히 해야 한다.

(2) ESSAY의 변화 분석

2016년 새로 바뀐 SAT에서 Essay의 변화를 다시 살펴보자.

(1) 2015년까지는 특정 주제에 대한 응시자의 생각을 표현하는 방식이었다.
(2) 2016년부터는 주어진 글에 대한 비평문을 작성하는 방식으로 바뀐다. 그리고 채점 기준까지 명확하게 발표했다. 주어진 글을 읽고 질문에 답하는 비평문을 쓰되 다음을 반드시 이용하라는 것이다.

- evidence, such as facts or examples, to support claims.
- Reasoning to develop ideas and to connect claims and evidence.
- stylistic or persuasive elements, such as word choice or appeals to emotion, to add power to the ideas expressed.

번역해 보면, 다음과 같다.

- 저자가 주장을 위해서 사용한 증거
- 저자가 개념/생각(idea)을 발전시키고 증거와 주장을 연결하는 데 사용한 논리성
- 저자가 표현한 개념/생각(idea)을 강화하기 위해 사용한 표현 방식 또는 설득의 요소(단어의 선택이나 감정적 호소 같은)

다시 말해, 분석적인 비평문을 쓰라는 얘기다. 매우 복잡해 보이는 요구이지만, 전년도까지의 에세이를 작성할 때도 이렇게 써야 했다.

2015년과 2016년의 차이는 본인 생각을 쓰느냐, 남의 생각을 읽고 분석/비판하는 글을 쓰느냐일 뿐, 본인의 생각을 쓰는 2015년 방식의 에세이에서도 (1) 증거(예)를 분명히 제시하고, (2) 증거와 주장을 제대로 잘 연결해 개념을 발전시켜야 하며, (3) 효과적인 표현을 사용하여 설득력을 강화해야 하는 것은 마찬가지였다. 그러므로 과거 방식의 에세이도 제대로 준비했다면 2016년 에세이의 준비가 된다. 유치하고 얕은 수법으로 에세이를 준비하는 학생이 아니라면 새로운 방식의 비평적 에세이를 두려워할 이유는 전혀 없다. 에세이의 종류와 관계없이 다음과 같이 쓰면 된다.

명확한 증거 제시 ➔ 증거와 주장의 논리적 연결 ➔ 연결할 때 효과적인 표현 방식 또는 설득 요소 사용

그럼 이런 훈련은 어떻게 하는 걸까? 답은 평소에 어떻게 읽느냐에 있다. 평소에 글을 읽을 때, 첫째로 무엇이 증거인지를 분명히 찾고, 둘째로 증거와 주장이 어떻게 연결돼 있는지를 확인하고, 셋째로 이 연결에 사용된 표현을 찾아내고 기록하는 훈련을 하면 된다. 매우 간단해 보이지만 실제로는 그리 쉽지 않다. 이유는 다음과 같다.

- 무엇이 증거이고 무엇이 주장인지 혼동되는 글이 많다.
- 증거와 주장을 연결하는 표현이 어려우면 어떻게 연결하고 있는지 이해가 안 되는 경우가 많다.
- 이 연결에 사용된 표현을 찾는 것은 그렇게 어렵지 않으나 그 표현이 왜 효과적인지, 또는 왜 설득력이 있는지를 이해하는 것은 자주 혼동될 수 있다. 특히 이런 표현이 문학적 요소 즉 은유(metaphor)를 사용할 때 더욱 그렇다.

위의 세 가지 문제를 극복하려면 다음과 같이 분석적으로 읽어야 한다.

- 증거와 주장에 사용되는 표현이 다르다는 것을 기억하자. 가장 쉬운 예로는 seem, may, appear, likely 같은 것이 있다. 이런 표현들이 사용되면 당연히 증거가 아니고 주장이다. 그럼 증거에 사용하는 표현은 어떤 것이 있을까? 또 가장 쉬운 예로는 역사적 사실이나 전문가 등의 주장을 인용하는 것이다. 모든 인용(quote)은 증거로 사용된 것이다.
- 증거와 주장에 사용되는 표현을 분류하고 정리하고 비교하고 적용하는 훈련을 게을리하지 말아야 한다. 이런 훈련은 글을 많이 읽은 학습자에게는 그리 어려운 일은 아니다.
- 증거와 주장이 분리되면, 증거와 주장을 연결하는 표현을 분석한다.

증거와 주장을 연결하는 표현을 찾는다는 것은 예가 없이는 이해하기 어려우므로, 네 가지 아주 쉬운 예를 들어 비교해 보자.(참고로 이렇게 쉬운 예는 실제 SAT에는 사용되지 않는다는 점을 밝혀 둔다.)

실전 연습 증거와 주장의 연결 분석

(A) Based on Dr. Lee's theory, one can easily tell why the monkey doesn't try to escape.

(B) Based on Dr. Lee's theory, it is impossible to postulate that the monkey doesn't try to escape because of fear.

(C) Based on Dr. Lee's theory, it is reasonable to postulate that the monkey doesn't try to escape because it is probably very risky to do so. The zoo is full of people who look anxious to watch many exotic animals.

(D) Based on Dr. Lee's theory, it is very safe to argue that the monkey doesn't try to escape obviously due to lack of opportunity. When in fear, it can't see when the door is left unlocked by mistake.

위 네 문장에서 가장 증거와 주장이 잘 연결된 경우는 어느 것일까? 간단한 분석을 보자.

(A) 원숭이가 도망가지 않는 이유가 무엇인지 설명하지 않고 있으므로 주장이 없는 셈이다.

(B) 공포 때문에 원숭이가 도망가지 않는다고 했다면 주장한 것이지만 그렇다고 볼 수는 없다고 했으므로 역시 주장은 없다.

(C) 지금까지의 내용 중에서는 가장 낫다. 그러나 원숭이가 도망가지 않는 이유가 위험하기 때문이라고 했는데, 왜 위험한지를 설명해야 할 위치에 있는 문장의 내용이 만족스럽지 못하다. 이국적인 동물을 구경하러 온 사람들로 동물원이 꽉 차 있다는 내용만으로는 뭐가 위험하다는 것인지가 분명하지 않다. 즉, 또 다른 설명이 뒤따라야 한다. 만일 이대로 설명이 끝난다면, 불명확한 설명 또는 불충분한 설명이라는 비난을 받게 된다.

(D) 그렇다면 이 연결은 어떠한가? 연결 자체는 큰 문제가 없어 보인다. 도망가지 않는 이유는 기회가 없기 때문이

며, 기회가 없는 이유는 공포에 사로잡히면 문이 언제 실수로 잠기지 않는지를 인지하지 못하기 때문이라고 했으므로 얼핏 제대로 연결된 것처럼 보인다. 그러나 이 내용만으로는 증거(Dr. Lee's theory)와 주장(in fear, can't see)의 명확한 관계를 알 수 없다. 이 박사가 펼치는 이론의 어느 부분이 이 주장을 설명하고 있는지를 밝혀야 한다. 그 이론이 self-explanatory(부가적인 설명이 없이도 이해되는) 경우가 아니라면, 이론의 내용이 이러저러하니 이렇게 저렇게 주장할 수 있다고 설명해야 한다.

그럼 다음의 두 가지 경우 중 어떤 경우가 제대로 된 설명인지 알아보자.

(D-1) Based on Dr. Lee's theory, it is very safe to argue that the monkey doesn't try to escape obviously due to lack of opportunity. When in fear, it can't see when the door is left unlocked by mistake. <u>She claims that many animals cannot think rationally in certain unexpected situations.</u>

(D-2) Based on Dr. Lee's theory, it is very safe to argue that the monkey doesn't try to escape obviously due to lack of opportunity. When in fear, it can't see when the door is left unlocked by mistake. <u>She argues that fear can work as an obstacle to the way most animals react to imminent danger.</u>

위의 두 연결 중, 두 번째 경우에 fear라는 표현이 사용되었으나 제대로 된 설명은 (D-1)이 다. 두 번째 경우에는 fear라는 단어만 사용되었을 뿐, 문이 실수로 잠기지 않는다는 내용과 관련된 내용이 없다. imminent danger는 문이 실수로 잠기지 않는다는 내용과 관계가 없는 정도가 아니고 정반대되는 내용이다. 문이 잠기지 않으면 도망가기에 좋은 기회일 수 있어도 위험할 수는 없기 때문이다. imminent(즉각적인)은 쓸데없는 생각을 하게 만들어서 시간 낭비를 유도하는, 글의 전체 흐름과 아무 상관 없는(totally irrelevant) 표현이다. 그러므로 다음과 같이 정리할 수 있다.

can't see (o) → obstacle (볼 수 없다는 것은 일종의 장애로 볼 수 있다.)
left unlocked (x) → danger (그러나 문이 잠기지 않은 것은 위험이 아니다.)

이에 비해 (D-1)은 다음과 같이 정리할 수 있다.

can't see (o) → can not think rationally
(제대로 볼 수 없는 것은 합리적으로 생각하지 못하기 때문일 수 있으므로)
left unlocked (o) → in certain unexpected situations
(문이 잠기지 않은 것은 흔히 발생하지는 않을 것이므로)

그럼, 마지막으로 설득력 있는 표현이란 어떤 것일까? 이 연결에 사용된 표현을 찾는 것은 그렇게 어렵지 않으나, 그 표현이 왜 효과적인지 또는 왜 설득력이 있는지를 이해하는 것은 자주 혼동될 수 있다. 특히 이런 표현이 문학적 요소, 즉 은유(metaphor)를 사용할 때 더욱 그렇다는 것을 다시 한 번 강조한다.
위의 예 (D-1)을 두 가지로 발전시켜 보자.

(F-1) Based on Dr. Lee's theory, it is very safe to argue that the monkey doesn't try to escape obviously due to lack of opportunity. When in fear, it can't see when the door is left unlocked by mistake. She claims that many animals can not think rationally in certain unexpected situations. In fact, some animals can easily confuse themselves by the conviction that a happy accident is never a possibility, especially when they are emotionally unstable.

(F-2) Based on Dr. Lee's theory, it is very safe to argue that the monkey doesn't try to escape obviously due to lack of opportunity. When in fear, it can't see when the door is left unlocked by mistake. She claims that many animals can not think rationally in certain unexpected situations. In fact, some animals can even get confused because of a sudden dreadful emotional attack, which can lead them unable to take full advantage of an opportunity.

위 두 글의 앞부분은 동일하다. 맨 뒤 두 줄을 서로 비교해서 어느 경우가 더 설득력 있게 설명하고 있는지, 그리고 어떤 스타일을 사용했는지 따져 보자. 이런 분석에 가장 필수적인 요소는 중요한 개념(key words)을 분리해 내는 것이다. key words는 다음과 같다.

(F-1) In fact, easily, confuse, conviction, a happy accident, never a possibility
(F-2) In fact, even, confused, unable

그리고 다른 단어/표현을 사용했지만 결국은 같은 의미인 단어/표현(paraphrased words and/or expressions)을 찾아본다.

(F-1)
unlocked = a happy accident
fear = emotionally unstable
(F-2)
fear = a sudden emotional attack
doesn't try to escape = unable to take full advantage
unlocked = an opportunity

(F-1)과 (F-2)의 공통된 내용을 살펴보면, 마지막 문장에서 모든 독자는 궁금한 점이 반드시 있어야 한다. 즉, 어떤 예상하지 상황(certain unexpected situations = in fear)에서는 이성적으로 생각하지(think rationally) 못한다고 했으므로 왜 그런지 궁금해야 하고 다음 내용에 설명되어 있어야 한다. 그런 관점으로 (F-1)과 (F-2)를 분석하면 어느 것이 더 설득력이 있는지는 분명해진다. paraphrased words and expressions는 결국은 같은 내용이므로 key words가 더 중요하다는 것은 설명할 필요도 없겠다.

key words 가운데에서도 가장 중요한 단어는 conviction이다. think rationally하지 못하는 이유가 a happy accident(=unlocked)는 절대로 일어나지 않을 것(never a possibility)이라고 생각하기 때문이므로 (F-1)은 think rationally하지 못하는 이유는 설명한 셈이다. 그런데 (F-2)는 공포에 사로잡히면(fear = a sudden emotional attack) 기회(an opportunity = unlocked)를 잡지(take full advantage) 못한다고

(unable)만 했으므로, 실제로 think rationally에 대한 설명은 없고, doesn't try to escape를 말만 바꾸어서 반복했을 뿐이다.

결론적으로 (F-1)은 conviction이 그 이유라고 제대로 설명했고, (F-2)는 전혀 그렇지 못했다.

그렇다면 이번에는 표현 방식(style)을 살펴보자. (F-1)은 어떤 표현 방식을 사용한 걸까? 소위 Direct Approach를 했다. think rationally하지 못하는 이유를, 문학적 기술(metaphor, symbolism, irony, paradox, simile, sarcasm 등) 따위를 사용하지 않고 직접적으로 설명했다. (F-2)와는 비교도 안 되는 좋은 설명이긴 하나 아직 부족하다. 설명하는 데 간접적인 방법을 사용하지 않은 이유는 여러 가지가 있을 수 있으나, 이 경우는 원인을 설명하기가 복잡했기 때문이다. 왜일까?

그렇다. 공포스러운 상황에서 운 좋은 일은 생기지 않는다는 conviction이 왜 생기는지도 설명해야 하기 때문에 간접적인 설명을 할 여유가 없었던 것이다. 결론적으로, 왜 conviction이 생기는지도 설명해야 하는 것이 맞다. 이런 계속적인 설명을 logical development라고 일컬으며, 에세이 채점의 가장 중요한 기준이다. 그러므로 이런 logical development가 없는 글은 좋은 글로 볼 수 없다.

어떤 SAT 응시자든지 본인의 글에서 주장에 대한 충분한 이유(위의 글을 이용해서 예를 들면, "think rationally 하지 못하는 이유는 무엇인가?" 또는 "conviction을 갖는 이유는 무엇인가?" 등)가 제대로 설명되어 있는지 그렇지 않은지를 스스로 깨닫는 능력이 배양되면, 에세이 출제 형식 따위는 문제가 되지 않는다.

평소에 글을 읽을 때도 이런 logical flow(위에서 말한 logical development)를 제대로 읽어 낼 수 있으면 글을 읽는 훈련은 곧 글을 쓰는 훈련이 되고, 논리적으로(logically) 분석적으로 (analytically) 생각하는 밑거름(foundation)이 된다.

심지어는 SAT의 문법 문제를 다루는 과정에서도 이 생각하는 훈련은 그대로 적용될 수 있으며, 그런 훈련이 고득점을 확보하는 데 가장 효과적이다. 이론(논리적 분석력의 배양)과 실제(SAT 고득점)는 절대 다르지 않다.

(3) GRAMMAR 영역의 변화 분석

이번에는 Grammar 영역의 변화와 대책을 살펴본다.
앞서 말했듯이 Grammar의 형식적 변화는 다음과 같다.

> Error Detection, Sentence Improvement, Paragraph Improvement가 하나로 통합되었으며, 개개의 문제에 따로 문제 설명이 있으면 내용과 관련된 문제이고(Old Sentence Improvement, Old Paragraph Improvement), 따로 설명이 없으면 단순한 Grammar 문제(Old Error Detection, Old Sentence Improvement)다.

즉, 모든 문제는 긴 지문의 일부가 되었고, 한 문장짜리 Grammar 문제는 사라졌다. 이것은 무엇을 의미할까? 단순한 문법 문제든 그렇지 않든 문맥이 있는 지문을 이용하겠다는 의도이다. SAT 문제를 어느 정도 연습한 학생들은 잘 알고 있겠지만 이전의 Paragraph Improvement 문제는 상대적으로 Error Detection이나 Sentence Improvement 문제보다 쉬웠다. 실제로 Writing 영역에서 650~700점 정도의 성적이 나오는 학생은 Paragraph Improvement에서는 거의 틀리지 않는다.

이런 불균형의 문제도 해결할 겸, Grammar(즉 Writing)와 Reading을 좀 더 연관지어 출제하려는 의도인 것이다. 즉, 단순한 문법 문제가 여전히 출제되지만, 2015년까지의 문제보다 훨씬 문맥, 즉 내용과 연관되어 문제의 난이도가 높아졌다는 의미이다.

Essay Writing에서도, Grammar에서도 내용을 이해하는 분석력이 이전보다 훨씬 중요해진 것이다. Sentence Completion을 없애고, 벌점제를 없애고, 지문의 내용에서 철학적이고 문학적인 요소를 대폭 줄여서 겉으로는 훨씬 쉬워진 것처럼 보이게 하고, 실제로는 Essay와 Grammar에서 Reading에 근거한 분석력을 강화함으로써 전반적으로 전혀 쉬워지지 않게 한 것이다. 도리어 분석력이 상대적으로 약한 학생에게는 더 어려워졌을 수도 있다. 난이도를 정리해 보면 다음과 같다.

(1) 단어/철학적 내용/문학적 표현을 극도로 싫어하는 학생에게는 NEW SAT가 유리할 수 있다.
(2) 그러나 그런 학생이라도 분석력이 너무 약하면 NEW SAT가 도리어 불리할 수 있다.
(3) 즉, (1)과 (2)의 강하고 약한 정도에 따라 유리해지기도 하고 불리해지기도 하게 될 것이 뻔하다.

Grammar에 출제된, 문맥을 이용한 문제를 하나 살펴보면 위의 상황은 분명해진다.

지문의 내용은 비교적 단순했다. 웅장한 도시를 디자인하겠다는 어느 건축가의 생각을 묘사한 글이었다. 지문에 언급된 세 개의 예 다음에 내용상 어울리는 네 번째 예를 고르라는 문제가 나왔다. 그런데 지문의 전체 내용은 웅장함이 초점인데, 그 세 개의 예 중 하나는 분명하게 세세함이 초점으로 보였다. 그리고 선택지에는 웅장함을 담고 있는 선택지도 있고 세세함을 묘사한 선택지도 있었다. 겉으로 볼 때는 말도 안 되는 문제이다. 도대체 어떻게 된 걸까?

비밀은 Perspective(관점)이다. 지문에 사용된 세세함을 묘사한 예는 세세함이 초점이 아니고, 도시의 웅장함 때문에 도시의 어떤 부분이 작게 보인다는 데 있었다. 그러므로 답은 웅장함이 초점인 선택지이다. 이런 Perspective의 문제는 2015년까지의 Critical Reading에서 가장 중요한 출제 경향 중의 하나였지만 Grammar에서는 중요하게 다룬 적이 별로 없었다.

결론적으로, NEW SAT는 Grammar에서도 분석적 Reading이 강화된 셈이다.

이제 NEW SAT는 다음 두 가지가 Old SAT보다 유리할 것인지 불리할 것인지를 결정한다고 보면 된다.

(1) 논리적 분석력
(2) 단어, 철학적 내용, 문학적 표현(metaphor, irony, figurative speech, sarcasm, contradiction 등)에 대한 이해력

위의 둘 중 어느 것이 더 강한지 또는 더 약한지가 모든 것을 결정한다.

(1) 이 (2)보다 더 강한 학생 → New SAT가 더 유리
(2) 이 (1)보다 더 강한 학생 → Old SAT가 더 유리

종합해 보면, 2016년에 바뀌는 SAT는 모든 영역에서 Reading에 근거한 분석력을 이용하도록 수정되었다고 보면 되겠다. Essay에서도, Grammar에서도 Reading을 이용한 분석력이 가장 중요한 요소가 되었다는 의미이다. Reading에서 분석력이 이전보다 중요해졌음은 말할 나위도 없다.

그러나 계속 강조하지만, 1993년에 영어 강의를 시작한 이후로 줄곧 강조해 오고 있지만, 이전까지의 SAT를 제대로 준비했다면, 논리적 분석력은 새로운 접근법이 아니다.

지금까지의 분석을 마무리하면, 다음과 같이 정리할 수 있겠다.

- 모든 영역에서 Reading이 중요해졌다.
- 제대로 읽고 이해하지 못하면 Essay도 Grammar도 제대로 할 수 없다는 것을 분명히 했다.
- 그리고 제대로 읽는다는 것은 논리적 분석력이 있어야 한다는 것을 강조한다.
- 과거에도 논리적 분석력이 가장 중요한 요인이었지만, Reading 지문의 성향 때문에 논리적 분석력이 뛰어난 학생도 제대로 실력을 발휘하지 못하는 경우가 많았다. 즉, 지문이 너무 특이한 관점을 가진 경우(철학적·문학적) 그랬다.
- 그러나 2016년 NEW SAT에서는 논리적 분석력이 뛰어나기만 하다면, 이전에 비해 상대적으로 특이한 성향의 지문(철학적·문학적)의 수가 줄었으므로 훨씬 유리하다. Reading, Grammar, Essay, 모두에서 그렇다.
- 물론 철학적인 내용과 문학적 표현을 좋아하고 익숙하지만 논리적 분석력이 떨어지는 학습자는 불리할 수 있다. 그러나 철학적인 내용과 문학적인 표현은 어려워하지만 논리적인 분석력은 뛰어난 학생은 얼마든지 있으나, 철학적인 내용과 문학적인 표현에 문제가 별로 없으면서 논리적인 분석력이 떨어지는 학생은 거의 없다.
- 2016년 새로 바뀐 SAT는 논리적 분석력은 뛰어나지만 지문의 내용에 심하게 영향을 받는 학생들을 구제하는 것이나 마찬가지이다.
- 결론적으로 2016년 NEW SAT에서 상대적으로 불리한 학생은 다음 경우들이다.

(1) 철학적 내용이나 문학적 표현에 크게 힘들어하지 않는 것은 아니지만, 그런 이유 때문이 아니고 영어 사용 능력 자체에 문제가 있어서 성적이 낮은 데다가 논리적 분석력까지 떨어지는 경우

(2) 철학적 내용이나 문학적 표현에 크게 영향을 받지 않으면서, 즉 그런 내용 때문에 성적에 큰 영향을 받지는 않으면서 논리적 분석력만 심하게 떨어지는 특이한 경우

(3) 글의 내용과 상관없이 대략적으로 글의 흐름을 잘 파악하는 편이지만, 논리적 분석력이 떨어지는 경우

3

분석을 토대로 한 NEW SAT 대비

Old든 New든 SAT는 단순한 영어 시험이 아니다. 제대로 준비하기 위해서는 자신을 잘 이해하고, 평소에 제대로 읽고 생각하는 훈련을 거듭해야 한다. New SAT에서는 또 Reading과 Essay Writing이 어떻게 긴밀하게 결합되어 있는지를 잘 이해해야 한다.

(1) Critical Reading에서 Reading으로

이전 SAT에는 Critical Reading이라는 영역이 있었고 이 영역은 Reading과 Sentence Completion으로 구성돼 있었다. 새로운 SAT에서는 Sentence Completion이 사라지고 Reading이 세분화되었다. Information and Ideas, Rhetoric, Synthesis가 그것이다. Sentence Completion이 사라졌기 때문에 일견 통합된 느낌이 들지만 사실은 더 세분화된 셈이다. 다른 시각에서 분류해 보면 확실히 알 수 있다.

1. Information(FACT: 사실, 객관적 정보) and Ideas(OPINION: 의견, 주관적 정보)
2. Rhetoric(OPINION: 의견, 주관적 정보)
3. Synthesis(FACT: 사실, 객관적 정보)

위의 분류를 자세히 살펴보면, 여러 형태의 방법으로 사실과 의견을 제대로 분석하는지를 평가하려는 것을 알 수 있다.

1. 사실과 의견을 섞어 놓고 분석력 평가 → Information and Ideas
2. 의견만을 분석적으로 평가 → Rhetoric
3. 사실만을 비교 분석 → Synthesis

이러는 과정에서 Science, Humanity, Social Science를 적당히 혼합하는 재치도 보인다.

1. 주로 과학적 분석
→ 도표 등이 많이 필요하다
→ Synthesis

2. 주로 인문학적 논리성
→ 주관성이 매우 강하다(특히 철학, 미학, 문학)
→ Rhetoric

3. 주로 사회과학적 접근
→ 인문학적 주관성과 과학적 논리성(특히 심리학, 경제학, 사회학, 인류학)이 얽혀 있다
→ Information and Ideas

게다가 문맥을 이용한 단어의 표현의 의미 추론을 강화함으로써 언어적 상상력을 강조했다. 정리하면 다음과 같다.

1. 객관적 정보(사실)와 주관적 정보(의견)를 구별하는 논리적 분석을 통해 학생들의 정보 분석력을 적절히 평가
2. 자연과학과 인문사회과학적 지문을 적절히 배합해서 지문의 종류에 치우치는 분석력 방지
3. 어려운 단어나 표현(결국 일종의 모르는 정보)을 문맥을 통해서 유추하도록 함으로써 언어적 상상력의 극대화

(2) Reading 이 강조된 문법으로
이전 SAT에는 다음과 같은 3가지 문법 영역이 있었다.

1. Error Detection
2. Sentence Improvement
3. Paragraph Improvement

그런데 1과 2가 통합되어 더 쉬워지고 3이 더 어려워졌다. 즉, 쉬워진 면도 있고 어려워진 면도 있는 셈이다. 무엇이 쉬워지고 무엇이 어려워진 걸까?

1. 쉬워진 내용
문맥과 관계없는 단순한 문법적 내용. 즉, 문장 하나만 놓고 문법을 따지는 경우
2. 어려워진 내용
문맥에 따라 문장의 내용이 달라지는 경우. 이때 문장의 내용이 달라지면서 문법이 달라지는 경우

1은 다른 시험(국내 내신, 토익, 텝스, 수능, GMAT)에서도 흔히 볼 수 있으므로 설명할 필요는 없겠다. 문제는 2의 경우인데, 이해하는 방법은 SAT에 왜 문법영역이 있는지를 살펴보면 사실 간단하다. SAT의 문법 영역은 Writing의 일부이다. 즉, 글을 제대로 쓸 수 있는지를 평가하기 위해 실제로 쓰게도 하고(Essay Writing), 에세이를 쓰게하는 것만으로 혹시 제대로 확인하지 못한 부분이 있는지도 따로 확인(Grammar)하겠다는 태도로 보면 된다. 이때 따로 확인하는 문법에 두 가지 종류가 있다.

1. 기술적인 측면
문장 하나 하나를 혼동되지 않도록 제대로 구성할 수 있는지를 묻는 문법. 이 경우 문맥은 필요 없고, 각각의 문장이 의미가 통하는지 확인한다.

2. 내용적인 측면

개개의 문장이 다른 문장과는 어울리는지를 분석한다. 문법이라는 개념을 넓게 이해해 보면 이 부분도 문법에 속한다고 볼 수 있다. 왜냐하면 문법이란 언어를 사용할 때의 일종의 약속을 말하는데, 각각의 문장에는 문제가 없더라도 문장과 문장의 관계가 내용상 어울리지 않는다면 이해에 문제가 생기므로 약속을 어긴 것으로 볼 수 있기 때문이다.

위의 두 가지 경우 중 두 번째 것을 이전 SAT에서는 Paragraph Improvement라고 불렀는데, 이 부분이 더 어려워졌다. 다시 말해서 Grammar 영역에 Reading이 이전보다 훨씬 강조된 것이다. 이 Reading-based Grammar를 해결하려면 평소에 읽기 습관을 잘 들여야 한다. 무엇을 읽든지 간에 다음의 관계를 파악하고, 어떤 경우든 그 관계가 보이지 않으면 잘못 읽고 있는 것이므로 다시 읽는다. 읽으면서 생각하는 습관이 없다면 매우 불리하지만 읽으면서 개개의 정보를 비교 분석하는 학생에게는 굉장히 쉬운 시험이 된 셈이다.

1. 단어와 단어의 관계
2. 문장과 문장의 관계
3. 문단과 문단의 관계
4. 개념과 개념의 관계(이 관계는 문제와 해결책 / 일반적 경우와 예외 / 확신과 의심 등 지문의 내용에 따라 무한하다.)

결론적으로 제대로 가르치는 학원이라면 Grammar 시간뿐 아니라 모든 SAT 시간에 다음과 같이 해야 한다.

1. Sentence-based Grammar에 이용되는 20가지 정도 되는 출제 패턴을 마치 손바닥 보듯이 익숙해지도록 한다. 이렇게 하기 위해서는 틀린 문제나 어려워하는 문제뿐만 아니라, 성적이 만족스럽지 못한 경우에는 모든 문제의 출제 패턴을 확인하고 정리해야 한다. 이 출제 경향은 뒤에 자세히 다룬다.
2. Reading-based Grammar를 위해서는, 문장을 보면 습관적으로 관계를 생각하도록 훈련한다. 다음의 예를 보자.

(ex) There are so many problems with his hypothesis. Typical historians couldn't link archeological evidence with the recent theorization.

위의 두 문장이 아무 관계도 없다면 이 글을 쓴 사람은 아마 제정신이 아닐 거고, 더 읽어 보면 관계가 명확하게 드러날 수도 있으나, 위의 두 문장만으로도 얼마든지 관계에 대한 추론은 가능하다. 이런 추론 연습이 충분히 훈련되지 않으면 성공적인 대학생활은 없다.

(A possible inference)
There are so many problems with his hypothesis. One of the problems is that typical historians couldn't link archeological evidence with the recent theorization. In other words, typical historians couldn't link archeological evidence with the recent theorization, based on his hypothesis.

(3) Reading이 강조된 에세이로

이전 SAT의 에세이는 주제(prompt, question)가 주어지면 그 주제에 맞도록 수험자의 생각을 쓰면 그만이었다. 문제는 몇 개의 예를 외우고 주제를 본인이 글을 쓰기 쉽도록 약간 바꾸고, 또 길게 쓰면 본인의 글쓰기 실력보다 훨씬 좋은 점수를 받을 수 있다는 것이었다. 실제로 7점 정도 받는 학생이 방금 언급된 방식을 이용하면 10-12점을 받는 경우가 속출했고, 상황이 이러니 위의 방법만 익히면 된다고 이 방법을 훈련시키는 준비서들 줄을 지어 출판되는 지경에 이르렀다. 놀라운 것은 이 중 다수가 미국인이 지은 책이라는 것이다.

그런데 2016년 3월부터 시행되는 SAT의 에세이는 비평서이다. 다른 사람이 쓴 글을 읽고 비평하는 글을 쓰는 것이므로 지금까지의 단순한 "몇 가지 외우기" 방법은 이제 더 이상 통하지 않는다. 게다가 채점 기준이 분명해졌으므로 누구나 에세이를 보면 몇 점 정도를 받을지 쉽게 평가할 수 있게 되었다. 즉, 분명히 에세이를 쓰는 것은 맞는데 Reading이 엄청나게 강조된 것이다. 채점 기준을 보면 왜 엄청나게 강조되었다고 말하는지 알 수 있다.

1. 읽은 글에 사용된 사실(Facts)을 추려내기.
즉, 저자가 사용한 사실과 그것을 통해 만들어낸 주장을 구별해서 사실만을 분리해 내라는 것이다. 이때 분리해 낸 사실의 수만큼 점수를 주겠다는 의미이다. 채점하기는 쉬워졌고, 쓰기는 어려워졌다. 읽어야 할 지문의 난이도를 높여, 무엇이 사실이고 어느 것이 주장인지 혼동하게 만들기만 하면 되는 것이 아닌가?

2. 사실과 주장 연결하기
어느 사실을 이용해서 어떤 주장을 했는지를 밝히라는 것이다. 예를 들어 3가지 사실과 3가지 주장이 있다면 어느 사실과 어느 주장이 짝을 이루냐는 것이다. 잘못 이해하면 매우 쉬울 것 같지만 지문에 irony(아이러니), metaphor(은유), sarcasm(빈정대기) 등의 rhetoric(수사학)이 얼마나 사용되느냐에 따라 상상을 초월할 수 있다.

3. 주장을 하는 과정에서 저자가 사용한 문체(style) 분석하기
주장을 하는 과정에서 저자가 감정에 호소했는지, 어떤 이론을 사용했는지 등을 자세히 밝히라는 것이다. 여기에는 2번에서와 같은 문제도 있고 또 다른 문제가 하나 더 있다. 저자가 사용된 style을 설명할 수는 있는데 무엇이라고 부르는지 모르면 안 된다는 것이다. 즉, 개개의 style에 대한 terminology가 중요해졌다.

그런데 제대로 된 비평서라면 한 가지가 더 있어야 한다. 3번에서 밝혀낸 그 저자의 style이 저자의 주장에 왜 효과적인지를 밝히는 것이 비평의 마지막 요소이다.

예를 들어 감정에 호소했다면 저자의 주장의 내용상 왜 합리적인 방법을 사용하지 않고 감정에 호소했는지를 밝히는 것이다. 즉, 감정에 호소하는 것이 저자의 주장의 내용과 왜 잘 맞는지를 밝히는 것이다. 이는 비평에서 빠져서는 안 되는 요소이다. 그런데 현재 왜 이 요소가 빠져 있는지는 확실하지 않다. 이런 비평서를 써 본 적이 별로 없는 학생들에게는 너무 어렵다고 판단한 것인지, 채점 상의 문제가 있는지는 아직 분명하지 않다.

어쨌든 이런 비평서를 제대로 쓰기 위해서 평소에 할 일은 다음과 같다.

1. 무엇을 읽든 사실과 의견을 분리하기
2. 분리가 힘들면 힘들 때마다 도움을 구하기. (예를 들면 네이버 카페 huntinglish로 오라.)

3. 주장할 때 사용되는 style의 종류와 이유를 미리 학습하기. (혼자서 힘들면 huntinglish로.)

(4) Reading이 강조된 math로

설명을 시작하기 전에 먼저 알아야 할 것이 있다. SAT의 math는 엄밀하게 말해서 우리 한국 사람들이 생각하는 그런 수학이 아니다.

SAT Subject나 AP의 수학은 우리가 생각하는 그런 수학이지만, SAT의 수학은 실제로는 언어사용능력평가의 일부일 뿐이다. 언어적 정보를 수학적 정보로 바꿀 수 있는지를 평면적으로 확인하는 간단한 평가에 불과하다.

2016년 NEW SAT 수학이 이전 SAT 수학보다 약간 어려워진 것은 사실이다. 그러나 그보다 훨씬 중요한 변화는 수학 문제에 사용되고 있는 언어적인 면이다. 질문이 훨씬 길어졌고 복잡해졌다. SAT 수학의 본질적인 기능인 언어적 정보의 수학적 정보로의 변환에 대한 평가를 좀 더 심도 있게 하겠다는 의도로 보인다.

결론적으로 수학은 약간 어려워졌고 영어는 훨씬 복잡해졌다. Reading, Grammar, Essay, Math 모든 영역에서 Reading이 이전보다 훨씬 강화된 것이다. 국내 학생들이 유럽이나 미국 학생들보다 더 심하기는 하지만, 전세계적으로 읽기를 점점 더 싫어하는 추세인 것을 볼 때 이를 막아 보려는 ETS와 College Board의 이런 노력은 어쩌면 당연한 것이지도 모른다.

어쨌든 SAT 준비라는 측면에서 보면, Reading 능력이 뛰어날수록 Math에서 유리하다고 말할 수 있겠다. 이전 SAT에서도 그랬지만 새 SAT에서는 더욱 더 그렇다. 아예 어떤 문제는 수학 시험인지 영어 시험인지가 혼동될 정도로 문제가 길다. 그렇다면 수학에 사용된 영어와 Reading에 이용되는 영어의 차이는 무엇일까?

차이는 Precision의 정도이다.

Reading에 사용된 영어 내용은 지문에 따라 다르기는 하지만 100퍼센트 이해를 해야만 문제를 풀 수 있는 경우는 드물다. 실제로 40~60퍼센트 정도만 이해되면 만점을 충분히 받을 수 있다. 물론 이 40~60퍼센트는 내용상 중요한 부분이므로, 글의 주된 흐름과 상대적으로 상관이 적은 40~60퍼센트를 이해하는 것은 문제 풀이에 도움이 되지 않는다. 글의 중요한 흐름과 상관이 적은 내용만 이해하고 있으면 지문의 주제를 오해하게 만들어서 도리어 방해가 되는 경우까지 있다.

그런데 SAT 수학의 질문에 사용된 영어는 100퍼센트 이해해야만 한다. 모든 표현이 문제를 푸는 데 필요하다. 질문이 매우 precise(정확하고 치밀하다)하다는 의미이다.

- Reading을 통해서
논리적이고 분석적으로 흐름을 판단하는 능력을 평가하고
- Grammar를 통해서
글에 나타난 모든 관계를 이해하는 능력을 평가하고
- Essay를 통해서

사실과 주장을 구별하고 저자의 주장의 흐름을 이해하는지 평가하고
- Math를 통해서

지문(수학적 지문)을 놓치는 내용 없이 치밀하게 분석하는지를 평가하겠다는 의도이다.

즉, 문제에 사용된 영어 표현을 모두 면밀히 검토하고 개개의 표현이 어떤 수학적 정보를 갖고 있는지를 이해한 다음, 모두 거기에 맞는 수학적 정보로 바꾸는 훈련을 해야 한다. 이때, Reading에 사용된 지문과는 달리 어떤 정보도 놓쳐서는 안 된다.

4

Reading 능력을 배양하는 실전 훈련의 예

(1) Reading/Essay 대처법 정리

1. 학교 교재, 소설, 잡지 등을 읽을 때 사실과 의견을 구별하는 훈련을 계속한다.
구별이 안 되면 글을 제대로 이해한 것이 아니라는 것을 깨닫고 더 노력하든지 도움을 받는다.

2. 각 문장과 문단, 개개의 개념 간의 관계를 확인한다.
일반적으로 사용되는 관계는 다음과 같다.

- cause and effect
- comparison and contrast
- generalization
- specification
- exemplification
- refutation
- self-refutation
- contradiction
- exception

3. 저자가 어떤 사실을 이용해서 어떤 주장을 했는지를 구별하는 훈련을 한다.
간혹 아무 사실(증거)도 사용하지 않고 주장만 하는 경우도 있으니 조심해야 한다. 지문의 내용이나 난이도에 따라서 사실과 주장을 구별하기 힘든 경우도 있다. 여유를 갖고 이런 훈련을 꾸준히 해야 한다. 대략 7학년부터 시작하는 것이 좋으며 9학년이 되었는데도 혼자서 할 수 없으면 반드시 전문가의 도움을 받아야 한다.

4. 저자가 주장을 하는 과정에서 사용한 문체(style)에 대한 감각이 생겨야 한다.
당연히 영어 문장을 이해하는 자체가 힘든 학생들에게는 거의 불가능한 일이라는 사실도 잊지 말아야 한다. 일반적으로 사용하는 style은 다음과 같다.

- Logical Approach
  Comparison and Contrast
  Cause and Effect
  Exemplification

- Emotional Approach

    Sympathy

    Frustration

    Doubt

    Suspicion

- Literary Approach

    Metaphor

    Simile

    Irony

    Sarcasm

    Figurative Speech

아직 New SAT Essay의 채점 기준에는 없지만 제대로 읽고 쓰려면, 그래서 미국 대학에서 전혀 문제가 없기 위해서는 위의 style이 주제를 전달하는 데 왜 효과적인지도 이해하고 설명할 수 있어야 한다

(2) Essay/Grammar 대처법 정리

1. 분석적으로 읽는 습관을 길러야 한다. (Context-based Grammar)

분석적으로 읽는 방법의 시작은 문장과 문장의 내용을 비교하는 것인데, 이 비교가 글쓰기 능력으로 발전하려면 다음과 같은 훈련을 지속적으로 해야 한다.

- 적어도 2개 이상의 문단이 있는 지문을 읽는다.
- 첫 두 문단의 관계를 정리한다(일반적 관계는 앞에서 이미 설명했다.).
- 그 관계를 글로 써 본다.
- 그 두 문단 중 첫 문단의 문장들을 살펴보고 관계가 불분명하거나 혼동되는 문장들을 찾아내서 관계를 글로 써 본다.
- 지문에 나타난 2개의 개념에 대해 위의 연습을 반복한다.
- 지문 내의 아무 문장이나 비교하여 관계를 살펴보고 정리한다.
- 각 단계에서 huntinglish에 의 답변과 제안을 숙독하고 이해가 어려운 내용은 다시 질문한다.

2. SAT에 출제되는 문법의 특징을 확실히 알고 있어야 한다. (No Reading-based Grammar)

SAT 문법 문제는 미국 대학생들의 실수 모음집이라고 보면 된다. 즉, SAT Grammar의 Reading-based Grammar가 아닌 문법 문제를 힘들어 한다는 것은, 대학 진학 후 기본적 Writing(시험, 과제 등)에 문제가 생길 것이라는 얘기다. 게다가 이런 문법 문제는 약간의 집중력만 있으면, 구별하기가 매우 쉽다. 그러므로 전반적인 Writing 능력도 물론 매우 중요하지만 우선 SAT의 Reading-based Grammar 문제가 아닌 문법 문제는 절대로 한 문제도 틀려서는 안 된다. 어떤 문제들이 출제되는지 살펴보자.

- Agreement

주어와 동사의 수가 같아야 한다. 단수는 단수와 복수와 연결된다. 문제는 주어가 길어지면 주어가 단수인지 복수인지 혼동되는 것인데, 평소에 긴 주어를 볼 때 마다 단수인지 복수인지 구별하는 연습을 해야 한다. 어느 정도 훈련이 되면 본인이 훈련이 더 이상 필요한지 아닌지 알게 된다. 이 글을 보면서 잘 모르겠으면 아직 훈련이 덜 된 상태이다.

(EX)
The phenomenon which is pursued by many mythologists over the last few decades are ⋯ (x)
The phenomenon which is pursued by many mythologists over the last few decades is ⋯ (o)

- Tense

누가 그까짓 시제에 관련된 문제를 틀리겠느냐고 우습게 생각하는 경우를 많이 본다. 그런데 쉬운 문제인데도, 문장의 흐름을 잘못 판단하게 되면 틀리는 경우가 의외로 굉장히 많다.

(EX)
Because he hated hiking alone, he will spend this weekend with his friends. (x)
Because he hates hiking alone, he will spend this weekend with his friends. (o)
Because he hated hiking alone, he would spend this weekend with his friends. (o)
Because he hates hiking alone, he would spend this weekend with his friends. (o)

위의 4개의 문장이 각각 왜 맞고 틀리는지 모르면 심각한 상황이라고 할 수 있는 정도로 쉬운 문장들이다.

- Parallelism

우리말로 흔히 병치라고 부르는 이 문장 현상은 크게 문법적인 경우와 의미적인 경우로 나뉜다. 다음은 어느 경우에 속하는지 구별해 보자.

(EX 1)
We need to talk and understand why what happened had to happen. (x)
We need to talk about and understand why what happened had to happen. (o)

(EX 2)
Korea's weather is very different from every African country. (x)
Korea's weather is very different from that of every African country. (o)

- Conjunction(Grammatical and Contextual)

접속사를 이용한 문제도 문법적인 경우와 의미적인 경우로 나뉜다.

(EX 1)
He always sounds as if he knows everything. (o)

He always sounds <u>like</u> he knows everything. (x)

She wouldn't help us <u>although</u> she has enough resources. (o)

She wouldn't help us <u>despite</u> she has enough resources. (x)

(EX 2)

She <u>wouldn't</u> help us <u>because</u> she has enough resources. (x)

She <u>wouldn't</u> help us <u>although</u> she has enough resources. (o)

• Colloquialism

SAT는 문어체만을 인정한다. 이 문어체/구어체의 구별은 흔히 접속사 문제와 깊은 관련이 있다.

(EX)

He always sounds <u>as if</u> he knows everything. (o) → Written English

He always sounds <u>like</u> he knows everything. (x) → Spoken English(Colloquial)

• Preposition(usages of verbs, idiomatic expressions, and simple mistakes)

전치사 문제도 역시 문법적인 문제와 의미상의 문제로 나뉜다.

(EX 1)

She wouldn't help us <u>although</u> all the help we have provided so far. (x)

She wouldn't help us <u>despite</u> all the help we have provided so far. (o)

They wandered around in <u>search for</u> the missing child. (x)

They wandered around in <u>search of</u> the missing child. (o)

They wandered around <u>searching of</u> the missing child. (x)

They wandered around <u>searching for</u> the missing child. (o)

(EX 2)

Since you have too much trouble with the recent case, I will personally <u>look for</u> the case. (x)

Since you have too much trouble with the recent case, I will personally <u>look into</u> the case. (o)

They wandered around <u>searching</u> the missing child. (x)

They wandered around <u>searching for</u> the missing child. (o)

• Inversion(in connection with Agreement)

SAT에서의 도치 문제는 거의 항상 주어/동사의 수의 일치와 관련 있다. 즉, 도치를 이용한 Agreement 문제가 대부분이다.

(EX)

Along the beautiful coast <u>lies</u> all <u>kinds</u> of trees whose colors and shapes are rather outlandish. (x)

Along the beautiful coast <u>lie</u> all <u>kinds</u> of trees whose colors and shapes are rather outlandish. (o)

그 외 가능한 출제 범주를 마저 살펴보면 다음과 같다.

- Active and Passive Voices(Grammatical and Contextual)
- Wordiness(if not changing the original intention)
- Parts of Speech(purely grammatical)
- Redundancy
- Pronoun
- Clarity
- Adverb/Conjunctive
- Diction
- Word Form(Spelling-related)
- Paired Structure
- Comparative and Superlative
- Idiomatic Expressions(a wide variety of)
- Original Intention

이러한 sentence-based Grammar의 출제 경향은 New(redesigned) SAT에서도 그대로 이용된다. New Official SAT Study Guide, 2015 edition에 그대로 나와 있다. 문맥을 이용하지 않는 이런 문법 문제는 단순한 연습으로 쉽게 만점이 가능하지만 context(reading)-based Grammar는 그렇게 쉽지 않으므로 이 둘을 구별하는 것이 우선 관건이다. 그런데 구별은 대부분 간단하다. 문제에 말로 부가적인 설명이 있으면 context(reading)-based Grammar이고, 문제 번호와 선택지(answer choices)밖에 없으면 sentence-based Grammar이다. 예외적인 경우도 있지만 우려할 정도는 아니다.

(3) logical analysis 실전 훈련

새로운 SAT를 제대로 준비하기 위해서는 logical analysis(논리적 분석력)가 생활화되어야 한다. 아래에 실례를 들어 설명한다.

> **실전 연습** logical analysis의 예—inference(추론)

Akira came directly, breaking all tradition. (p. 334, The Official SAT Study Guide, 2015 edition)

위의 문장만 보고 아래 내용을 추론할 수 없다면 SAT를 준비하거나 치르는데 큰 문제가 있다고 볼 수 있다.

inference 1)
직접 왔는데 모든 전통을 깼다고 했으므로 여기서 말하는 이 전통은 무엇인가 간접적인 특징을 지니고 있는 것이 분명하다.

inference 2)

그러므로 이 문장 다음에는 그 간접적인 특징이 무엇인지 언급되어 있어야 한다.

지문을 계속 읽다 보면 a go-between이라는 표현이 보이고, 두 사람이 의사를 전달할 때 가운데에서 일종의 의사전달을 위한 심부름꾼이라는 걸 쉽게 알 수 있게 된다. 즉, Akira는 이런 go-between(=indirect)을 이용하지 않은 것이다(=direct). 이 정도의 추론은 1에서 10까지의 난이도로 보면 1~2 정도의 수준이다. 이런 추론은 글의 흐름을 빠르게 판단하는데 도움이 되는 것 이외의 또 다른 중요성을 지니는데, 그것은 "Akira came directly…."라는 문장과 a go-between이라는 표현과의 관계(여기서 a go-between은 첫 문장에 대한 specification이다)를 알려준다는 데 있다. 계속 강조하고 있지만 영어로 쓰인 글을 제대로(logical analysis) 읽으려면 다음 연습을 꾸준히 해야 한다.

1. prediction
2. connection
3. comparison and contrast
4. wrong inference

inference 3)

아마도 그 간접적인 면과 전체 글의 주제가 관련성이 있을 가능성이 크다.

이 글은 소설이어서 이 소설 전체를 읽어 보면 주제가 분명하겠지만 official guide에 출제된 부분만으로는 분명하지 않다. 출제된 부분만 분석해 보면 전통을 깨고 직접 미래 신부의 어머니를 찾아 온 Akira와 미래 신부의 어머니인 Chie, 그리고 Chie와 딸인 Naomi와의 미묘한 심리적 갈등에 더 중점을 두고 있다. 단, 논리적으로 중요한 부분이 남아 있기는 한데, 출제된 지문의 마지막 부분에 Chie가 Akira의 집안을 무시하는 발언을 하는 부분이다. 즉 위에 언급한 comparison and contrast and/or wrong inference 연습이 필요해진다. 전통을 어긴 것과 낮은 신분의 집안인 것이 무슨 관계냐는 것이다. 이때 잊지 말아야 할 것은 아무 관계도 없을 수도 있으나, 없더라도 없다는 증거가 지문에 있어야 한다는 것이다.

전통을 깨고 직접 찾아온 것과 별로 영향력이 없는 집안의 자녀인 것이 관계가 있을까, 없을까? 어떻게 알아내는 걸까? 만일 관계가 없다면 "있는 척"하는 문제를 출제할 수 있다. 이런 예상을 미리 해 보는 것도 logical analysis에 큰 도움이 된다. 모든 '생각하기'는 전부 도움이 된다는 것을 잊지 말자. 지문을 다시 읽되 '전통을 깨고 직접 찾아 온' 것과 '그저 그런 집안'의 자손인 것이 관계가 있는지 없는지를 확인하려는 분명한 목적이 있음을, 지금은 그 목적밖에 없음을 절대 잊지 말아야 한다.

이렇게 지문을 읽을 때 우선적으로 중요한 것은 fact(사실)와 argument(주장)을 구별하는 것이다. 그럼 이 경우에 중요한 것은 fact와 argument 중 어느 것일까? 그저 그런 집안의 자손이라는 것은 Chie의 '생각'이므로 Chie의 argument가 초점이다. 그러므로 읽으면서 Chie의 주장에만 집중해야 한다. 물론 '사실'이 '의견'을 추론하는 데 도움이 되는 경우가 있기는 하나, 관계 없는 사실을 도움이 된다고 착각하게 되면 Wrong Inference(잘못된 추론)의 경우이며 이런 상황을 예측하고 이에 대한 문제를 만든다는 것을 잊지 말자. 이제 지문을 다시 읽을 준비가 되었다.

1. Chie thought him only the wind; fact는 아니지만 전통을 깬 것과 집안을 낮게 보는 것을 연결시키지는 못한다.
2. Chie was reluctant to go to her guest; Chie가 Akira에 대해 부정적이라는 것을 분명히 나타내고는 있지만 전통을 깬 것과 집안에 대한 태도를 연결시킬 근거는 되지 못함.
3. She saw his reflection like a dark double; 위의 2와 마찬가지 경우.
4. Chie felt herself starting to like him; 긍정적인 태도이므로 사용 불가.
5. That's how she viewed him, as a child; 위의 2와 마찬가지 경우.
6. Suddenly she felt the dampness of the night; 위의 2와 마찬가지 경우.
7. The sight of Naomi's clear eyes, her dark brows gave her(=Chie) Strength. Maybe his hopes were preposterous; 위의 2와 마찬가지 경우.

결론적으로 Chie의 부정적인 태도는 얼마든지 찾을 수 있으나 지문 어디에도 전통을 깬 것과 Chie가 무시하는 가문의 자손인 것이 어떤 관계인지는 나와 있지 않다. 즉 이 두 가지 정보는 부정적인 기능을 한다는 점에서는 공통점이 있으나 특정한 별다른 관계(cause and effect, specification, generalization)는 없다. 그러므로 이 두 정보 간에 어떤 관계가 있다는 내용은 모두 Wrong Inference가 된다. 굳이 관계를 찾자면, 전통을 깨고 직접 찾아옴으로써 부정적인 결과(결혼 반대)를 초래할 것이라는 예측(prediction, foreboding)을 하게 한 다음, 게다가 가문도 좋지 않다는 종지부를 찍은 것이다. 그러므로 굳이 따지면 일종의 foreboding 또는 omen(나쁜 징조)의 구실을 했다고 볼 수 있다. 그러고는 반전을 잊지 않는다.

Naomi turned to go back into the house, then stopped. "Mother." "Yes?" "I mean to have him"

그리고는 Chie의 반응을 보여 주지 않음으로써 독자를 호기심에 빠뜨린다. 지금까지의 내용으로는 Chie는 이 결혼에 부정적인 것이 분명한데, 딸이 이렇게 강하게 나오면 어떻게 대처할지까지를 예측할 정도의 근거나 정보를 주지는 않음으로써 독자의 추측을 기술적으로 제한하고 있다.

이런 게 분석이다. 어떻게 기술적으로 제한했는지 위의 1~7에서 찾지 못한다면 큰일이다. 답은 4와 7이다. 왜일까? Chie 태도는 전반적으로 부정적이지만 4처럼 긍정적인 면도 있고 7처럼 자신 없는 면도 있다. 즉, 딸이 너무 강하게 나오면 이 부정적인 태도가 약해질 가능성이 없다고는 자신할 수 없다. 그러나 전반적으로는 부정적이고, 날씨에 대한 묘사도 모두 부정적인 분위기를 자아내고 있으므로 너무 희망적일 수는 없겠다.

이제 남은 것은 날씨에 대한 어떤 묘사가 부정적인 분위기를 자아내는지 얼마나 효과적인지 분석하는 것이며, 이쯤 되면 학생들은 지문에 집중할 수 있게 된다. 이런 게 공부다

(결론) 지문의 맨 처음에 쓰인 한 문장만으로 글의 흐름을 판단하는 독자가 있는가 하면 몇 개의 문단을 읽고서도 흐름을 판단하지 못하는 사람이 있는 이유가 여기에 있다. 직접 알려준 것이나 마찬가지인 이 숨어 있는 내용을 추론하는 것이 logical analysis의 시작이다.

이번엔 약간 더 어려운 예를 살펴보자.

| 실전 연습 | logical analysis-Example 2 |

GAME of THRONES
TIME talks 2016 with the most surprising couple in politics(Bush and Clinton)(TIME: Aug. 3, 2015)

위의 문장을 읽고도 지문에서 어떤 정보를 찾아야 하는지 추론하지 못한다면 심각한 상황이다. 두 가지 가능성이 있겠다.

    1. 두 전직 대통령이 각자 따로 대단한(amazing) 인물들인 경우
    2. 따로는 별로지만 모이면 amazing한 경우

2번 경우라면 모여서 어떤 점이 amazing한지를 설명해야 한다. 아직 둘 중 어느 경우인지 추론하지 못하는 사람은 SAT를 치를 것을 다시 생각하는 것이 좋다. 문제는 2번 경우라면 왜 이 둘을 couple이라고 불렀는지이다. 대통령은 한 번에 한 사람이므로 여기서의 couple은 둘이 대통령일 때를 가리키는 것이 아님을 알 수 있다. 그렇다면 언제를 가리키는 것인가? 이제 글의 흐름은 사실상 분명해졌다. 이 정도까지 느끼는 데 걸리는 시간은 다음과 같다.

    old SAT Critical Reading 기준 750 이상 = 5-10초
    old SAT Critical Reading 기준 700 이상 = 10-20분
    old SAT Critical Reading 기준 600 이상 = 1-3시간
    old SAT Critical Reading 기준 600 미만 = forever
    (주의) 유출 문제로 연습한 학생들은 제외

2번, 따로는 별로지만 모이면 amazing한 경우라면 모여서 어떤 점이 amazing한지를 설명해야 한다. "Somewhere on this how July day, Jeb Bush and Hillary Clington are thuming each other over jobs and economic policy,"라는 소제목으로 기사는 시작한다. 그러나 바로 다음에 나오는 본문의 내용은 이렇다.

but in a cool Dallas office, George W. Bush is sharing a sofa with Bill Clington to talk about how to handle the 2016 race.

즉 이들은 누가 이기느냐가 관심사가 아니다. 관심사는 how to handle the 2016 race이다. 이 부분이 바로 amazing한 것이고 이제 기사는 이 부분을 자세히 설명할 것이다. 그러므로 지금까지 key words and phrases는 amazing couple / how to handle the 2016 race이다.
37쪽의 사진 아래에 이런 내용이 눈에 띈다.

At least for this stage of journey, the Bush-Clington interests are aligned.

이 부분은 읽고도 무슨 생각을 해야 하는지 잘 모르겠다면, 그런데 10학년 이상이라면 사태는 심각하다.

1. 무슨 journey인가? race를 가리키는 것인가? 그럴 수도 있지만 그보다는 Bush-Clington는 talk을 가리킨다고 보는 것이 합리적이다. 이 기사의 초점은 Jeb과 Hillary가 아니기 때문이다.

2. aligned된 것과 how to handle 2016 race와 무슨 관계인가? 읽다 보면 clues to unprecedented predicament라는 표현이 보인다. 여기서 글의 흐름을 예측해 보자(Prediction). 어떤 글이든지 읽으면서 계속적으로 두 개의 문장, 단어, 개념의 관계를 이해하려고 해야 하고(Connection), 다음에는 무슨 내용이 나올지 예측해야 하며(Prediction), 저자가 무엇을 비교하고 있는지 깨달아야 하며(Comparison and Contrast), 비교하는 과정에서 원인과 결과에 대해 설명하는지 눈여겨 봐야 한다(Cause and Effect). 이 네 가지가 읽기의 기본이다. 읽으면서 이런 분석을 하지 않았다면 지금까지 엉터리로 읽었다는 것을 잊지 말자.

그렇다면 clues to unprecedented predicament 와 how to handle 2016 race 의 관계는 무엇인가? 이 기사가 그리 어려운 내용이 아니라면 unprecedented predicament 때문에 이 둘이 how to handle 2016 race에 대한 대화를 나눌 필요가 생긴 것이 분명하다고 Prediction할 수 있겠다.

잘못된 Prediction이 전혀 아무것도 prediction 못하는 것보다 낫다. 본인의 Prediction과 실제 글의 흐름을 비교하는 것도 좋은 연습이며, 글을 읽는 힘을 기르는 데 큰 힘이 된다.

《이 내용은 엑스퍼트프렙 블로그(blog.naver.com/kei4379)의 컬럼 '계관웅 유학사냥'으로, 계속 연재되고 있습니다.》

The Redesigned SAT
Practice Tests

TEST 1

Test 1

Reading | 65 minutes, 50 questions

DIRECTIONS

Each passage below is followed by a number of questions. After reading each passage, choose the best answer to each question based on what is stated or implied in the passage.

Questions 1-10 are based on the following passage.

There is some confusion in the use of the terms "nutrient," "plant food," etc., as applied to the nutrition and growth of plants. Strictly speaking, these terms ought probably to be limited in their
5 application to the organized compounds within the plant which it uses as sources of energy and of metabolizable material for the development of new cells and organs during its growth.

Botanists quite commonly use the terms in this
10 way. But students of the problems involved in the relation of soil elements to the growth of plants, including such practical questions as are involved in the maintenance of soil productivity and the use of commercial fertilizers for the growing of
15 economic plants, or crops, are accustomed to use the terms "plant foods," or "mineral nutrients," to designate the chemical elements and simple gaseous compounds which are supplied to the plant as the raw material from which its food and
20 tissue-building materials are synthetized. Common usage limits these terms to the soil elements; but there is no logical reason for segregating the raw materials derived from the soil from those derived from the atmosphere.

25 The essential difference between these raw materials for plant syntheses and the organic compounds which are produced within the plants and used by them, and by animals, as food, is that the former are inorganic and can furnish only
30 materials but no energy to the organism; while the latter are organic and supply both materials and potential energy. It would probably be the best practice to confine the use of the word "food" to materials of the latter type, and several attempts
35 have been made to limit its use in this way and to apply some such term as "intake" to the simple raw materials which are taken into the organism and utilized by it in its synthetic processes. But the custom of using the words "food," or "nutrient," to
40 represent anything that is taken into the organism and in any way utilized by it for its nourishment has been followed so long and the newer terms are themselves so subject to criticism that they have not yet generally supplanted the loosely used word
45 "food."

If such use is permitted, however, it is necessary to recognize that only the green parts of green plants can use this inorganic "food," and that the colorless plants must have organic food.

50 To avoid this confusion, the suggestion has recently been made that all of the intake of plants and animals shall be considered as food, but that those forms which supply both materials and potential energy to the organism shall be
55 designated as synergic foods, while those which contain no potential energy shall be known as anergic foods. On this basis, practically all of the food of animals, excepting the mineral salts and water, and all of the organic compounds which
60 are synthetized by plants and later used by them for further metabolic changes, are synergic foods; while practically all of the intake of green plants is anergic food.

It is with the latter type of food materials
65 that this chapter is to deal; while the following

and all subsequent chapters deal with the organic
compounds which are synthetized by plants
and contain potential energy and are, therefore,
capable of use as synergic food by either the plants
70 themselves or by animals. It will be understood,
therefore, that in this chapter the word "food" is
used to mean the anergic food materials which
are taken into and used by green plants as the raw
materials for the synthesis of organic compounds,
75 with the aid of solar energy, or that of previously
produced synergic foods. In all later chapters,
the term "food" will be used to mean the organic
compounds which serve as the synergic food for
the green parts of green plants and as the sole
80 supply of nutrient material for the colorless parts
of green plants and for parasitic or saprophytic
forms.

1

What would be the best title of the passage?

A) The differences between green plants and their colorless counterparts

B) The ways food is utilized within different kinds of plants

C) How a certain definition affects some interpretation

D) Possible differences between organic and inorganic food

2

Which of the following is the primary conflict described in the passage?

A) conflicting ways food can be observed

B) complications involved in looking at a certain phenomenon

C) problems distinguishing what is green and what is not

D) problems distinguishing what is organic and what is inorganic

3

Which of the following gives the most direct evidence for the answer to the previous question?

A) Lines 28-32 ("and used…energy.")

B) Lines 32-35 ("It would…this way")

C) Lines 51-55 ("that all…foods,")

D) Lines 56-63 ("contain…food")

Test 1

4

According to the passage, what is the difference between organic crude material and inorganic counterpart?

A) one provides integral substances
B) the way energy is taken advantage of
C) the variety of functions they serve in plant
D) the fact that energy is produced to secure the production of one of the two

5

Which of the following gives the most direct evidence for the answer to the previous question?

A) Lines 28-32 ("and used…energy.")
B) Lines 32-35 ("It would…this way")
C) Lines 51-55 ("that all…foods,")
D) Lines 56-63 ("contain…food")

6

Which of the following does such use refer to?

A) "loosely using the word 'food'." (Lines 44-45)
B) "criticism" (Line 43)
C) "the custom of using the words 'food,' or 'nutrient,'" (Lines 38-39)
D) using "the newer terms" (Line 42)

7

Which of the following is most consistent with the author's attitude?

A) Only the green parts of green plants can use this inorganic "food."
B) Colorless plants must have organic food.
C) Traditional use of such terms as "food" must be respected.
D) However terms such as food and intake are used, they must be used with caution.

8

Which of the following gives the most direct evidence for the answer to the previous question?

A) "so long" (Line 41) and "criticism" (Line 43)
B) "custom" (Line 39) and "nourishment" (Line 41)
C) "must" and "organic" (Line 49)
D) "best practice" (Lines 32-33) and "limit (Line 35)

9

Which of the following is a suggested solution to the main problem of the passage?

A) introducing a novel concept of food to designate new kinds of food
B) redefining the connection between "intake" and "food"
C) classifying a pivotal concept in a novel fashion.
D) making a compromise between traditional and modern ways of defining biological terms

Test 1

10

What is the role of the last paragraph compared to the passage as a whole?

A) reiteration

B) conclusion

C) changing the main direction

D) additional information

Test 1

Questions 11-20 are based on the following passage.

Spain, as everyone knows, was the country behind the discovery of America. Few people know, however, what an important part the beautiful city of Granada played in that famous event. It was in
5 October, 1492, that Columbus first set foot on the New World and claimed it for Spain. In January of that same year another territory had been added to that same crown; for the brave soldier-sovereigns, Ferdinand and Isabella, had conquered
10 the Moorish kingdom of Granada in the south and made it part of their own country. Nearly eight hundred years before, the dark-skinned Moors had come over from Africa and invaded the European peninsula which lies closest to the Straits
15 of Gibraltar, and the people of that peninsula had been battling fiercely ever since to drive them back to where they came from. True, the Moor had brought Arabian art and learning with him, but he had brought also the Mohammedan religion,
20 and that was intolerable not only to the Spaniards but to all Europeans. No Christian country could brook the thought of this Asiatic creed flourishing on her soil, so Spain soon set to work to get rid of it. This war between the two religions began
25 in the north near the Bay of Biscay whither the Christians were finally pushed by the invaders. Each century saw the Moors driven a little farther south toward the Mediterranean, until Granada, where the lovely Sierra Nevadas rise, was the last
30 stronghold left them. Small wonder, then, that when Granada was finally taken the Spanish nation was supremely happy. Small wonder that they held a magnificent fete in their newly-won city in the "Snowy Mountains." The vanquished Moorish
35 king rode down from his mountain citadel and handed its keys to Ferdinand and Isabella. Bells pealed, banners waved, and the people cheered wildly as their victorious sovereigns rode by. And yet, so we are told by a writer who was present,
40 in the midst of all this rejoicing one man stood aside, sad and solitary. While all the others felt that their uttermost desire had been granted in acquiring the Moorish kingdom, he knew that he could present them with a far greater territory
45 than Granada if only they would give him the chance. What were these olive and orange groves beside the tropic fertility of the shores he longed to reach, and which he would have reached long ere this, he told himself regretfully, if only they had
50 helped him! What was the Christianizing of the few Moors who remained in Spain compared with the Christianizing of all the undiscovered heathen across the Atlantic! And so on that eventful January 2, 1492, when a whole city was delirious with joy,
55 "There was crying in Granada when the sun was going down, Some calling on the Trinity some calling on Mahoun. Here passed away the Koran therein the Cross was borne. And here was heard the Christian bell and there the Moorish horn."

Mahoun = Mohammad / Muhammad / Muhammed

Test 1

11

The point of the passage could have been a lot clearer should which of the following be known?

A) the main reason why Columbus suffered

B) the primary conflict between moors and Europeans

C) why the people of Granada were exhilarated

D) the exact role the city of Granada played in the discovery of the new world

12

According to the passage, why was Spanish royalty probably reluctant to go with Columbus's plan?

A) because it was preposterous

B) because the royal government was faced with other more urgent matters

C) because he asked too much as a reward for the possible success of his plan

D) because he was a foreigner

13

As used in line 22, "brook" most nearly means

A) embrace

B) resent

C) picture

D) bear

14

As used in line 38, "sovereigns" most nearly means

A) independent people

B) absolution

C) queens

D) rulers

15

According to the passage, why was the one man sad as explained?

A) because he was not satisfied with the victory mentioned

B) because he was anxious about the possible outcomes of the victory mentioned

C) because he thought some people were near-sighted

D) because he could easily find the new world

16

Which choice best explains the answer to the previous question?

A) He could have given the people of Spain much more than the victory mentioned in the passage.

B) He has given the people of Granada something to go on with.

C) His plan could have been more religiously satisfying.

D) The people of Granada could have benefited more than from the victory mentioned in the passage.

49

Test 1

17

Which choice gives the best evidence for the answer to the previous question?

A) "compared with the Christianizing of all the undiscovered heathen across the Atlantic!" (Lines 51-53)

B) "beside the tropic fertility of the shores he longed to reach, and which he would have reached long ere this" (Lines 47-49)

C) "a far greater territory than Granada" (Lines 44-45)

D) "And so on that eventful January 2, 1492, when a whole city was delirious with joy, (Lines 53-54)

18

What could be the best topic of the passage?

A) Why Columbus was upset about the victory of Granada

B) Columbus's responses to Christianity and Islam

C) The religious conflict in Granada and its impact on Columbus

D) How a specific historical event at a historical location might have affected an important historical figure

19

According to the passage, what can be said about the invasion of Granada by the Moors?

A) It only created a severe religious conflict.

B) It made a cultural contribution to Christians.

C) It was a source of Columbus's ambition to set sail on a journey to the new world.

D) Directly because of it, Columbus had a hard time getting his plans implemented.

20

Which of the following gives the best interpretation of the last sentence of the passage?

A) The religious conversion of the moors had failed.

B) The religious conflict had not totally disappeared.

C) There were some Moors still residing in the area even after the victory.

D) It was impossible for the Christians to accept other religions.

Test 1

Questions 21-30 are based on the following passage.

The story of our world is a story that is still very imperfectly known. A couple of hundred years ago men possessed the history of little more than the last three thousand years. What happened before that time was a matter of legend and speculation. Over a large part of the civilized world it was believed and taught that the world had been created suddenly in 4004 B.C., though authorities differed as to whether this had occurred in the spring or autumn of that year. This fantastically precise misconception was based upon a too literal interpretation of the Hebrew Bible, and upon rather arbitrary theological assumptions connected therewith. Such ideas have long since been abandoned by religious teachers, and it is universally recognized that the universe in which we live has to all appearances existed for an enormous period of time and possibly for endless time. Of course there may be deception in these appearances, as a room may be made to seem endless by putting mirrors facing each other at either end. But that the universe in which we live has existed only for six or seven thousand years may be regarded as an altogether exploded idea. The earth, as everybody knows nowadays, is a spheroid, a sphere slightly compressed, orange fashion, with a diameter of nearly 8,000 miles. Its spherical shape has been known at least to a limited number of intelligent people for nearly 2,500 years, but before that time it was supposed to be flat, and various ideas which now seem fantastic were entertained about its relations to the sky and the stars and planets. We know now that it rotates upon its axis (which is about 24 miles shorter than its equatorial diameter) every twenty-four hours, and that this is the cause of the alternations of day and night, that it circles about the sun in a slightly distorted and slowly variable oval path in a year. Its distance from the sun varies between ninety-one and a half millions at its nearest and ninety-four and a half million miles. About the earth circles a smaller sphere, the moon, at an average distance of 239,000 miles. Earth and moon are not the only bodies to travel round the sun. There are also the planets, Mercury and Venus, at distances of thirty-six and sixty-seven millions of miles; and beyond the circle of the earth and disregarding a belt of numerous smaller bodies, the planetoids, there are Mars, Jupiter, Saturn, Uranus and Neptune at mean distances of 141, 483, 886, 1,782, and 1,793 millions of miles respectively.

These figures in millions of miles are very difficult for the mind to grasp. It may help the reader's imagination if we reduce the sun and planets to a smaller, more conceivable scale. If, then, we represent our earth as a little ball of one inch diameter, the sun would be a big globe nine feet across and 323 yards away, that is about a fifth of a mile, four or five minutes' walking. The moon would be a small pea two feet and a half from the world. Between earth and sun there would be the two inner planets, Mercury and Venus, at distances of one hundred and twenty-five and two hundred and fifty yards from the sun. All round and about these bodies there would be emptiness until you came to Mars, a hundred and seventy-five feet beyond the earth; Jupiter nearly a mile away, a foot in diameter; Saturn, a little smaller, two miles off; Uranus four miles off and Neptune six miles off.

Then nothingness and nothingness except for small particles and drifting scraps of attenuated vapour for thousands of miles. The nearest star to earth on this scale would be 40,000 miles away. These figures will serve perhaps to give one some conception of the immense emptiness of space in which the drama of life goes on. For in all this enormous vacancy of space we know certainly of life only upon the surface of our earth. It does not penetrate much more than three miles down into the 4,000 miles that separate us from the centre of our globe, and it does not reach more than five miles above its surface. Apparently all the limitlessness of space is otherwise empty and dead. The deepest ocean dredgings go down to five miles. The highest recorded flight of an aeroplane is little more than four miles. Men have reached to seven miles up in balloons, but at a cost of great suffering. No bird can fly so high as five miles, and small birds and insects which have been carried up by aeroplanes drop off insensible far below that level.

Test 1

21

What could be the best title of the passage?

A) The earth in many perspectives
B) The world in space
C) The earth as a place for the living
D) The world in its heavenly habitat

22

As used in line 31, "fantastic" most nearly means

A) splendid
B) fantasized
C) wrong
D) fabulous

23

According to the passage, what kind of role is played by mirrors in a room?

A) imagination
B) caution
C) foreboding
D) diversion

24

Why does the author say "precise" when s/he talks about a certain misconception?

A) to reveal previously hidden elements
B) to stress the degree of misconception
C) to emphasize a certain accuracy
D) to allude to an irony suggested by the situation in general

25

Which choice gives the best evidence for the cause of a "shorter" (Line 34) axis as explained in the passage?

A) "flat" (Line 31)
B) "compressed" (Line 26)
C) "enormous" (Line 77)
D) "alternations" (Line 36)

26

According to the passage, which choice is the best approximation of the number of heavenly bodies in the solar system?

A) nine
B) just a few
C) a lot more than a dozen
D) countless

27

Which choice gives the best evidence for the answer to the previous question?

A) "Mars, Jupiter, Saturn, Uranus and Neptune" (Line 49)
B) "a belt of numerous smaller bodies" (Lines 47-48)
C) "not the only bodies to travel round the sun." (Lines 43-44)
D) "at mean distances of 141, 483, 886, 1,782, and 1,793 millions of miles respectively." (Lines 51-52)

Test 1

28

What is the author trying to do in the second paragraph?

A) put the reader in perspective

B) help the reader see precisely what is happening outside the earth

C) explain in detail what is happening around the sun

D) provide clues to what might happen if anything goes wrong

29

Which choice gives the best evidence for the answer to the previous question?

A) "These figures in millions of miles are very difficult for the mind to grasp." (Lines 52-53)

B) "It may help the reader's imagination if we reduce the sun and planets to a smaller, more conceivable scale." (Lines 53-55)

C) "For in all this enormous vacancy of space we know certainly of life only upon the surface of our earth." (Lines 76-78)

D) "Apparently all the limitlessness of space is otherwise empty and dead." (Lines 82-84)

30

According to the passage, what is the probable reason why the author mentioned ocean dredgings and aeroplane?

A) to show a contrast between limitlessness and limitations

B) to provide a few pieces of evidence for the previous argument

C) to supply some of the possible causes of the previous claim

D) to argue for examinable consequences of a previously mentioned hypothesis

Test 1

Questions 31-40 are based on the following passage.

We may all agree about aesthetics, and yet differ about particular works of art. We may differ as to the presence or absence of the quality x. My immediate object will be to show that significant
5 form is the only quality common and peculiar to all the works of visual art that move me; and I will ask those whose aesthetic experience does not tally with mine to see whether this quality is not also, in their judgment, common to all works
10 that move them, and whether they can discover any other quality of which the same can be said. Also at this point a query arises, irrelevant indeed, but hardly to be suppressed: "Why are we so profoundly moved by forms related in a particular
15 way?" The question is extremely interesting, but irrelevant to aesthetics. In pure aesthetics we have only to consider our emotion and its object: for the purposes of aesthetics we have no right, neither is there any necessity, to pry behind the object
20 into the state of mind of him who made it. Later, I shall attempt to answer the question; for by so doing I may be able to develop my theory of the relation of art to life. I shall not, however, be under the delusion that I am rounding off my theory of
25 aesthetics. For a discussion of aesthetics, it need be agreed only that forms arranged and combined according to certain unknown and mysterious laws do move us in a particular way, and that it is the business of an artist so to combine and
30 arrange them that they shall move us. These moving combinations and arrangements I have called, for the sake of convenience and for a reason that will appear later, "Significant Form." A third interruption has to be met. "Are you forgetting
35 about colour?" someone inquires. Certainly not; my term "significant form" included combinations of lines and of colours. The distinction between form and colour is an unreal one; you cannot conceive a colourless line or a colourless space;
40 neither can you conceive a formless relation of colours. In a black and white drawing the spaces are all white and all are bounded by black lines; in most oil paintings the spaces are multi-coloured and so are the boundaries; you cannot imagine a
45 boundary line without any content, or a content without a boundary line. Therefore, when I speak of significant form, I mean a combination of lines and colours (counting white and black as colours) that moves me aesthetically. Some people
50 may be surprised at my not having called this "beauty." Of course, to those who define beauty as "combinations of lines and colours that provoke aesthetic emotion," I willingly concede the right of substituting their word for mine. But most of
55 us, however strict we may be, are apt to apply the epithet "beautiful" to objects that do not provoke that peculiar emotion produced by works of art. Everyone, I suspect, has called a butterfly or a flower beautiful. Does anyone feel the same kind
60 of emotion for a butterfly or a flower that he feels for a cathedral or a picture? Surely, it is not what I call an aesthetic emotion that most of us feel, generally, for natural beauty. I shall suggest, later, that some people may, occasionally, see in nature
65 what we see in art, and feel for her an aesthetic emotion; but I am satisfied that, as a rule, most people feel a very different kind of emotion for birds and flowers and the wings of butterflies from that which they feel for pictures, pots, temples
70 and statues. Why these beautiful things do not move us as works of art move is another, and not an aesthetic, question. For our immediate purpose we have to discover only what quality is common to objects that do move us as works of art. In the
75 last part of this chapter, when I try to answer the question— "Why are we so profoundly moved by some combinations of lines and colours?" I shall hope to offer an acceptable explanation of why we are less profoundly moved by others.

Test 1

31

What would be the best title of the passage?

A) The immediate and distant object
B) Esthetics in works of art
C) What significant form does in esthetics
D) The difference between esthetics and works of art.

32

Which of the following is most likely the author's intention for writing this passage?

A) to attempt to explain how an individual artwork is perceived within the boundary of esthetics
B) to show the superiority of esthetics to the way each artwork differently moves different people
C) to compare and contrast the concept of esthetics and the physical objects of art
D) to defy the traditional perception of esthetics and art

33

Which of the following is the most essential contrast throughout the passage?

A) some commonality and corresponding particularity
B) esthetics and art
C) specialists and generalists
D) depth and superficiality

34

According to the author, which of the following might be the best definition of art?

A) something that has something in common with other things, but in a different way with a different consequence
B) something that is too abstract to define in simple words or expressions
C) an enterprise for which there should be two approaches: immediate and distant
D) something that creates double standard

35

What is the most probable role of the author's immediate object in relation to the two immediately previous sentences?

A) to make an effective compromise
B) to create a slow diversion
C) to propose a reluctant solution
D) to suggest a hidden goal

36

Which of the following is the best assessment about significant form?

A) an inevitable compromise needed to deal with an old problem
B) a link by which to solve the previously mentioned problem
C) any combination of lines and colors
D) whatever is considered beautiful is composed of

Test 1

37

Which of the following is the closest in meaning to "tally with" as used in line 8?

A) record

B) count

C) match

D) respond to

38

According to the passage, what does "this quality" (Line 8) refer to?

A) significant form

B) esthetic experience

C) the fact that some people's esthetic experience does not tally with the author's

D) my immediate object

39

According to the passage, which of the following is the best inference about the author's long-term objective as compared with the immediate objective mentioned in the passage?

A) finding insignificant form

B) finding insignificant lines and colors

C) appreciating different effects of the concept used as the author's immediate object

D) illustrating the comparison and contrast related to commonality and diversity

40

Which of the following gives the most direct evidence for the answer to the previous question?

A) "My immediate object will be to show…also, in their judgment," (Lines 3-4)

B) "In pure aesthetics…there any necessity," (Lines 16-19)

C) "Some people may…called this 'beauty.'" (Lines 49-51)

D) "For our immediate purpose…why we are less profoundly moved by others." (Lines 72-79)

Questions 41-50 are based on the following passage.

We observe today not a victory of party but a celebration of freedom—symbolizing an end as well as a beginning—signifying renewal as well as change. For I have sworn before you and Almighty
5 God the same solemn oath our forebears prescribed nearly a century and three quarters ago.

The world is very different now. For man holds in his mortal hands the power to abolish all forms of human poverty and all forms of human
10 life. And yet the same revolutionary beliefs for which our forebears fought are still at issue around the globe—the belief that the rights of man come not from the generosity of the state but from the hand of God.

15 We dare not forget today that we are the heirs of that first revolution. Let the word go forth from this time and place, to friend and foe alike, that the torch has been passed to a new generation of Americans—born in this century, tempered by
20 war, disciplined by a hard and bitter peace, proud of our ancient heritage—and unwilling to witness or permit the slow undoing of those human rights to which this Nation has always been committed, and to which we are committed today at home and
25 around the world.

Let every nation know, whether it wishes us well or ill, that we shall pay any price, bear any burden, meet any hardship, support any friend, oppose any foe to assure the survival and the
30 success of liberty.

This much we pledge—and more.

To those old allies whose cultural and spiritual origins we share, we pledge the loyalty of faithful friends. United, there is little we cannot do in a
35 host of cooperative ventures. Divided, there is little we can do—for we dare not meet a powerful challenge at odds and split asunder.

To those new states whom we welcome to the ranks of the free, we pledge our word that one
40 form of colonial control shall not have passed away merely to be replaced by a far more iron tyranny. We shall not always expect to find them supporting our view. But we shall always hope to find them strongly supporting their own freedom—and to
45 remember that, in the past, those who foolishly sought power by riding the back of the tiger ended up inside.

To those people in the huts and villages of half the globe struggling to break the bonds of mass
50 misery, we pledge our best efforts to help them help themselves, for whatever period is required— not because the Communists may be doing it, not because we seek their votes, but because it is right. If a free society cannot help the many who are
55 poor, it cannot save the few who are rich.

To our sister republics south of our border, we offer a special pledge—to convert our good words into good deeds—in a new alliance for progress—to assist free men and free governments
60 in casting off the chains of poverty. But this peaceful revolution of hope cannot become the prey of hostile powers. Let all our neighbors know that we shall join with them to oppose aggression or subversion anywhere in the Americas. And
65 let every other power know that this hemisphere intends to remain the master of its own house.

To that world assembly of sovereign states, the United Nations, our last best hope in an age where the instruments of war have far outpaced
70 the instruments of peace, we renew our pledge of support—to prevent it from becoming merely a forum for invective—to strengthen its shield of the new and the weak—and to enlarge the area in which its writ may run.

Test 1

41

Why did the author talk about the power?

A) in order to show some possible dreadful consequences

B) because there is hope despite its negative aspects

C) in order to emphasize its ambiguity

D) because its negative aspects surpass its positive aspects

42

Which of the following is the best interpretation of the second paragraph in connection with the first paragraph?

A) generalization

B) specification

C) cause and effect

D) comparison and contrast

43

Why did the author mention that first revolution?

A) to improve the strength of the present revolution

B) to stress the necessity of a certain kind of continuity

C) because the present revolution is not as powerful as the first one was

D) because the author is ashamed of the current generation who are incapable of maintaining the revolution that began long ago

44

What does "the word" (Line 16) refer to?

A) revolution

B) heirs

C) linguistic approach

D) revolutionary concept

45

Which of the following is most directly related with the concept of "torch" (Line 18)?

A) democracy

B) revolution

C) human rights

D) history

46

What's probably the most direct role of "bitter peace" (Line 20) in the passage as a whole?

A) to emphasize the difficulties involved in dealing with the present reality

B) to demonstrate the differences between it and war

C) to instill foreboding about a possibly dreadful future.

D) to emphasize the need of revolution

New SAT Reading Prep

Test 1

47

According to the passage, which of the following is most consistent with the author's argument?

A) America as a nation will not tolerate the weakening of human rights.

B) Wars can irreversibly change the nature of a certain group of people.

C) Challenge is part of America's tradition.

D) America will cherish human rights for decades to come.

48

Which of the following gives the best evidence to support the answer to the previous question?

A) 1st paragraph

B) 2nd paragraph

C) 3rd paragraph

D) 4th paragraph

49

What is the author's attitude toward freedom?

A) He will never make any compromise that jeopardizes it.

B) He cares more about getting it than about defending it.

C) He is rather pessimistic about it.

D) Poor people living in the countryside need more help defending it than rich people living in urban areas.

50

Which of the following gives the best evidence to support the answer to the previous question?

A) 3rd paragraph

B) 4th paragraph

C) 5th paragraph

D) 6th & 7th paragraph

STOP

TEST 2

Test 2

Reading | 65 minutes, 52 questions

DIRECTIONS

Each passage below is followed by a number of questions. After reading each passage, choose the best answer to each question based on what is stated or implied in the passage.

Questions 1-10 are based on the following passage.

When in the Course of human events, it becomes necessary for one people to dissolve the political bands which have connected them with another, and to assume among the powers of the
[5] earth, the separate and equal station to which the Laws of Nature and of Nature's God entitle them, a decent respect to the opinions of mankind requires that they should declare the causes which impel them to the separation.

[10] We hold these truths to be self-evident, that all men are created equal, that they are endowed by their Creator with certain unalienable Rights, that among these are Life, Liberty and the pursuit of Happiness.—That to secure these
[15] rights, Governments are instituted among Men, deriving their just powers from the consent of the governed, —That whenever any Form of Government becomes destructive of these ends, it is the Right of the People to alter or to abolish
[20] it, and to institute new Government, laying its foundation on such principles and organizing its powers in such form, as to them shall seem most likely to effect their Safety and Happiness. Prudence, indeed, will dictate that Governments
[25] long established should not be changed for light and transient causes; and accordingly all experience hath shewn, that mankind are more disposed to suffer, while evils are sufferable, than to right themselves by abolishing the forms to which they
[30] are accustomed. But when a long train of abuses and usurpations, pursuing invariably the same Object evinces a design to reduce them under absolute Despotism, it is their right, it is their duty, to throw off such Government, and to provide new
[35] Guards for their future security. Such has been the patient sufferance of these Colonies; and such is now the necessity which constrains them to alter their former Systems of Government. The history of the present King of Great Britain is a history
[40] of repeated injuries and usurpations, all having in direct object the establishment of an absolute Tyranny over these States. To prove this, let Facts be submitted to a candid world.

He has refused his Assent to Laws, the most
[45] wholesome and necessary for the public good.

He has forbidden his Governors to pass Laws of immediate and pressing importance, unless suspended in their operation till his Assent should be obtained; and when so suspended, he has utterly
[50] neglected to attend to them.

He has refused to pass other Laws for the accommodation of large districts of people, unless those people would relinquish the right of Representation in the Legislature, a right
[55] inestimable to them and formidable to tyrants only.

He has called together legislative bodies at places unusual, uncomfortable, and distant from the depository of their public Records, for the sole
[60] purpose of fatiguing them into compliance with his measures.

Test 2

1

Which of the following can be inferred about "separation" (Line 9) in the passage?

A) In order to achieve it, the laws of nature and of nature's God must be understood in advance.

B) In order for that to happen, why it must happen must also be revealed because whoever needs it requires others' agreement.

C) It cannot be accomplished by human enterprise alone.

D) The cause of it cannot be separated from that of occupying a land.

2

Which of the following is the closest in meaning to "assume" as used in line 4?

A) speculate

B) contemplate

C) apprehend

D) take

3

Which of the following cannot be implied from the first paragraph?

A) the reason for severing a relationship

B) the reason some new link can be forged

C) prerequisites for some link to be broken

D) the way in which politics and religion are connected

4

Which of the following is most likely to be part of truths?

A) Sometimes people need to dissolve the political bands connecting them with others.

B) Due to their political differences, a group of people must sometimes separate itself from another.

C) Disconnecting two political groups necessitates that the cause of the disconnection be known.

D) Most political collaborations are undesirable.

5

According to the passage, what can be said about the equality of men?

A) It depends on a person's nationality.

B) It is a product of individuality.

C) It is directly related to America's Declaration of Independence.

D) Political separation is a prerequisite for both human and national equality.

6

Which of the following is the best interpretation of the pursuit of happiness?

A) It is one of the scores of rights that cannot be taken away by a whim of the government.

B) Being one of the most integral rights it can never be taken away.

C) Its existence depends directly on the other two unalienable rights.

D) It is involved with the source of power necessary to justify a political disconnection.

Test 2

7

Which of the following is a prerequisite for "Life" and "Liberty" (Line 13)?

A) pursuit of Happiness

B) a certain form of mutual understanding

C) agreement among the governed

D) manipulation of the people by the governors

8

Which of the following is consistent with the author's arguments?

A) Without the three fundamental rights, no government can be founded.

B) The people's right to fight against repressive governments is more important than liberty in general.

C) As a right, Life is as important as any other right.

D) The people have a right to change their government if that change will result in improvements in their lives.

9

Which of the following serves as direct evidence for the answer to the previous question?

A) Lines 1-9 ("When…separation.")

B) Lines 10-13 ("We hold…Liberty")

C) Lines 14-17 ("That to…the governed,")

D) Lines 19-22 ("it is…shall seem")

10

In context, what is the author trying to say by "Laws" (Line 44)?

A) English laws

B) international laws

C) common sense

D) politically advanced laws

New SAT Reading Prep

Questions 11-20 are based on the following passage.

Like every concrete political conception, Fascism is thought and action. It is action with an inherent doctrine which, arising out of a given system of historic forces, is inserted in it and works on it from within. It has therefore a form co-related to the contingencies of time and place; but it has at the same time an ideal content which elevates it into a formula of truth in the higher region of the history of thought. There is no way of exercising a spiritual influence on the things of the world by means of a human will-power commanding the wills of others, without first having a clear conception of the particular and transient reality on which the will-power must act, and without also having a clear conception of the universal and permanent reality in which the particular and transient reality has its life and being. To know men we must have a knowledge of man; and to have a knowledge of man we must know the reality of things and their laws. There can be no conception of a State which is not fundamentally a conception of Life. It is a philosophy or intuition, a system of ideas which evolves itself into a system of logical contraction, or which concentrates itself in a vision or in a faith, but which is always, at least virtually, an organic conception of the world.

Fascism would therefore not be understood in many of its manifestations (as, for example, in its organisations of the Party, its system of education, its discipline) were it not considered in the light of its general view of life. A spiritualised view. To Fascism the world is not this material world which appears on the surface, in which man is an individual separated from all other men, standing by himself and subject to a natural law which instinctively impels him to lead a life of momentary and egoistic pleasure. In Fascism man is an individual who is the nation and the country. He is this by a moral law which embraces and binds together individuals and generations in an established tradition and mission, a moral law which suppresses the instinct to lead a life confined to a brief cycle of pleasure in order, instead, to replace it within the orbit of duty in a superior conception of life, free from the limits of time and space a life in which the individual by self-abnegation and by the sacrifice of his particular interests, even by death, realises the entirely spiritual existence in which his value as a man consists.

It is therefore a spiritual conception, itself also a result of the general reaction of the Century against the languid and materialistic positivism of the Eighteenth Century. Anti-positivist, but positive: neither sceptical nor agnostic, neither pessimistic nor passively optimistic, as are in general the doctrines (all of them negative) which place the centre of life outside of man, who by his free will can and should create his own world for himself. Fascism wants a man to be active and to be absorbed in action with all his energies; it wants him to have a manly consciousness of the difficulties that exist and to be ready to face them. It conceives life as a struggle, thinking that it is the duty of man to conquer that life which is really worthy of him: creating in the first place within himself the (physical, moral, intellectual) instrument with which to build it. As for the individual, so for the nation, so for mankind. Hence the high value of culture in all its forms (art, religion, science) and the supreme importance of education. Hence also the essential value of labour, with which man conquers nature and creates the human world (economic, political, moral, intellectual).

This positive conception of life is evidently an ethical conception. And it comprises the whole reality as well as the human activity which domineers it. No action is to be removed from the moral sense; nothing is to be in the world that is divested of the importance which belongs to it in respect of moral aims. Life, therefore, as the Fascist conceives it, is serious, austere, religious; entirely balanced in a world sustained by the moral and responsible forces of the spirit. The Fascist disdains the "easy" life.

Fascism is a religious conception in which man is considered to be in the powerful grip of a superior law, with an objective which transcends the particular individual and elevates him into a fully conscious member of a spiritual society. Anyone who has stopped short at the mere consideration of opportunism in the religious policy of the Fascist Regime, has failed to understand that Fascism, besides being a system of government, is also a system of thought.

11

What could be the best title of the passage?

A) The history of fascism

B) The philosophy of fascism

C) Fascism as a philosophy

D) Different perspectives of a concept

12

According to the passage, what can be said about the "form" (Line 5) of fascism?

A) It possesses impractical content that brings fascism a recipe of truth in theory.

B) It is impossible to spiritually influence the world using human will-power without using this form.

C) It is a philosophy or intuition, a system of ideas which evolves itself into a system of logical contraction, or which concentrates itself in a vision or in a faith.

D) It can change depending upon when and where fascism is practiced.

13

Which choice gives the best evidence for the answer to the previous question?

A) "It has at the same time an ideal content which elevates it into a formula of truth in the higher region of the history of thought." (Lines 6-9)

B) "It has therefore a form co-related to the contingencies of time and place." (Lines 5-6)

C) "There is no way of exercising a spiritual influence on the things of the world by means of a human will-power commanding the wills of others." (Lines 9-12)

D) "It is action with an inherent doctrine which, arising out of a given system of historic forces, is inserted in it and works on it from within." (Lines 2-5)

14

Why did the author argue that fascism cannot be understood by looking at its approach to education?

A) because it is a blatant lie

B) because it is a living conception of the world and the world can change

C) because it is based on intuition

D) because it usually has dreadful consequences

15

Which choice gives the best evidence for the answer to the previous question?

A) "but which is always, at least virtually, an organic conception of the world" (Lines 25-26)

B) "It is a philosophy or intuition, a system of ideas which evolves itself into a system of logical contraction, or which concentrates itself in a vision or in a faith." (Lines 23-25)

C) "There can be no conception of a State which is not fundamentally a conception of Life." (Lines 20-22)

D) "to have a knowledge of man we must know the reality of things and their laws" (Lines 19-20)

16

According to the passage, what is the connection between the various conceptions of fascism?

A) a simple listing of each conception in turn

B) a series of conceptions leading to a final conception

C) one conception to be elaborated on by another conception

D) a conception that serves as a foundation for all other conceptions

Test 2

17

According to the passage, why is fascism a spiritual conception?

A) because each person in a fascist country is an embodiment of the nation itself

B) because everybody in fascism is in absolutely spiritual surroundings in which his or her worth is suited for the surroundings

C) because people in fascist societies believe that their value consists of their metaphysical essence

D) because people in fascism are not really alone in their ideology

18

Which choice gives the best evidence for the answer to the previous question?

A) "He is this by a moral law which embraces and binds together individuals and generations in an established tradition and mission," (Lines 39-41)

B) "by self-abnegation and by the sacrifice of his particular interests, even by death, realises the entirely spiritual existence in which his value as a man consists." (Lines 46-50)

C) "a moral law which suppresses the instinct to lead a life confined to a brief cycle of pleasure in order, instead, to replace it within the orbit of duty in a superior conception of life, free from the limits of time and space" (Lines 41-46)

D) "itself also a result of the general reaction of the Century against the languid and materialistic positivism of the Eighteenth Century." (Lines 51-54)

19

As used in lines 47, "abnegation" most nearly means

A) denial
B) offering
C) retreat
D) diffidence

20

According to the last paragraph of the passage, in Fascism, that Fascism is a religious conception can be translated that

A) Fascism is much more than just a system of control.

B) According to fascist ideology people must have their own religion.

C) Only religious people can belong to a fascist society.

D) In a fascist society nobody should be opportunistic about the religious policies of fascism.

New SAT Reading Prep

Test 2

Questions 21-30 are based on the following passage.

I call our world Flatland, not because we call it so, but to make its nature clearer to you, my happy readers, who are privileged to live in Space. Imagine a vast sheet of paper on which straight
[5] Lines, Triangles, Squares, Pentagons, Hexagons, and other figures, instead of remaining fixed in their places, move freely about, on or in the surface, but without the power of rising above or sinking below it, very much like shadows—
[10] only hard with luminous edges— and you will then have a pretty correct notion of my country and countrymen. Alas, a few years ago, I should have said "my universe:" but now my mind has been opened to higher views of things. In such
[15] a country, you will perceive at once that it is impossible that there should be anything of what you call a "solid" kind; but I dare say you will suppose that we could at least distinguish by sight the Triangles, Squares, and other figures, moving
[20] about as I have described them. On the contrary, we could see nothing of the kind, not at least so as to distinguish one figure from another. Nothing was visible, nor could be visible, to us, except Straight Lines; and the necessity of this I will
[25] speedily demonstrate. Place a penny on the middle of one of your tables in Space; and leaning over it, look down upon it. It will appear a circle. But now, drawing back to the edge of the table, gradually lower your eye (thus bringing yourself more and
[30] more into the condition of the inhabitants of Flatland), and you will find the penny becoming more and more oval to your view, and at last when you have placed your eye exactly on the edge of the table (so that you are, as it were, actually a
[35] Flatlander) the penny will then have ceased to appear oval at all, and will have become, so far as you can see, a straight line. The same thing would happen if you were to treat in the same way a Triangle, or a Square, or any other figure cut out
[40] from pasteboard. As soon as you look at it with your eye on the edge of the table, you will find that it ceases to appear to you as a figure, and that it becomes in appearance a straight line. Take for example an equilateral Triangle— who represents
[45] with us a Tradesman of the respectable class. Figure 1 represents the Tradesman as you would see him while you were bending over him from above; figures 2 and 3 represent the Tradesman, as you would see him if your eye were close to the level,
[50] or all but on the level of the table; and if your eye were quite on the level of the table (and that is how we see him in Flatland) you would see nothing but a straight line. When I was in Spaceland I heard that your sailors have very similar experiences
[55] while they traverse your seas and discern some distant island or coast lying on the horizon. The far-off land may have bays, forelands, angles in and out to any number and extent; yet at a distance you see none of these (unless indeed your sun
[60] shines bright upon them revealing the projections and retirements by means of light and shade), nothing but a grey unbroken line upon the water. Well, that is just what we see when one of our triangular or other acquaintances comes towards
[65] us in Flatland. As there is neither sun with us, nor any light of such a kind as to make shadows, we have none of the helps to the sight that you have in Spaceland. If our friend comes closer to us we see his line becomes larger; if he leaves us it
[70] becomes smaller; but still he looks like a straight line; be he a Triangle, Square, Pentagon, Hexagon, Circle, what you will— a straight Line he looks and nothing else. You may perhaps ask how under these disadvantageous circumstances we are able to
[75] distinguish our friends from one another: but the answer to this very natural question will be more fitly and easily given when I come to describe the inhabitants of Flatland. For the present let me defer this subject, and say a word or two about the
[80] climate and houses in our country.

Test 2

21
What could be the best title for the passage?

A) The merits of living on land that is flat

B) A comparison and contrast between Flatland and Spaceland

C) The difficulties associated with living in Flatland

D) The nature of Flatland

22
According to the author, why does a person look like a flat line?

A) because of perspective

B) because the observer is in space

C) because the observer is on a flat land

D) because of the way the observer looks at things

23
According to the passage, which choice will determine whether or not an island and a ship look the same?

A) their shapes

B) their distance from the observer

C) the observer's reasoning

D) their surroundings

24
Why does the author call his world flatland?

A) because this is actually the real shape of his world

B) because the readers live happily in Space

C) because the readers lack imagination even though they enjoy having certain rights

D) because the readers must be informed of something about the world

25
What is the role of quotations around the word "solid" (Line 17) in the passage?

A) emphasis

B) indicating a dual meaning

C) irony

D) showing some level of misunderstanding

26
Which choice gives the best evidence for the answer to the previous question?

A) "but I dare say you will suppose that we could at least distinguish by sight the Triangles, Squares, and other figures, moving about as I have described them." (Lines 17-20)

B) "On the contrary, we could see nothing of the kind, not at least so as to distinguish one figure from another." (Lines 20-22)

C) "the necessity of this I will speedily demonstrate." (Lines 24-25)

D) "but now my mind has been opened to higher views of things." (Lines 13-14)

New SAT Reading Prep   70

Test 2

27

In context, which choice most nearly means the same as "solid" as used in line 17?

A) hardened
B) unmistakable
C) distinguishable
D) strong

28

It can be inferred that in Flatland one way to tell apart objects of different shapes would be to

A) look at them from a distance
B) be helped by sunlight shining on them
C) find a solid object
D) get really close to the objects being observed

29

According to the passage, why does the author mention Pentagon?

A) to talk about a specific characteristic of some shape
B) to expound on the difficulties involved in distinguishing specific shapes
C) to explain how the shape of an object is of no help when attempting to distinguish one from another
D) to describe the universal problem of too much geometric complication

30

The answer to which question gives the best evidence for the answer to the previous question?

A) Question 22
B) Question 24
C) Question 27
D) Question 28

71

Test 2

Questions 31-42 are based on the following passage.

In 'What was the Gunpowder Plot? The Traditional Story tested by Original Evidence,' Father Gerard has set forth all the difficulties he found while sifting the accessible evidence, and
5 has deduced from his examination a result which, though somewhat vague in itself, leaves upon his readers a very distinct impression that the celebrated conspiracy was mainly, if not altogether, a fiction devised by the Earl of Salisbury for the
10 purpose of maintaining or strengthening his position in the government of the country under James I. Such, at least, is what I gather of Father Gerard's aim from a perusal of his book. Lest, however, I should in any way do him an injustice,
15 I proceed to quote the summary placed by him at the conclusion of his argument:—

"The evidence available to us appears to establish principally two points: that the true history of the Gunpowder Plot is now known to
20 no man, and that the history commonly received is certainly untrue. "It is quite impossible to believe that the Government were not aware of the Plot long before they announced its discovery. "It is difficult to believe that the proceedings of
25 the conspirators were actually such as they are related to have been. "It is unquestionable that the Government consistently falsified the story and the evidence as presented to the world, and that the points upon which they most insisted prove upon
30 examination to be the most doubtful. "There are grave reasons for the conclusion that the whole transaction was dexterously contrived for the purpose which in fact it opportunely served, by those who alone reaped benefit from it, and who
35 showed themselves so unscrupulous in the manner of reaping."

No candid person, indeed, can feel surprise that any English Roman Catholic, especially a Roman Catholic priest, should feel anxious to wipe
40 away the reproach which the plot has brought upon those who share his faith. Not merely were his spiritual predecessors subjected to a persecution borne with the noblest and least self-assertive constancy, simply in consequence of what is now
45 known to all historical students to have been the entirely false charge that the plot emanated from, or was approved by the English Roman Catholics as a body, but this false belief prevailed so widely that it must have hindered, to no slight extent, the
50 spread of that organization which he regards as having been set forth by divine institution for the salvation of mankind. If Father Gerard has gone farther than this, and has attempted to show that even the handful of Catholics who took part in
55 the plot were more sinned against than sinning, I, for one, am not inclined to condemn him very harshly, even if I am forced to repudiate alike his method and his conclusions. Erroneous as I hold them, Father Gerard's conclusions at least call for
60 patient inquiry. Up to this time critics have urged that parts at least of the public declarations of the Government were inconsistent with the evidence, and have even pointed to deliberate falsification. Father Gerard is, as far as I know, the first to
65 go a step farther, and to argue that much of the evidence itself has been tampered with, on the ground that it is inconsistent with physical facts, so that things cannot possibly have happened as they are said to have happened in confessions attributed
70 to the conspirators themselves. I can only speak for myself when I say that after reading much hostile criticism of Father Gerard's book— and I would especially refer to a most able review of it, so far as negative criticism can go, in the Edinburgh
75 Review of January last— I did not feel that all difficulties had been removed, or that without further investigation I could safely maintain my former attitude towards the traditional story. It is, indeed, plain, as the Edinburgh Review has
80 shown, that Father Gerard is unversed in the methods of historical inquiry which have guided recent scholars. Yet, for all that, he gives us hard nuts to crack; and, till they are cracked, the story of Gunpowder Plot cannot be allowed to settle
85 down in peace. It seems strange to find a writer so regardless of what is, in these days, considered the first canon of historical inquiry, that evidence worth having must be almost entirely the evidence of contemporaries who are in a position to know
90 something about that which they assert.

Test 2

31

What is the role of the first paragraph in relation to the rest of the passage?

A) aside
B) background
C) introduction
D) generalization

32

What is the author's intention for writing this passage?

A) to criticize some general problems common among reviewers of historical events
B) to depict how the government had falsified certain evidence
C) to attempt to give a fair and unbiased review of a historical commentary
D) to demonstrate what was wrong with the Gunpowder plot

33

According to the author, what might be Father Gerard's problem?

A) His bottom lines need patient investigation.
B) His method is not compatible with his conclusions.
C) He is simply not qualified to conduct a historical investigation.
D) He made the mistake of giving us a very difficult assignment to handle.

34

Which of the following provides the best evidence for the answer to the previous question?

A) "Father Gerard is unversed in the methods of historical inquiry which have guided recent scholars." (Lines 80-82)
B) "It is unquestionable that the Government consistently falsified the story and the evidence as presented to the world, and that the points upon which they most insisted prove upon examination to be the most doubtful." (Lines 26-30)
C) "Yet, for all that, he gives us hard nuts to crack." (Lines 82-83)
D) "Erroneous as I hold them, Father Gerard's conclusions at least call for patient inquiry." (Lines 58-60)

35

According to the passage, who must be his spiritual predecessors?

A) spiritual leaders of old times
B) previous Roman Catholic priests
C) most religious people
D) those who might be persecuted for religious reasons

73

36

Which of the following is strongly suggested by the first sentence of the third paragraph of the passage?

A) The plot was a protestant blasphemy.
B) The plot was devised by Roman Catholics.
C) The consequences of the plot probably worked against the Roman Catholic creed.
D) The plot was designed to attack the main articles of faith held by Roman Catholics.

37

According to the passage, what is most likely to be the primary principle when someone is making a historical investigation?

A) Almost every piece of evidence must be contemporary.
B) Only contemporaries can produce any worthwhile evidence.
C) Only contemporaries who have expertise relevant to the evidence they are dealing with can offer valid opinions.
D) It is frequently ignored by people like Father Gerald.

38

Which of the following provides the best evidence for the answer to the previous question?

A) "till they are cracked, the story of Gunpowder Plot cannot be allowed to settle down in peace." (Lines 83-85)
B) "the first canon of historical inquiry, that evidence worth having must be almost entirely the evidence of contemporaries who are in a position to know something about that which they assert." (Lines 87-90)
C) "It seems strange to find a writer so regardless of what is, in these days, considered the first canon of historical inquiry," (Lines 85-87)
D) "Father Gerard is unversed in the methods of historical inquiry which have guided recent scholars." (Lines 80-82)

39

In context, what is the author probably trying to say in the second sentence of the third paragraph of the passage?

A) The plot did not do anything wrong.
B) It was an injustice that those involved in the plot were unfairly persecuted rather than fairly prosecuted.
C) Roman Catholic priests should not be the only ones who are prosecuted.
D) Students of History usually have false understanding of the plot.

Test 2

40

According to the passage, which of the following is the best appreciation of the author's attitude toward Father Gerald's conclusions?

A) hard to grasp

B) ill-conceived

C) with no practical evidence

D) patient

41

According to the passage, probably why does the author say "hard nut to crack"?

A) because Father Gerald has made the case very difficult to solve

B) because he raised important suspicions regarding certain fabrications

C) because the Catholics involved in the plot were the worst sinners of their time

D) because the case is unlikely to be solved in the foreseeable future

42

Which of the following provides the best evidence for the answer to the previous question?

A) "till they are cracked,…down in peace." (Lines 83-85)

B) "that Father Gerard is…recent scholars." (Lines 80-82)

C) "I did not feel that all difficulties had been removed, or…towards the traditional story." (Lines 75-78)

D) "the first to go a step farther,… conspirators themselves." (Lines 64-70)

Test 2

Questions 43-52 are based on the following passage.

Psychological warfare is waged before, during, and after war; it is not waged against the opposing psychological warfare operators; it is not controlled by the laws, usages, and customs of war; and it
5 cannot be defined in terms of terrain, order of battle, or named engagements. It is a continuous process. Success or failure is often known only months or years after the execution of the operation. Yet success, though incalculable, can be
10 overwhelming; and failure, though undetectable, can be mortal. Psychological warfare does not fit readily into familiar concepts of war. Military science owes much of its precision and definiteness to its dealing with a well-defined subject, the
15 application of organized lawful violence. The officer or soldier can usually undertake his task of applying mass violence without having to determine upon the enemy. The opening of war, recognition of neutrals, the listing of enemies,
20 proclamation of peace— such problems are considered political, and outside the responsibility of the soldier. Even in the application of force short of war, the soldier proceeds only when the character of the military operation is prescribed by
25 higher (that is, political) authorities, and after the enemies are defined by lawful and authoritative command. In one field only, psychological warfare, is there endless uncertainty as to the very nature of the operation. Psychological warfare, by the
30 nature of its instruments and its mission, begins long before the declaration of war. Psychological warfare continues after overt hostilities have stopped. The enemy often avoids identifying himself in psychological warfare; much of the
35 time, he is disguised as the voice of home, of God, of the church, of the friendly press. Offensively, the psychological warfare operator must fight antagonists who never answer back— the enemy audience. He cannot fight the one enemy who is
40 in plain sight, the hostile psychological warfare operator, because the hostile operator is greedily receptive to attack. Neither success nor defeat are measurable factors. Psychological strategy is planned along the edge of nightmare.
45 In a formal approach to this mysterious part of the clean-cut process of war, it might be desirable to start with Euclidian demonstrations, proceeding from definition to definition until the subject-matter had been delimited by logic.
50 Alternatively it might be interesting to try a historical approach, describing the development of psychological warfare through the ages. The best approach is perhaps afforded by a simplification of both a logical and historical approach. For
55 concrete examples it is most worthwhile to look at instances of psychological warfare taken out of history down to World War II. Then the definitions and working relationships can be traced and with these in mind— a somewhat more
60 detailed and critical appraisal of World Wars I and II organizations and operations can be undertaken. If a historian or philosopher picks up this book, he will find much with which to quarrel, but for the survey of so hard-to-define a subject, this
65 may be a forgivable fault. Psychological warfare and propaganda are each as old as mankind; but it has taken modern specialization to bring them into focus as separate subjects. The materials for their history lie scattered through thousands of
70 books and it is therefore impossible to brief them. Any reader contemplating retirement from the army to a sedentary life is urged to take up this subject. A history of propaganda would provide not only a new light on many otherwise odd or
75 trivial historical events; it would throw genuine illumination on the process of history itself. There are however numerous instances which can be cited to show applications of psychological warfare.

Test 2

43

What could be the best title of the passage?

A) The nature of a certain intriguing war enterprise

B) The reasons for the complications of psychological warfare

C) The relation between war and psychological warfare

D) The history of psychological warfare

44

Which of the following is true of the connection between war and the soldier?

A) Soldiers usually resort to using force short of actually going to war.

B) Soldiers have absolutely nothing to with problems during war, which are not concerned with military force.

C) During a war soldiers are probably not likely to be involved in psychological warfare.

D) Conducting psychological warfare is not a clear-cut matter.

45

According to the passage, which of the following is true of the connection between war and psychological warfare?

A) The duration of psychological warfare depends on that of the corresponding war.

B) Psychological warfare necessarily lasts longer than the war itself.

C) Psychological warfare must stop if the enemy ceases its war effort.

D) In terms of the results produced psychological warfare is more effective than war itself.

46

Which choice gives the best evidence for the answer to the previous question?

A) "Offensively, the psychological warfare operator must fight antagonists who never answer back" (Lines 36-38)

B) "Psychological warfare; much of the time, he is disguised as the voice of home, of God, of the church, of the friendly press" (Lines 34-36)

C) "In one field only, psychological warfare, is there endless uncertainty as to the very nature of the operation." (Lines 27-29)

D) "Psychological warfare, by the nature of its instruments and its mission, begins long before the declaration of war. Psychological warfare continues after overt hostilities have stopped." (Lines 29-33)

47

Which of the following can be most likely be inferred about psychological warfare?

A) Before declaring war, a nation must prepare the details of how the war is going to be conducted.

B) Before declaring war nations must have prepared a detailed plan of how the war is going to be conducted.

C) Psychological warfare is much more complicated than war itself.

D) Psychological warfare requires more labor than war itself.

Test 2

48

Which choice gives the best evidence for the answer to the previous question?

A) "Military science owes much of its precision and definiteness to its dealing with a well-defined subject, the application of organized lawful violence." (Lines 12-15)

B) "He cannot fight the one enemy who is in plain sight, the hostile psychological warfare operator, because the hostile operator is greedily receptive to attack." (Lines 39-43)

C) "In one field only, psychological warfare, is there endless uncertainty as to the very nature of the operation." (Lines 27-29)

D) "Psychological warfare, by the nature of its instruments and its mission, begins long before the declaration of war." (Lines 29-31)

49

According to the passage, which of the following is most similar to psychological warfare?

A) The strategy of a kid who takes full advantage of a math book in order to pass a test.

B) A governmental plan to spread the rumor that a newly proposed medical plan will definitely work this time.

C) A national undertaking to collect money for the construction of shelters in preparation for heavy bombing during a war.

D) A government's plan to infiltrate a heavily guarded missile factory of a friendly nation.

50

Which choice gives the best evidence for the answer to the previous question?

A) "Neither success nor defeat are measurable factors." (Lines 42-43)

B) "A history of propaganda would provide not only a new light on many otherwise odd or trivial historical events." (Lines 73-75)

C) "Offensively, the psychological warfare operator must fight antagonists who never answer back" (Lines 36-38)

D) "There are however numerous instances which can be cited to show applications of psychological warfare." (Lines 76-78)

51

As used in line 24, "prescribed" most nearly means

A) cured
B) dictated
C) commended
D) depicted

52

According to the passage, which of the following is a trait of psychological warfare?

A) Its greatest enemy is those who don't respond.
B) It advances as quickly as history progresses.
C) Its precision relies on the application of military strategy.
D) Its objectives might go beyond just winning a war.

STOP

TEST 3

Test 3

Reading | 65 minutes, 51 questions

DIRECTIONS

Each passage below is followed by a number of questions. After reading each passage, choose the best answer to each question based on what is stated or implied in the passage.

Questions 1-10 are based on the following passage.

There were three great European nations in ancient days, each of which furnished history with a hero: the Greeks, the Carthaginians, and the Romans.

Alexander was the hero of the Greeks. He was [line 5] King of Macedon, a country lying north of Greece proper. He headed an army of his countrymen, and made an excursion for conquest and glory into Asia. He made himself master of all that quarter of the globe, and reigned over it in Babylon, till he [line 10] brought himself to an early grave by the excesses into which his boundless prosperity allured him. His fame rests on his triumphant success in building up for himself so vast an empire, and the admiration which his career has always excited [line 15] among mankind is heightened by the consideration of his youth, and of the noble and generous impulses which strongly marked his character.

The Carthaginian hero was Hannibal. We class the Carthaginians among the European nations [line 20] of antiquity; for, in respect to their origin, their civilization, and all their commercial and political relations, they belonged to the European race, though it is true that their capital was on the African side of the Mediterranean Sea. Hannibal [line 25] was the great Carthaginian hero. He earned his fame by the energy and implacableness of his hate. The work of his life was to keep a vast empire in a state of continual anxiety and terror for fifty years, so that his claim to greatness and glory rests on the [line 30] determination, the perseverance, and the success with which he fulfilled his function of being, while he lived, the terror of the world.

The Roman hero was Caesar. He was born just [line 35] one hundred years before the Christian era. His renown does not depend, like that of Alexander, on foreign conquests, nor, like that of Hannibal, on the terrible energy of his aggressions upon foreign foes, but upon his protracted and dreadful contests [line 40] with, and ultimate triumphs over, his rivals and competitors at home. When he appeared upon the stage, the Roman Empire already included nearly all of the world that was worth possessing. There were no more conquests to be made. Caesar did, [line 45] indeed, enlarge, in some degree, the boundaries of the empire; but the main question in his day was, who should possess the power which preceding conquerors had acquired.

The Roman Empire, as it existed in those [line 50] days, must not be conceived of by the reader as united together under one compact and consolidated government. It was, on the other hand, a vast congeries of nations, widely dissimilar in every respect from each other, speaking various [line 55] languages, and having various customs and laws. They were all, however, more or less dependent upon, and connected with, the great central power. Some of these countries were provinces, and were governed by officers appointed and sent out by the [line 60] authorities at Rome. These governors had to collect the taxes of their provinces, and also to preside over and direct, in many important respects, the administration of justice. They had, accordingly, abundant opportunities to enrich themselves while [line 65] thus in office, by collecting more money than

they paid over to the government at home, and by taking bribes to favor the rich man's cause in court. Thus the more wealthy and prosperous provinces were objects of great competition among aspirants
70 for office at Rome. Leading men would get these appointments, and, after remaining long enough in their provinces to acquire a fortune, would come back to Rome, and expend it in intrigues and maneuvers to obtain higher offices still.
75 Whenever there was any foreign war to be carried on with a distant nation or tribe, there was always a great eagerness among all the military officers of the state to be appointed to the command. They each felt sure that they should
80 conquer in the contest, and they could enrich themselves still more rapidly by the spoils of victory in war, than by extortion and bribes in the government of a province in peace. Then, besides, a victorious general coming back to Rome always
85 found that his military renown added vastly to his influence and power in the city. He was welcomed with celebrations and triumphs; the people flocked to see him and to shout his praise. He placed his trophies of victory in the temples, and entertained
90 the populace with games and shows, and with combats of gladiators or of wild beasts, which he had brought home with him for this purpose in the train of his army. While he was thus enjoying his triumph, his political enemies would be
95 thrown into the back ground and into the shade; unless, indeed, some one of them might himself be earning the same honors in some other field, to come back in due time, and claim his share of power and celebrity in his turn. In this case,
100 Rome would be sometimes distracted and rent by the conflicts and contentions of military rivals, who had acquired powers too vast for all the civil influences of the Republic to regulate or control.

1

What could be the best title of the passage?

A) The three greatest ancient nations
B) The three heroes in the greatest ancient nations
C) The history of Caesar
D) How Caesar rose to power

2

According to the passage, why did the author probably mention three heroes?

A) to talk about their significant differences
B) to stress the similarity that some nations have
C) to emphasize the differences between Caesar and the other two heroes
D) to lead into a more important topic

3

Which of the following is the main difference between Alexander and Hannibal?

A) Only one of them conquered a vast land area.
B) Only one of them had to deal mostly with domestic problems rather than having to invade foreign nations.
C) Only one of them had a horrific image.
D) They had dissimilar reasons for their conquest.

Test 3

4

Which of the following is the main difference between Alexander and Caesar?

A) Only one of them conquered a vast land area.

B) Only one of them had to deal with more of domestic problems than having to invade foreign nations.

C) Only one of them had a horrific image.

D) They had dissimilar reasons for their conquests.

5

According to the passage, of all the differences mentioned, which difference is most outstanding and why?

A) Alexander's, because he conquered the largest land area.

B) Hannibal's, because he had the most horrible image of all.

C) Caesar's, because he was born just one hundred years before the Christian era.

D) Caesar's, because he was in a significantly different circumstance than the other two who were in a more typical situation.

6

Which of the following is true of the Roman Empire?

A) Some of the nations in it had political independence.

B) The central government possessed absolute power in every aspect of life.

C) Although its nations had many differences, they had one thing in common.

D) The nations were different from each other in every way except for the central government.

7

As used in line 53, "congeries" most nearly means

A) aggregate

B) host

C) collectivity

D) congregation

8

According to the passage, in Roman Empire probably who would get the most profit?

A) the officials in the central government at Rome

B) the king of each nation conquered by Rome

C) the governors sent to the provinces by Rome

D) the officials at Rome bribed by the governors appointed for the conquered nations

New SAT Reading Prep

Test 3

9

Which choice gives the best evidence for the answer to the previous question?

A) "after remaining long enough in their provinces to acquire a fortune," (Lines 71-72)

B) "These governors had to collect the taxes of their provinces, and also to preside over and direct, in many important respects, the administration of justice." (Lines 60-63)

C) "They were all, however, more or less dependent upon, and connected with, the great central power." (Lines 56-57)

D) "they paid over to the government at home, and by taking bribes to favor the rich man's cause in court." (Lines 66-67)

10

According to the passage, which of the following is true of victorious generals returning to Rome?

A) They were welcomed because everyone knew they would try to acquire political power.

B) Their influence as war generals was surpassed by their role in entertaining the populace.

C) Most of them showed their strength by fighting with gladiators or with wild beasts.

D) They considered war a way of gaining wealth.

Questions 12-20 are based on the following passage.

The raw materials from which the food and tissue-building compounds of plants are synthesized include carbon dioxide, oxygen, water, nitrogen, phosphorus, sulfur, potassium,
5 calcium, magnesium, and iron. The two gases first mentioned are derived directly from the air, through the respiratory organs of the plant. Water is taken into the plant chiefly from the soil, through its fibrous roots. All the other elements
10 in the list are taken from the soil, nitrogen being derived from decaying organic matter (the original source of the nitrogen is, however, the atmosphere, from which the initial supply of nitrogen is obtained by direct assimilation by certain bacteria
15 and perhaps other low forms of plant life), and the remaining ones from the mineral compounds of the soil.

Carbon dioxide and oxygen, being derived from the air, are always available to the leaves and
20 stems of growing plants in unlimited supply; but the supply available to a seed when germinating in the soil, or to the roots of a growing farm crop, may sometimes become inadequate, especially in soils of a very compact texture, or "water-logged"
25 soils. In such cases, the deficiency of these gaseous food elements may become a limiting factor in plant growth.

Water is often a limiting factor in plant growth. Experiments which have been repeated
30 many times and under widely varying conditions show that when water is supplied to a plant in varying amounts, by increasing the percentage of water in the soil in which the plant is growing by regular increments up to the saturation point, the
35 growth of the plant, or yield of the crop, increases up to a certain point and then falls off because the excess of water reduces the supply of air which is available to the plant roots. Hence, abundance of water is, in general, a most essential factor in plant
40 growth.

Under normal conditions of air and moisture supply, however, the plant food elements which may be considered to be the limiting factors in the nutrition and growth of plants are the chemical
45 elements mentioned in the list above.

The plant food materials which are taken from the soil by a growing plant must enter it by osmosis through the semi-permeable membranes which constitute the epidermis of the root-hairs,
50 and circulate through the plant either carried in solution in the sap or by osmosis from cell to cell. Hence, they must be in water-soluble form before they can be utilized by plants. Obviously, therefore, only those compounds of these elements
55 in the soil which are soluble in the soil water are available as plant food. The greater proportion of the soil elements are present there in the form of compounds which are so slightly soluble in water as to be unavailable to plants. The processes
60 by which these practically insoluble compounds become gradually changed into soluble forms are chiefly the "weathering" action of air and water (particularly if the latter contains carbonic acid) and the action of the organic acids resulting from
65 decaying animal or vegetable matter or secreted by living plants.

Test 3

11

What would be the best title of the passage?

A) Diverse chemical elements comprising plant food
B) Sources of plant food elements
C) Plant food elements
D) Indispensable chemical elements in plant growth

which cannot be one of the 'chemical elements'.

12

Why were different chemical elements mentioned in the first paragraph?

A) to show the variety involved
B) to demonstrate the similarities between them
C) to delve into some biological differences
D) to establish some foundation for classification

13

What is the role of the second paragraph in connection to the first one?

A) cause and effect
B) specification
C) exemplification
D) comparison and contrast

14

According to the passage, which of the following is true of oxygen and water?

A) They come from the same source.
B) They function in practically the same fashion.
C) They might have different availability.
D) Too much of either can work against the growth of a plant.

15

Which of the following is the most direct evidence for the answer to the previous question?

A) limiting factor
B) in varying amounts
C) always available
D) reduces the supply of air

16

According to the passage, which of the following is the most unique feature of water in plant growth?

A) It is a constant limiting factor.
B) It inhibits the increment pattern of plant growth.
C) Its amount must vary to fit the needs of plant growth.
D) The efficiency of its role has to do with other essential element.

Test 3

17

What would be the most probable reason the author said "however" (Line 12)?

A) because there are many limiting factors

B) because the definition of certain elements is dictated by some surrounding conditions

C) because the author didn't like the way the previous paragraph ends

D) because water is not the most important limiting factor

18

Which of the following is the most direct evidence for the answer to the previous question?

A) limiting factor

B) in varying amounts

C) always available

D) under normal conditions

19

Why did the author mention "osmosis" (Line 51)?

A) to show one of many possible ways for nutrients to be absorbed into plants

B) to set up a criterion by which to improve efficiency

C) to talk about availability and limitation of a certain intake, which provides a criterion for classifying plant foods

D) to show how insoluble some elements in water are, the solubility of which gives a significant ingredient of plant food classification

20

What is the role of the last paragraph in the passage as a whole?

A) a solution to the problem presented by the passage

B) a very cautious conclusion

C) a decent elaboration of a concept proposed in the rest of the passage

D) adding a new perspective to the previous discussion

Test 3

Questions 21-30 are based on the following passage.

The appearances in the heavens have from earliest historic ages filled men with wonder and awe; then they gradually became a source of questioning, and thinkers sought for explanations of the daily and nightly phenomena of sun, moon and stars. Scientific astronomy, however, was an impossibility until an exact system of chronology was devised. Meanwhile men puzzled over the shape of the earth, its position in the universe, what the stars were and why the positions of some shifted, and what those fiery comets were that now and again appeared and struck terror to their hearts. In answer to such questions, the Chaldean thinkers, slightly before the rise of the Greek schools of philosophy, developed the idea of the seven heavens in their crystalline spheres encircling the earth as their center. This conception seems to lie back of both the later Egyptian and Hebraic cosmologies, as well as of the Ptolemaic. Through the visits of Greek philosophers to Egyptian shores this conception helped to shape Greek thought and so indirectly affected western civilization. Thus our heritage in astronomical thought, as in many other lines, comes from the Greeks and the Romans reaching Europe (in part through Arabia and Spain), where it was shaped by the influence of the schools down to the close of the Middle Ages when men began anew to withstand authority in behalf of observation and were not afraid to follow whither their reason led them. But not all Greek philosophers, it seems, either knew or accepted the Babylonian cosmology. According to Plutarch, though Thales (640?-546? B.C.) and later the Stoics believed the earth to be spherical in form, Anaximander (610-546? B.C.) thought it to be like a "smooth stony pillar," Anaximenes (6th cent.) like a "table." Beginning with the followers of Thales or perhaps Parmenides (?-500 B.C.), as Diogenes Laërtius claims, a long line of Greek thinkers including Plato (428?-347? B.C.) and Aristotle (384-322 B.C.) placed the earth in the center of the universe. Whether Plato held that the earth "encircled" or "clung" around the axis is a disputed point; but Aristotle claimed it was the fixed and immovable center around which swung the spherical universe with its heaven of fixed stars and its seven concentric circles of the planets kept in their places by their transparent crystalline spheres. The stars were an even greater problem. Anaximenes thought they were "fastened like nails" in a crystalline firmament, and others thought them to be "fiery plates of gold resembling pictures." But if the heavens were solid, how could the brief presence of a comet be explained? Among the philosophers were some noted as mathematicians whose leader was Pythagoras (c. 550 B.C.). He and at least one of the members of his school, Eudoxus (409?-356? B.C.), had visited Egypt, according to Diogenes Laërtius, and had in all probability been much interested in and influenced by the astronomical observations made by the Egyptian priests. On the same authority, Pythagoras was the first to declare the earth was round and to discuss the antipodes. He too emphasized the beauty and perfection of the circle and of the sphere in geometry, forms which became fixed for 2000 years as the fittest representations of the perfection of the heavenly bodies. There was some discussion in Diogenes' time as to the author of the theory of the earth's motion of axial rotation. Diogenes gives the honor to Philolaus (5th cent. B.C.) one of the Pythagoreans, though he adds that others attribute it to Icetas of Syracuse (6th or 5th cent. B.C.). Cicero, however, states the position of Hicetas of Syracuse as a belief in the absolute fixedness of all the heavenly bodies except the earth, which alone moves in the whole universe, and that its rapid revolutions upon its own axis cause the heavens apparently to move and the earth to stand still. Other thinkers of Syracuse may also have felt the Egyptian influence; for one of the greatest of them, Archimedes (c. 287-212 B.C.), stated the theory of the earth's revolution around the sun as enunciated by Aristarchus of Samos. (Perhaps this is the "hearth-fire of the universe" around which Philolaus imagined the earth to whirl.) In Arenarius, a curious study on the possibility of expressing infinite sums by numerical denominations as in counting the sands of the universe, Archimedes writes: "For you have known that the universe is called a sphere by several astrologers, its center the center of the earth, and its radius equal to a line drawn from the

87

center of the sun to the center of the earth. This
was written for the unlearned, as you have known
from the astrologers…

21

What would be the best title of the passage?

A) Astrological developments in ancient times

B) The development of astronomical thought

C) How Plato affected modern astronomy

D) The way Greek philosophers influenced modern science

22

What is the organization of the first sentence of the passage?

A) generalization and specification

B) comparison and contrast

C) cause and effect

D) transition in perspective

23

According to the passage, what was Greek philosophers' attitude toward Babylonian cosmology?

A) A few of them were not interested.

B) Some of them didn't try hard enough to truly comprehend it.

C) Some of them appeared not to agree with it.

D) Its conceptualization was particularly difficult for them to grasp.

24

In context, which of the following is most probably the reason the Chaldean thinkers developed a multiple heaven theory?

A) because they did not know how to time certain astronomical events

B) because it was the best way for them to overcome their terror

C) because they had to answer some of their questions properly

D) because some horrible heavenly objects kept reappearing

25

Which choice gives the best evidence for the answer to the previous question?

A) "This conception seems to lie back of both the later Egyptian and Hebraic cosmologies, as well as of the Ptolemaic." (Lines 17-19)

B) "Scientific astronomy, however, was an impossibility until an exact system of chronology was devised." (Lines 6-8)

C) "Meanwhile men puzzled over the shape of the earth, its position in the universe, what the stars were and why the positions of some shifted, and what those fiery comets were that now and again appeared and struck terror to their hearts" (Lines 8-13)

D) "Through the visits of Greek philosophers to Egyptian shores this conception helped to shape Greek thought and so indirectly affected western civilization." (Lines 19-23)

26

Which of the following is true of Babylonian cosmology?

A) At the time of its inception it was less scientific than other approaches.

B) It had an influence far beyond the realm of scientific curiosity

C) It served as the foundation of Western civilization.

D) It was difficult for outsiders to understand, leading many to misunderstand it.

27

Which of the following gives the most direct evidence for the answer to the previous question?

A) not all Greek philosophers

B) so indirectly affected western civilization

C) men began anew to withstand authority

D) spherical in form

28

According to the passage, which of the following is probably the reason stars were bigger problems?

A) because they were obviously much greater in number than the earth

B) because their movements were more complicated than that of the earth

C) because of an unexplainable anomaly

D) because there was a big conflict between astronomy and mathematics

Test 3

29

Which of the following gives the most direct evidence for the answer to the previous question?

A) "Pythagoras was the first to declare the earth was round" (Lines 63-64)

B) "the fittest representations of the perfection of the heavenly bodies." (Lines 67-68)

C) "how could the brief presence of a comet be explained?" (Lines 53-54)

D) "Cicero, however, states the position of Hicetas of Syracuse as a belief in the absolute fixedness of all the heavenly bodies except the earth," (Lines 74-77)

30

Which of the following most directly shows the same attitude as displayed by enunciated?

A) Egyptian influence

B) curious

C) revolutions

D) the unlearned

31

Which of the following is not the strategy the author is using to convey his or her argument in the passage?

A) generalization and specification

B) comparison and contrast

C) cause and effect

D) exception and refutation

Questions 32-41 are based on the following passage.

Electricity, next to Deity, is the most remarkable entity in the universe. Its marvelous and varied powers and utilities create a new epoch in scientific thought and discovery. Its study is
[5] replete with new and fascinating ideas and scientific theories. It contains the story of the universe more sublime than an epic, more wonderful than a romance. It organized the machinery of the worlds, and holds the secrets of nature and the mysteries
[10] of life in its invisible grasp. Electricity is the right hand of Deity, the tongue of the Spirit, the Word of Omnipotent power, the protean cosmic force and creative machinery of the universe. At the divine fiat it seized all atoms and space, it shook
[15] the ether into nebula, the nebula into worlds, the worlds into constellations, the constellations into a universe. It shaped planets and rounded suns and hurled them forth to circle in the chorus of the singing spheres. It gave form and functions to
[20] all matter from the rounded pebble to the stars; from the raindrop to the surging seas; from the chirping cricket to the sporting leviathan; from the helpless infant to the giant man. It is the messenger and executive of Creative Will to all
[25] created things. It is the ambassador of spirit to matter, the autocrat of communication between all the faculties of mind and all the functions of physical existence. It is the law of affinity in matter, of selection in atoms, and whispers to the body
[30] the intuitions of the Spirit and guides insensate worlds to do the will of Creative Omnipotence. Electricity is the wonderful medium and agent by which mind acts upon matter and works the miracle of life and growth. This mightiest servant
[35] of God and man, this genii greater than Aladdin's lamp, impresses all laws upon nature, and makes the universe obedient to the will of Deity, as man's body is obedient to the dictates of man's mind. This inscrutable word of power from the source of
[40] all power is beginning to supply the human race with an inexhaustible force that will revolutionize the earth and link all nations together as one family in a millennium of peace and good will. Human life seems to throb, pulsate, gleam and
[45] glow in this marvelous current of existence, which causes illumination, transportation, telegraphy, photography, surgery, horticulture, agriculture, metallurgy and manufacture to step forth as master magicians to work miracles for the comfort and
[50] happiness of mankind. Every new discovery, every step in the progress of electrical science conquers time, destroys distances, diffuses knowledge, dissipates ignorance, encourages friendship and draws men and nations closer and closer by
[55] physical ties and spiritual affinities. Where once noisy ponderous mechanism pounded the rocks to release the metals, electrical science with her unseen but resistless currents instantly separate the ore and the dross. Where the soot-begrimed
[60] engineer seizes the heavy iron throttle, she cleanly and softly touches a tiny button and the miracle is wrought— the heavy steed of steel receives its life not from smoking, hissing, fussing steam, but from an energy as silent as light and as potent
[65] as Omnipotence. This invisible electrical energy, without brush or color, paints the gorgeous beauties of the rainbow, and photographs in every ray of light and on every human eye the moving panorama of every passing scene. It telegraphs
[70] between mind and matter, between soul and body, between suns and planets, and gives life and energy to all the varied functions of this electric magnetic universe. This strange, miraculous power has taken its place as the supreme force of all forces,
[75] the ultimate elemental force from which all other physical forces are derived, and, without fuel or expense, flies with its burdens swifter than the flight of eagles. It is the last and greatest progeny of man genius and discovery, the seventh daughter
[80] of science, who dips her wand in the impossible and miraculous until miracles become prolific and common. Its power and expression are universal and its character and process superlatively grand. Its theatre of action is the universe and it comes
[85] to earth as the voice of Deity and the word of His Omnipotence. This science of the impossible, this daughter of miracles, is destined to outstrip all past achievements. The ponderous and noisy mechanisms will pass away, the barren rocks will
[90] change into most precious things, the sunlight will be converted into reservoirs of power, and every raindrop and waterfall, ocean tide and wind current, will reveal exhaustless sources of wealth and energy.

Test 3

32

What would be the best title of the passage?

A) The practical uses of electricity

B) What electricity can and cannot do

C) The miraculous and ambivalent power of electricity

D) An incredible agent in the Universe

33

According to the passage, what can be said about electricity?

A) There will be no scientific outcome greater than that of electricity.

B) Its influence is as great as that of God.

C) It is the earliest and most significant scientific discovery.

D) It and God play complementary roles in human history.

34

Which of the following is the best interpretation of the author's attitude toward electricity?

A) overwhelmed

B) exhilarated

C) overzealous

D) detached

35

Which of the following gives the least evidence for the answer to the previous question?

A) "This strange, miraculous power…the flight of eagles." (Lines 73-78)

B) "This mightiest servant…to the will of Deity," (Lines 34-37)

C) "Every new discovery,…physical ties and spiritual affinities." (Lines 50-55)

D) "Electricity, next to Deity, is the most remarkable entity in the universe." (Lines 1-2)

36

According to the context, what does the author most likely mean by mind acts upon matter?

A) Mind produces changes in the states of matter.

B) People employ mind to create useful things from matter.

C) Some people take advantage of matter with a mind to do things that would be totally incredible or impossible without God's help.

D) Mind can work wonders, sometimes even in the realm of the gods.

Test 3

37

According to the passage, which of the following is NOT true of electricity?

A) It must be the most integral element that God works with.

B) It is the most important tool used by God to govern the Universe.

C) It serves God, but not man.

D) Without it, it might be hard for mind to act upon matter.

38

As used in line 39, "inscrutable" most likely means

A) mysterious

B) splendid

C) docile

D) devine

39

Which of the following is mostly likely the role of "current" (Line 45)?

A) irony

B) sarcasm

C) metaphor

D) duality

40

If turned out to be true, which of the following would most directly undermine the author's argument?

A) Electricity is absolutely essential for the development of any inventions, in the future, near or distant.

B) Because of the many advances in electrical science and engineering, weapons have become more sophisticated and deadly.

C) Some people are hardcore atheists while others are uncommitted agnostics.

D) Some countries are not advanced enough to take full advantage of the advances in electrical science.

41

Which of the following gives the best evidence for the answer to the previous question?

A) "This mightiest servant…the will of Deity," (Lines 34-37)

B) "an inexhaustible force…and good will." (Lines 41-43)

C) "Human life seems…, metallurgy and manufacture" (Lines 44-48)

D) "the heavy steed…potent as Omnipotence." (Lines 62-65)

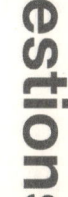

93

Questions 42-51 are based on the following passage.

   As happens in all the sciences in which Geometry is applied to matter, the demonstrations concerning Optics are founded on truths drawn from experience. Such are that the rays of light
5 are propagated in straight lines; that the angles of reflexion and of incidence are equal; and that in refraction the ray is bent according to the law of sines, now so well known, and which is no less certain than the preceding laws. The majority
10 of those who have written touching the various parts of Optics have contented themselves with presuming these truths. But some, more inquiring, have desired to investigate the origin and the causes, considering these to be in themselves
15 wonderful effects of Nature. In which they advanced some ingenious things, but not however such that the most intelligent folk do not wish for better and more satisfactory explanations. Wherefore I here desire to propound what I have
20 meditated on the subject, so as to contribute as much as I can to the explanation of this department of Natural Science, which, not without reason, is reputed to be one of its most difficult parts. I recognize myself to be much indebted
25 to those who were the first to begin to dissipate the strange obscurity in which these things were enveloped, and to give us hope that they might be explained by intelligible reasoning. But, on the other hand I am astonished also that even here
30 these have often been willing to offer, as assured and demonstrative, reasonings which were far from conclusive. For I do not find that any one has yet given a probable explanation of the first and most notable phenomena of light, namely why it is
35 not propagated except in straight lines, and how visible rays, coming from an infinitude of diverse places, cross one another without hindering one another in any way. I shall therefore essay in this book, to give, in accordance with the principles
40 accepted in the Philosophy of the present day, some clearer and more probable reasons, firstly of these properties of light propagated rectilinearly; secondly of light which is reflected on meeting other bodies. Then I shall explain the phenomena
45 of those rays which are said to suffer refraction on passing through transparent bodies of different sorts; and in this part I shall also explain the effects of the refraction of the air by the different densities of the Atmosphere. Thereafter I shall examine the
50 causes of the strange refraction of a certain kind of Crystal which is brought from Iceland. And finally I shall treat of the various shapes of transparent and reflecting bodies by which rays are collected at a point or are turned aside in various ways. From
55 this it will be seen with what facility, following our new Theory, we find not only the Ellipses, Hyperbolas, and other curves which Mr. Des Cartes has ingeniously invented for this purpose; but also those which the surface of a glass lens
60 ought to possess when its other surface is given as spherical or plane, or of any other figure that may be. It is inconceivable to doubt that light consists in the motion of some sort of matter. For whether one considers its production, one sees that here
65 upon the Earth it is chiefly engendered by fire and flame which contain without doubt bodies that are in rapid motion, since they dissolve and melt many other bodies, even the most solid; or whether one considers its effects, one sees that when light is
70 collected, as by concave mirrors, it has the property of burning as a fire does, that is to say it disunites the particles of bodies. This is assuredly the mark of motion, at least in the true Philosophy, in which one conceives the causes of all natural effects in
75 terms of mechanical motions. This, in my opinion, we must necessarily do, or else renounce all hopes of ever comprehending anything in Physics. And as, according to this Philosophy, one holds as certain that the sensation of sight is excited only
80 by the impression of some movement of a kind of matter which acts on the nerves at the back of our eyes, there is here yet one reason more for believing that light consists in a movement of the matter which exists between us and the luminous body.

Test 3

42

What could be the best title of the passage?

A) The physical characteristics of rays
B) The reason for which rays move rectilinearly
C) The significance of the rectilinear motion of rays
D) Certain traits of light
E) The importance of matter in the movement of light

43

According to the passage, in which aspect of light is the author most interested in?

A) that it needs matter to propagate
B) what happens when it propagates
C) that the rules of Geometry govern its movement
D) that studying it has led to improvements in the field of Optics

44

What is the author's general attitude?

A) inquisitive
B) subjective
C) authoritative
D) qualified

45

According to the author, what is the connection between "light" and "matter"?

A) irrelevant
B) inclusive
C) unclear
D) inseparable

46

According to the passage, which of the following is a case in which exploring physics would become futile?

A) when physicists lose hope
B) when it is not possible to explain any natural effect using physical movements
C) when excited light possesses traits similar to fire
D) when collecting light using a concave mirror no longer exhibits the property of burning fire

47

Which of the following gives the best evidence for the answer to the previous question?

A) "one considers its effects…the particles of bodies." (Lines 68-72)
B) "the sensation of sight…at the back of our eyes," (Lines 79-82)
C) "in which one conceives…mechanical motions." (Lines 73-75)
D) "This, in my opinion,…in Physics." (Lines 75-77)

Test 3

48

According to the passage, which choice can be logically added to the end of the passage?

A) a wider varieties of light motions

B) a wider varieties of light

C) a way to corroborate the author's argument

D) a way to refute a possible counterargument against the author's

49

Which choice would the author be most likely to agree with?

A) Light must be some kind of matter.

B) Without matter, light cannot exist.

C) A light source must exist as a form of matter.

D) Matter is the cause of light.

50

According to the passage, why did the author probably mention the connection between Optics and experience along with the connection between Geometry and matter?

A) in order to introduce a more detailed topic

B) in order to introduce the connection between Optics and matter

C) in order to talk about how Optics was invented

D) in order to establish some background for a further explanation of why light must move through matter

51

Which choice gives the best evidence for the answer to the previous question?

A) "the ray is bent according to the law of sines," (Lines 7-8)

B) "it is not propagated except in straight lines," (Lines 34-35)

C) "light which is reflected on meeting other bodies." (Lines 43-44)

D) "majority of those who have written touching the various parts of Optics have contented themselves with presuming these truths." (Lines 9-12)

STOP

TEST 4

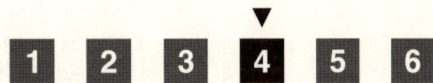

Test 4

Reading | **65 minutes, 51 questions**

DIRECTIONS

Each passage below is followed by a number of questions. After reading each passage, choose the best answer to each question based on what is stated or implied in the passage.

Questions 1-10 are based on the following passage.

Archimedes writes: "For you have known that the universe is called a sphere by several astrologers, its center the center of the earth, and its radius equal to a line drawn from the center of
5 the sun to the center of the earth. This was written for the unlearned, as you have known from the astrologers…. [Aristarchus of Samos] concludes that the world is many times greater than the estimate we have just given. He supposes that the fixed stars
10 and the sun remain motionless, but that the earth following a circular course, revolves around the sun as a center, and that the sphere of the fixed stars having the same sun as a center, is so vast that the circle which he supposes the earth to follow in
15 revolving holds the same ratio to the distance of the fixed stars as the center of a sphere holds to its circumference." These ancient philosophers realized in some degree the immensity of the universe in which the earth was but a point. They held that the
20 earth was an unsupported sphere the size of which Eratosthenes (c. 276-194 B.C.) had calculated approximately. They knew the sun was far larger than the earth, and Cicero with other thinkers recognized the insignificance of earthly affairs in
25 the face of such cosmic immensity. They knew too about the seven planets, had studied their orbits, and worked out astronomical ways of measuring the passage of time with a fair amount of accuracy. Hipparchus and other thinkers had discovered the
30 fact of the precession of the equinoxes, though there was no adequate theory to account for it until Copernicus formulated his "motion of declination." The Pythagoreans accepted the idea of the earth's turning upon its axis, and some
35 even held the idea of its revolution around the motionless sun. Others suggested that comets had orbits which they uniformly followed and therefore their reappearance could be anticipated. Why then was the heliocentric theory not definitely accepted?
40 In the first place, such a theory was contrary to the supposed facts of daily existence. A man did not have to be trained in the schools to observe that the earth seemed stable under his feet and that each morning the sun swept from the east to set at night
45 in the west. Sometimes it rose more to the north or to the south than at other times. How could that be explained if the sun were stationary? Study of the stars was valuable for navigators and for surveyors, perhaps, but such disturbing theories should not be
50 propounded by philosophers. Cleanthes, according to Plutarch, "advised that the Greeks ought to have prosecuted Aristarchus the Samian for blasphemy against religion, as shaking the very foundations of the world, because this man endeavoring to save
55 appearances, supposed that the heavens remained immovable and that the earth moved through an oblique circle, at the same time turning about its own axis." Few would care to face their fellows as blasphemers and impious thinkers on behalf of
60 an unsupported theory. Eighteen hundred years later Galileo would not do so, even though in his day the theory was by no means unsupported by observation. Furthermore, one of the weaknesses of the Greek civilization militated strongly against
65 the acceptance of this hypothesis so contrary to

the evidence of the senses. Experimentation and the development of applied science was practically an impossibility where the existence of slaves made manual labor degrading and shameful. Men might
[70] reason indefinitely; but few, if any, were willing to try to improve the instruments of observation or to test their observations by experiments. At the same time another astronomical theory was developing which was an adequate explanation for the
[75] phenomena observed up to that time. This theory of epicycles and eccentrics worked out by Apollonius of Perga (c. 225 B.C.) and by Hipparchus (c. 160 B.C.) and crystallized for posterity in Ptolemy's great treatise on astronomy, the Almagest, (c. 140
[80] A.D.) became the fundamental principle of the science until within the last three hundred years. The theory of the eccentric was based on the idea that heavenly bodies following circular orbits revolved around a center that did not coincide
[85] with that of the observer on the earth. That would explain why the sun appeared sometimes nearer the earth and sometimes farther away. The epicycle represented the heavenly body as moving along the circumference of one circle (called the epicycle)
[90] the center of which moves on another circle (the deferent). With better observations additional epicycles and eccentric were used to represent the newly observed phenomena till in the later Middle Ages the universe became a "—Sphere with
[95] Centric and Eccentric scribbled o'er, Cycle and Epicycle, Orb in Orb"—

1

According to the passage, which of the following exemplifies earthly affairs?

A) the size of the earth
B) the distance between the earth and the Sun
C) the orbit of the earth
D) the revolution of the earth around the sun

2

In context, which of the following most clearly shows the author's intention for mentioning daily existence?

A) to show that it is impossible to verify whether it is valid or not
B) to imply that sometimes, it cannot be used as a basis for theorization.
C) to indicate that experiencing it can be a very subjective
D) to explain that, in most cases, without it, theorization is impossible, especially in the realm of science

3

According to the passage, which of the following is NOT a direct obstacle to fully accepting the heliocentric theory?

A) the theory of epicycles
B) the observations of a navigator on a vessel at sea
C) everyday experience
D) religion

Test 4

4

Which of the following provides the best evidence for the answer to the previous question?

A) "such a theory was contrary to the supposed facts of daily existence." (Lines 41-42)

B) "At the same time another astronomical theory was developing" (Lines 72-74)

C) "seemed stable under his feet" (Line 44)

D) "Sometimes it rose more to the north or to the south than at other times." (Lines 46-47)

5

In context, why was using applied science almost out of the question?

A) Performing the procedures necessary in the applied science was regarded as shameful.

B) Philosophers did not have the instruments necessary to conduct accurate scientific experiments.

C) Slaves could not work in the field of science.

D) Getting involved in applied science was considered blasphemous.

6

Which of the following provides the most direct evidence for the answer to the previous question?

A) "Few would care to face their fellows as blasphemers" (Lines 58-59)

B) "an adequate explanation for the phenomena observed up to that time." (Lines 74-75)

C) "on behalf of an unsupported theory." (Lines 59-60)

D) "where the existence of slaves made manual labor degrading and shameful." (Lines 68-69)

7

Why does the author probably mention within the last three hundred years?

A) A major breakthrough must have occurred around that time.

B) There must have been some reason why the Almagest could no longer serve as a fundamental basis for a meaningful theory.

C) Something happened to the idea of eccentric theory so that it was no longer dependable.

D) Heliocentric theorists couldn't defend themselves against blasphemous criticism.

8

Which of the following would be the best way to comprehend the connection between the heliocentric and the eccentric theory?

A) They were compatible with each other to a certain degree.

B) They could have worked in harmony with each other in that one could have taken care of the other's weaknesses.

C) Although both were related to the concept of a center, they were referring to different centers.

D) They were both correct, but they were applied in the wrong manner.

9

As used in line 78, "crystallized" most nearly means

A) solidified

B) concentrated

C) clarified

D) clear to understand

Test 4

10

According to the passage, what would be the correct attitude of a modern astronomer toward the Almagest?

- A) absolutely inspiring
- B) mostly suspicious
- C) somewhat correct
- D) extremely doubtful

Questions 11-20 are based on the following passage.

He has dissolved Representative Houses repeatedly, for opposing with manly firmness his invasions on the rights of the people.

He has refused for a long time, after such
[5] dissolutions, to cause others to be elected; whereby the Legislative powers, incapable of Annihilation, have returned to the People at large for their exercise; the State remaining in the mean time exposed to all the dangers of invasion from
[10] without, and convulsions within.

He has endeavoured to prevent the population of these States; for that purpose obstructing the Laws for Naturalization of Foreigners; refusing to pass others to encourage their migrations hither,
[15] and raising the conditions of new Appropriations of Lands.

He has obstructed the Administration of Justice, by refusing his Assent to Laws for establishing Judiciary powers.

[20] He has made Judges dependent on his Will alone, for the tenure of their offices, and the amount and payment of their salaries.

He has erected a multitude of New Offices, and sent hither swarms of Officers to harrass our
[25] people, and eat out their substance.

He has kept among us, in times of peace, Standing Armies without the Consent of our legislatures.

He has affected to render the Military
[30] independent of and superior to the Civil power.

He has combined with others to subject us to a jurisdiction foreign to our constitution, and unacknowledged by our laws; giving his Assent to their Acts of pretended Legislation:

[35] For Quartering large bodies of armed troops among us:

For protecting them, by a mock Trial, from punishment for any Murders which they should commit on the Inhabitants of these States:

[40] For cutting off our Trade with all parts of the world:

For imposing Taxes on us without our Consent:

For depriving us in many cases, of the benefits
[45] of Trial by Jury:

For transporting us beyond Seas to be tried for pretended offences

For abolishing the free System of English Laws in a neighbouring Province, establishing
[50] therein an Arbitrary government, and enlarging its Boundaries so as to render it at once an example and fit instrument for introducing the same absolute rule into these Colonies:

Test 4

11

As used in line 1, "dissolved" most nearly means

A) divided
B) solved
C) annihilated
D) destroyed

12

What can be said about Representative Houses?

A) They resisted the power of the King but only in moderation.
B) They could not resist as strongly as they had wanted to.
C) They defied the King's interference with determination.
D) They tried to make a compromise.

13

Why is State mentioned in the passage?

A) to show how the King perceives his power over it.
B) to imply the importance of the absence of Representative Houses
C) to speculate on the impact of the King's enterprise against the population of the States
D) to predict the future of the States without Representative Houses

14

Which of the following provides the best evidence for the answer to the previous question?

A) "Annihilation" (Line 6)
B) "convulsions" (Line 10)
C) "manly firmness" (Line 2)
D) "at large" (Line 7)

15

Which of the following is NOT what the King did to hamper a certain social phenomenon?

A) hindered immigration
B) created some new restrictions
C) inhibited some legal institutions
D) created a general sense of injustice

16

Which of the following is the best interpretation of what the King did to obstruct the justice system of the States?

A) What he did was intentional from the beginning.
B) His actions were not limited to a specific aspect of the system.
C) Controlling the general population was his top priority.
D) Manipulating judges' incomes was the most effective measure he took to accomplish his goal.

Test 4

17

Which of the following is what the author means by substance?

A) privacy

B) freedom

C) economy

D) history

18

According to the passage, what can be said about the military created by the King?

A) It derived its power from the ordinary citizens.

B) Its power surpasses that of citizens by a huge margin.

C) The citizenry was probably not involved in establishing it.

D) It was an obstacle to the conduct of normal civil life.

19

The author describes King's attitude regarding the military as.

A) hostile

B) aggressive

C) arrogant

D) agitated

20

Which of the following is the best evidence for the answer to the previous question?

A) "affected" (Line 20)

B) "render" (Line 20)

C) "independent" (Line 21)

D) "superior" (Line 21)

Test 4

Questions 21-31 are based on the following passage.

Finally, to those nations who would make themselves our adversary, we offer not a pledge but a request: that both sides begin anew the quest for peace, before the dark powers of destruction
5　unleashed by science engulf all humanity in planned or accidental self-destruction.

We dare not tempt them with weakness. For only when our arms are sufficient beyond doubt can we be certain beyond doubt that they will
10　never be employed.

But neither can two great and powerful groups of nations take comfort from our present course—both sides overburdened by the cost of modern weapons, both rightly alarmed by the steady spread
15　of the deadly atom, yet both racing to alter that uncertain balance of terror that stays the hand of mankind's final war.

So let us begin anew—remembering on both sides that civility is not a sign of weakness, and
20　sincerity is always subject to proof. Let us never negotiate out of fear. But let us never fear to negotiate.

Let both sides explore what problems unite us instead of belaboring those problems which divide
25　us.

Let both sides, for the first time, formulate serious and precise proposals for the inspection and control of arms—and bring the absolute power to destroy other nations under the absolute control of
30　all nations.

Let both sides seek to invoke the wonders of science instead of its terrors. Together let us explore the stars, conquer the deserts, eradicate disease, tap the ocean depths, and encourage the arts and
35　commerce.

Let both sides unite to heed in all corners of the earth the command of Isaiah—to "undo the heavy burdens . . . [and] let the oppressed go free."

And if a beachhead of cooperation may push
40　back the jungle of suspicion, let both sides join in creating a new endeavor, not a new balance of power, but a new world of law, where the strong are just and the weak secure and the peace preserved.

45　All this will not be finished in the first one hundred days. Nor will it be finished in the first one thousand days, nor in the life of this administration, nor even perhaps in our lifetime on this planet. But let us begin.

50　In your hands, my fellow citizens, more than mine, will rest the final success or failure of our course. Since this country was founded each generation of Americans has been summoned to give testimony to its national loyalty. The graves of
55　young Americans who answered the call to service surround the globe.

Now the trumpet summons us again—not as a call to bear arms, though arms we need—not as a call to battle, though embattled we are—but a
60　call to bear the burden of a long twilight struggle, year in and year out, "rejoicing in hope, patient in tribulation"—a struggle against the common enemies of man: tyranny, poverty, disease, and war itself.

65　Can we forge against these enemies a grand and global alliance, North and South, East and West, that can assure a more fruitful life for all mankind? Will you join in that historic effort?

In the long history of the world, only a few
70　generations have been granted the role of defending freedom in its hour of maximum danger. I do not shrink from this responsibility—I welcome it. I do not believe that any of us would exchange places with any other people or any other generation. The
75　energy, the faith, the devotion which we bring to this endeavor will light our country and all who serve it—and the glow from that fire can truly light the world.

And so, my fellow Americans: ask not what
80　your country can do for you—ask what you can do for your country.

My fellow citizens of the world: ask not what America will do for you, but what together we can do for the freedom of man.

85　Finally, whether you are citizens of America or citizens of the world, ask of us here the same high standards of strength and sacrifice which we ask of you. With a good conscience our only sure reward, with history the final judge of our deeds, let us go
90　forth to lead the land we love, asking His blessing and His help, but knowing that here on earth God's work must truly be our own.

Test 4

21

What is the author's attitude toward negotiations related to the control of deadly weapons?

A) Beyond doubt he is totally against them.

B) Everything depends on certain conditions being met in advance.

C) He welcomes them wholeheartedly, but with certain conditions.

D) He is not fearful of them for his own unique reasons

22

According to the passage, what is the role of science in the author's argument?

A) It is an obstacle that stands in the way of negotiating controls on weapons.

B) It provides a unique opportunity to start peace talks and negotiations on arms control.

C) It is something that must be balanced for the sake of world peace.

D) It is a field in which many positive advances can be made.

23

Why does the author want to deal with deadly weapons from a position of confidence?

A) because the author is afraid of them

B) because war would be inevitable without it

C) because dealing with them without it would be too expensive

D) because dealing with them without it might be uncomfortable

24

Which of the following is the most direct evidence for the answer to the previous question?

A) "But neither can two great and powerful groups of nations take comfort from our present course" (Lines 11-12)

B) "Let both sides unite to heed in all corners of the earth the command of Isaiah—to "undo the heavy burdens . . . [and] let the oppressed go free." (Lines 36-38)

C) "the strong are just and the weak secure and the peace preserved." (Lines 42-44)

D) "For only when our arms are sufficient beyond doubt can we be certain beyond doubt that they will never be employed." (Lines 7-10)

25

In the context of the passage what is the most probable role of beachhead?

A) extreme criticism

B) genuine hope

C) irony

D) playfulness

New SAT Reading Prep　　106

26

According to the passage, what is the most significant difference between "a new balance of power" and "a new world of law"? (Lines 41-42)

A) Combining the two is a solution to many of the world's problems.

B) Only one of the two can guarantee what the author is aiming for.

C) The former might be a by-product of the old world.

D) One of them might not be easy to achieve because of the jungle of suspicion.

27

In context, what does the first one hundred days signify?

A) a period of time during the author's administration

B) the first half of the duration of any significant change

C) a period shorter than one thousand days

D) a relatively short period of time

28

Why did the author say "more than mine" (Lines 50-51)?

A) because what the author wants to accomplish is not a job for one person

B) because the author knows he is not strong enough to do the job required

C) because the author needs the collaboration of his fellow citizens

D) because the achievement of the author's goal do not depend on just old Americans

29

Which of the following is the best evidence for the answer to the previous question?

A) "The graves of young Americans who answered the call to service surround the globe." (Lines 54-56)

B) "a beachhead of cooperation may push back the jungle of suspicion," (Lines 39-40)

C) "Since this country was founded each generation of Americans has been summoned to give testimony to its national loyalty." (Lines 52-54)

D) "nor in the life of this administration, nor even perhaps in our lifetime on this planet. But let us begin." (Lines 47-49)

30

Which of the following is the main goal of the passage?

A) to achieve world peace in order to maintain civilization as it is

B) to encourage a certain group of people to become part of an attempt to maintain something of consequence

C) to defend freedom around the world at all cost

D) to secure world peace by using only peaceful means

31

Which of the following is the best evidence for the answer to the previous question?

A) "only a few generations have been granted the role of defending freedom in its hour of maximum danger." (Lines 69-71)

B) "My fellow citizens of the world: ask not what America will do for you, but what together we can do for the freedom of man." (Lines 82-84)

C) "knowing that here on earth God's work must truly be our own." (Lines 91-92)

D) "Let us never negotiate out of fear. But let us never fear to negotiate." (Lines 20-22)

Questions 32-41 are based on the following passage.

As everybody knows nowadays, the knowledge we possess of life before the beginnings of human memory and tradition is derived from the markings and fossils of living things in the stratified rocks,
5 We find preserved in shale and slate, limestone, and sandstone, bones, shells, fibres, stems, fruits, footmarks, scratchings and the like, side by side with the ripple marks of the earliest tides and the pittings of the earliest rain-falls. It is by the
10 sedulous examination of this Record of the Rocks that the past history of the earth's life has been pieced together. That much nearly everybody knows to-day. The sedimentary rocks do not lie neatly stratum above stratum; they have been
15 crumpled, bent, thrust about, distorted and mixed together like the leaves of a library that has been repeatedly looted and burnt, and it is only as a result of many devoted lifetimes of work that the record has been put into order and read. The whole
20 compass of time represented by the record of the rocks is now estimated as 1,600,000,000 years. The earliest rocks in the record are called by geologists the Azoic rocks, because they show no traces of life. Great areas of these Azoic rocks lie uncovered
25 in North America, and they are of such a thickness that geologists consider that they represent a period of at least half of the 1,600,000,000 which they assign to the whole geological record. Let me repeat this profoundly significant fact. Half the
30 great interval of time since land and sea were first distinguishable on earth has left us no traces of life. There are ripplings and rain marks still to be found in these rocks, but no marks nor vestiges of any living thing. Then, as we come up the record, signs
35 of past life appear and increase. The age of the world's history in which we find these past traces is called by geologists the Lower Palæozoic age. The first indications that life was astir are vestiges of comparatively simple and lowly things: the shells
40 of small shellfish, the stems and flowerlike heads of zoophytes, seaweeds and the tracks and remains of sea worms and crustacea. Very early appear certain creatures rather like plant-lice, crawling creatures which could roll themselves up into balls as the
45 plant-lice do, the trilobites. Later by a few million years or so come certain sea scorpions, more mobile and powerful creatures than the world had ever seen before. None of these creatures were of very great size. Among the largest were certain of
50 the sea scorpions, which measured nine feet in length. There are no signs whatever of land life of any sort, plant or animal; there are no fishes nor any vertebrated creatures in this part of the record. Essentially all the plants and creatures which have
55 left us their traces from this period of the earth's history are shallow-water and intertidal beings. If we wished to parallel the flora and fauna of the Lower Palæozoic rocks on the earth today, we should do it best, except in the matter of size, by
60 taking a drop of water from a rock pool or scummy ditch and examining it under a microscope. The little crustacea, the small shellfish, the zoophytes and algæ we should find there would display a quite striking resemblance to these clumsier, larger
65 prototypes that once were the crown of life upon our planet. It is well, however, to bear in mind that the Lower Palæozoic rocks probably do not give us anything at all representative of the first beginnings of life on our planet. Unless a creature has bones
70 or other hard parts, unless it wears a shell or is big enough and heavy enough to make characteristic footprints and trails in mud, it is unlikely to leave any fossilized traces of its existence behind. Today there are hundreds of thousands of species of small
75 soft-bodied creatures in our world which it is inconceivable can ever leave any mark for future geologists to discover. In the world's past, millions of millions of species of such creatures may have lived and multiplied and flourished and passed
80 away without a trace remaining. The waters of the warm and shallow lakes and seas of the so-called Azoic period may have teemed with an infinite variety of lowly, jelly-like, shell-less and boneless creatures, and a multitude of green scummy plants
85 may have spread over the sunlit intertidal rocks and beaches. The Record of the Rocks is no more a complete record of life in the past than the books of a bank are a record of the existence of everybody in the neighbourhood. It is only when a species
90 begins to secrete a shell or a spicule or a carapace or a lime-supported stem, and so put by something for the future, that it goes upon the Record. But in rocks of an age prior to those which bear any

fossil traces, graphite, a form of uncombined
95 carbon, is sometimes found, and some authorities
consider that it may have been separated out
from combination through the vital activities of
unknown living things.

32

What could be the best title of the passage?

A) The varieties of life on earth

B) Fossils as the primary source for tracing the history of life on earth

C) Life on earth

D) Evolution of life on earth

33

As used in line 10, "sedulous" most nearly means

A) cautious

B) meticulous

C) diligent

D) analytical

34

According to the passage, which of the following is true about the traces left by past life forms?

A) They are haphazard all through the history of the earth.

B) They continue to be discovered and at an increasing rate.

C) They seem to be concentrated in a certain time period.

D) They are very accurate indications of how long ago life came into being on Earth.

Test 4

35

Which choice gives the best evidence for the answer to the previous question?

A) "As everybody knows nowadays, the knowledge we possess of life before the beginnings of human memory and tradition is derived from the markings and fossils of living things in the stratified rocks," (Lines 1-4)

B) "Very early appear certain creatures rather like plant-lice, crawling creatures which could roll themselves up into balls as the plant-lice do, the trilobites." (Lines 42-45)

C) "Then, as we come up the record, signs of past life appear and increase." (Lines 34-35)

D) "The age of the world's history in which we find these past traces is called by geologists the Lower Palæozoic age." (Lines 35-37)

36

As used in line 33, "vestiges" most nearly means

A) image
B) amount
C) number
D) trace

37

According to the passage, what can be learned from shells of small shellfish?

A) that life on Earth has existed for a very long time.
B) that fossils are the first sign of life on Earth
C) that fossils are very useful
D) that there are a wide varieties of fossils

38

Which choice gives the best evidence for the answer to the previous question?

A) "The first indications that life was astir are vestiges of comparatively simple and lowly things:" (Lines 37-39)

B) "We find preserved in shale and slate, limestone, and sandstone, bones, shells, fibres, stems, fruits, footmarks, scratchings and the like," (Lines 5-7)

C) "it wears a shell or is big enough and heavy enough to make characteristic footprints and trails in mud," (Lines 70-72)

D) "The little crustacea, the small shellfish, the zoophytes and algæ we should find there would display a quite striking resemblance to these clumsier," (Lines 61-64)

39

Which of the following might be the best interpretation of the author's attitude?

A) authoritative
B) mainly speculative
C) detached
D) emotional

Test 4

40

Which choice gives the best evidence for the answer to the previous question?

A) "We find preserved in shale and slate, limestone, and sandstone, bones, shells, fibres, stems, fruits," (Lines 5-7)

B) "There are ripplings and rain marks still to be found in these rocks, but no marks nor vestiges of any living thing." (Lines 32-34)

C) "The first indications that life was astir are vestiges of comparatively simple and lowly things:" (Lines 37-39)

D) "Essentially all the plants and creatures which have left us their traces from this period of the earth's history are shallow-water and intertidal beings." (Lines 54-56)

41

What is the general organization of the passage?

A) presenting a misconception followed by a number of examples to be refuted later in the passage

B) proving a general statement by supporting it with a fair amount of elaboration and providing an interesting conclusion

C) proposing a theory supported by a substantial amount of detail which eventually leads to a new topic

D) supplying unclear information to be clarified by facts as the passage progresses

Questions 42-51 are based on the following passage.

The history of European civilization is the history of a certain political institution which united and expressed Europe, and was governed from Rome. This institution was informed at its very origin by the growing influence of a certain definite and organized religion: this religion it ultimately accepted and, finally, was merged in. The institution— having accepted the religion, having made of that religion its official expression, and having breathed that religion in through every part until it became the spirit of the whole— was slowly modified, spiritually illumined and physically degraded by age. But it did not die. It was revived by the religion which had become its new soul. It re-arose and still lives. This institution was first known among men as Republica; we call it today "The Roman Empire." The Religion which informed and saved it was then called, still is called, and will always be called "The Catholic Church." Europe is the Church, and the Church is Europe. It is immaterial to the historical value of this historical truth whether it be presented to a man who utterly rejects Catholic dogma or to a man who believes everything the Church may teach. A man remote in distance, in time, or in mental state from the thing we are about to examine would perceive the reality of this truth just as clearly as would a man who was steeped in its spirit from within and who formed an intimate part of Christian Europe. The Oriental pagan, the contemporary atheist, some supposed student in some remote future, reading history in some place from which the Catholic Faith shall have utterly departed, and to which the habits and traditions of our civilization will therefore be wholly alien, would each, in proportion to his science, grasp as clearly as it is grasped today by the Catholic student who is of European birth, the truth that Europe and the Catholic Church were and are one thing. The only people who do not grasp it (or do not admit it) are those writers of history whose special, local, and temporary business it is to oppose the Catholic Church, or who have a traditional bias against it. These men are numerous, they have formed, in the Protestant and other anti-Catholic universities, a whole school of hypothetical and unreal history in which, though the original workers are few, their copyists are innumerable: and that school of unreal history is still dogmatically taught in the anti-Catholic centres of Europe and of the world. Now our quarrel with this school should be, not that it is anti-Catholic—that concerns another sphere of thought— but that it is unhistorical. To neglect the truth that the Roman Empire with its institutions and its spirit was the sole origin of European civilization; to forget or to diminish the truth that the Empire accepted in its maturity a certain religion; to conceal the fact that this religion was not a vague mood, but a determinate and highly organized corporation; to present in the first centuries some non-existent "Christianity" in place of the existent Church; to suggest that the Faith was a vague agreement among individual holders of opinions instead of what it historically was, the doctrine of a fixed authoritative institution; to fail to identify that institution with the institution still here today and still called the Catholic Church; to exaggerate the insignificant barbaric influences which came from outside the Empire and did nothing to modify its spirit; to pretend that the Empire or its religion have at any time ceased to be— that is, to pretend that there has ever been a solution of continuity between the past and the present of Europe— all these pretensions are parts of one historical falsehood. In all by which we Europeans differ from the rest of mankind there is nothing which was not originally peculiar to the Roman Empire, or is not demonstrably derived from something peculiar to it.

Test 4

42

What would be the best title of the passage?

A) Religion in Europe

B) The significance of the Roman Empire in the history of Europe

C) Several factors necessary for processing the history of Europe and Roman Empire

D) History, religion and the Roman Empire in Europe

43

According to the passage, what is the connection between the Church and the Roman Empire in Europe?

A) They were intertwined with each other so strongly that they dictated every major aspect of European history.

B) One of them was inconceivable without the other.

C) The Church survived in Europe with the help of Roman Empire.

D) The Roman Empire had a strong faith in the Catholic Church.

44

Which of the following provides the best evidence for the answer to the previous question?

A) "Europe is the Church, and the Church is Europe." (Lines 20-21)

B) "It was revived by the religion which had become its new soul." (Lines 13-15)

C) "The Religion which informed and saved it was then called, still is called, and will always be called "The Catholic Church." (Lines 17-19)

D) "But it did not die." (Line 13)

45

As used in line 21, "immaterial" most nearly means

A) spiritual

B) metaphysical

C) unsubstantial

D) priceless

46

In talking about the historical value of the true connection between Europe and Church, why were two very different men mentioned?

A) to illustrate how people's opinions might differ depending on their historical era

B) to create an extreme contrast

C) to emphasize the universal importance of the historical value

D) to show the difference between the genuine historical value and people's perception of it

New SAT Reading Prep 114

Test 4

47

As used in line 54, "unhistorical" most nearly means

A) not historically organized
B) not famous
C) false
D) not imaginative

48

How does the author view those who deny that the Roman Empire with its institutions and its spirit was the sole origin of European civilization?

A) immature
B) liars
C) vague
D) not authoritative

49

Which of the following provides the best evidence for the answer to the previous question?

A) "neglect the truth" "diminish the truth" "conceal the fact" (Lines 54-59)
B) "the Empire accepted in its maturity a certain religion;" (Lines 58-59)
C) "pretend that there has ever been a solution of continuity between the past and the present of Europe" (Lines 73-75)
D) "a determinate and highly organized corporation" (Lines 60-61)

50

In context, which of the following could work against the author by using the same strategy employed by the author?

A) "a traditional bias against it" (Line 44)
B) "in proportion to his science" (Lines 36-37)
C) "that school of unreal history is still dogmatically taught" (Lines 49-50)
D) "the Catholic Faith shall have utterly departed" (Lines 33-34)

51

Which of the following could be the best interpretation of the author's attitude?

A) perceptive
B) qualified
C) authoritative
D) scientific

STOP

TEST 5

Test 5

Reading | 65 minutes, 52 questions

DIRECTIONS

Each passage below is followed by a number of questions. After reading each passage, choose the best answer to each question based on what is stated or implied in the passage.

Questions 1-10 are based on the following passage.

Analyses of the tissues of plants show that they contain all of the elements that are to be found in the soil on which they grew. Any of these elements which are present in the soil in soluble form are
5 carried into the plants with the soil water in which they are dissolved, whether they are needed by the plant for its nutrition or not. But in the case of those elements which are not taken out of the sap to be used by the plant cells in their activities,
10 the total amount taken from the soil is much less than is that of the elements which are used in the synthetic processes of the plant. Hence, much larger proportions of some elements than of others are taken from the soil by plants. The
15 proportions of the different elements which are used by plants as raw materials for the manufacture of the products needed for their growth varies with the different species; but a certain amount of each of the so-called "essential elements" (see below) is
20 necessary to every plant, because each such element has a definite role which it performs in the plant's growth. A plant cannot grow to maturity unless a sufficient supply of each essential element comes to it from the soil.
25   From the standpoint of their relative value as raw materials for plant food, the elements which are present in the soil may be divided into three classes; namely, the non-essential, the essential and abundant, and the critical elements.
30   The first class includes silicon, aluminium, sodium, manganese, and certain other rarer elements which sometimes are found in soils of some special type, or unusual origin. These elements seem to have no role to play in the
35 nutrition of plants; although silicon is always present in plant ash and sodium salts are found in small quantities in all parts of practically all plants. Nearly all species of plants can be grown to full maturity in the entire absence of these elements
40 from their culture medium. Occasional exceptions to this statement in the case of special types of plants are known, and are of interest in special studies of plant adaptations, but need not be considered here.
45   The second group includes iron, calcium, magnesium, and, generally, sulfur. All of these elements are essential for plant growth, but are usually present in the soil in ample quantities to insure a sufficient supply in available form for all
50 plant needs. Recent investigations have shown, however, that there are many soils in which sulfur is present in such limited quantities that many agricultural crops, when grown on these soils, respond favorably to the application of sulfur-
55 containing fertilizers. In such cases, sulfur is a "critical" element.
   The "critical" elements are those which are essential to the growth of all plants and which are present in most soils in relatively small proportions
60 and any one may, therefore, be the limiting factor in plant growth so far as plant food is concerned. These are nitrogen, phosphorus, potassium, and (possibly) sulfur.

Test 5

1

What could be the best title for the passage?

A) The value of the soil elements as plant food

B) The role of the soil elements in plant synthesis.

C) Why some elements are essential to plant survival

D) The water solubility of elements essential for plant nutrition

2

Which of the following is true of the elements in soil?

A) The classification of them depends on their relative availability in soil.

B) The criterion for the classification of them is crystal clear.

C) A certain classification sometimes depends on the availability of relevant element to that classification.

D) Their availability in soil is directly related to their value.

3

According to the passage, what is the connection between essential elements and limiting factors?

A) Some essential elements may well be limiting factors.

B) Whether some elements are essential or not has no relevance to whether they are limiting factors.

C) Some of the limiting factors can be essential elements.

D) When certain essential elements lose one of their characteristics, they can become limiting factors.

4

Which of the following is the most direct evidence for the answer to the previous question?

A) "relative value" (Line 25) and "essential to the growth" (Line 58)

B) "in relatively small proportions and any one may, therefore, be the limiting factor in plant growth" (Lines 59-61)

C) "the essential and abundant, and the critical elements." (Lines 28-29)

D) "unusual origin" (Line 33) and "a definite role" (Line 21)

Test 5

5

Which of the following questions is not clearly answered by the passage?

A) What is the connection between essential elements and limiting factors?

B) Why are essential elements readily available in soil?

C) What is the connection between essential and critical elements?

D) What is the function of non-essential elements?

6

Which of the following pieces of evidence might prove that non-essential elements might have something to do with plant growth?

A) "Occasional exceptions" (Line 40)

B) "entire absence" (Line 39)

C) "unusual origin" (Line 33)

D) "grow to maturity" (Line 22)

7

Which of the following might work as the best logical analysis for the answer to the previous question?

A) Quantity makes quality more significant.

B) Nature doesn't put things where they are not needed.

C) No value, no use.

D) There are only three different kinds of elements.

8

Which of the following might be the best assessment about non-essential elements?

A) They may well be relatively more available than essential elements.

B) They might be indirectly related with plant growth.

C) Their availability might have a lot to do with their significance.

D) Their apparent role in some cases might be due to specific adaptations in the certain plants.

9

Which of the following is the most direct evidence for the answer to the previous question?

A) "plant adaptations" (Line 43)

B) "special types" (Line 41)

C) "other rarer elements" (Line 31)

D) "special studies" (Lines 42-43)

10

Why most probably might the author not be interested in the significance of certain elements?

A) because no plant needs them to fully develop

B) because they do not exist in any significant amount in soil

C) because the special plants that need them are not rare enough

D) because their role in most plants' growth is not biologically evident, yet

Questions 11-20 are based on the following passage.

For taking away our Charters, abolishing our most valuable Laws, and altering fundamentally the Forms of our Governments:

For suspending our own Legislatures, and
5 declaring themselves invested with power to legislate for us in all cases whatsoever.

He has abdicated Government here, by declaring us out of his Protection and waging War against us.

10 He has plundered our seas, ravaged our Coasts, burnt our towns, and destroyed the lives of our people.

He is at this time transporting large Armies of foreign Mercenaries to complete the works
15 of death, desolation and tyranny, already begun with circumstances of Cruelty & perfidy scarcely paralleled in the most barbarous ages, and totally unworthy the Head of a civilized nation.

He has constrained our fellow Citizens taken
20 Captive on the high Seas to bear Arms against their Country, to become the executioners of their friends and Brethren, or to fall themselves by their Hands.

He has excited domestic insurrections
25 amongst us, and has endeavoured to bring on the inhabitants of our frontiers, the merciless Indian Savages, whose known rule of warfare, is an undistinguished destruction of all ages, sexes and conditions.

30 In every stage of these Oppressions We have Petitioned for Redress in the most humble terms: Our repeated Petitions have been answered only by repeated injury. A Prince whose character is thus marked by every act which may define a Tyrant, is
35 unfit to be the ruler of a free people.

Nor have We been wanting in attentions to our Brittish brethren. We have warned them from time to time of attempts by their legislature to extend an unwarrantable jurisdiction over us.
40 We have reminded them of the circumstances of our emigration and settlement here. We have appealed to their native justice and magnanimity, and we have conjured them by the ties of our common kindred to disavow these usurpations,
45 which, would inevitably interrupt our connections and correspondence. They too have been deaf to the voice of justice and of consanguinity. We must, therefore, acquiesce in the necessity, which denounces our Separation, and hold them, as we
50 hold the rest of mankind, Enemies in War, in Peace Friends.

We, therefore, the Representatives of the united States of America, in General Congress, Assembled, appealing to the Supreme Judge of the
55 world for the rectitude of our intentions, do, in the Name, and by Authority of the good People of these Colonies, solemnly publish and declare, That these United Colonies are, and of Right ought to be Free and Independent States; that they are
60 Absolved from all Allegiance to the British Crown, and that all political connection between them and the State of Great Britain, is and ought to be totally dissolved; and that as Free and Independent States, they have full Power to levy War, conclude
65 Peace, contract Alliances, establish Commerce, and to do all other Acts and Things which Independent States may of right do. And for the support of this Declaration, with a firm reliance on the protection of divine Providence, we mutually pledge to each
70 other our Lives, our Fortunes and our sacred Honor.

Test 5

11

Which of the following is probably NOT part of the actions of "he" as described in the passage?

A) territorial invasion

B) legal obstruction

C) organizational interference

D) military monopoly

12

According to the passage, what is most likely the nature of "his" military actions?

A) inhumane

B) treacherous

C) unparalleled

D) captivating

13

Why did the author refer to a barbarous age?

A) because s/he was afraid of what was happening in the present age

B) in order to make a comparison between this age and another barbarous age

C) in order to emphasize how bad the situation was in a certain era

D) because the nature of the English regime had traditionally been compared to that of savages

14

In context, which of the following is the best interpretation of the attitude of the American resistance to the English?

A) It was mainly military in nature.

B) It was evenly balanced between diplomatic and aggressive in nature.

C) It displayed constant enterprise of a somewhat peaceful nature.

D) Unsuccessful at times but with some exceptions.

15

Which of the following is the best evidence for the answer to the previous question?

A) "these unsurpations" (Line 44)

B) "In every stage…Petitioned…most humble terms:" (Lines 30-31)

C) "attentions to our Brittish brethren" (Lines 36-37)

D) "warned them…of attempts" (Lines 37-38)

16

According to the passage, what can be said about the British response to American resistance?

A) retaliatory in nature

B) compromising if necessary

C) brutal at all cost

D) more severe than the resistance against it

17

Which of the following is the best evidence for the answer to the previous question?

A) "constrained" "taken captive" (Lines 19-20)

B) "paralleled" "totally unworthy" (Lines 17-18)

C) "humble" "repeated injury" (Line 31, 33)

D) "insurrections" "merciless" (Line 24, 26)

18

In context, what is the author's attitude toward British public?

A) hostile

B) enthusiastic

C) apathetic

D) affectionate

19

Which of the following is the best evidence for the answer to the previous question?

A) "unwarrantable jurisdiction" (Line 39)

B) "Petitioned for Redress" (Line 31)

C) "marked...a Tyrant" (Line 34)

D) "our Brittish brethren" (Line 37)

20

What is the connection of the last paragraph to the passage as a whole?

A) reiteration

B) specification

C) a novel conclusion

D) generalization

Test 5

Questions 21-32 are based on the following passage.

The editor of these essays was busy in the autumn of last year collating the opinions attached by different people to the word 'progress'. One Sunday afternoon he happened to be walking
5 with two friends in Oxford, one a professor of philosophy, the other a lady. The professor of philosophy declared that to him human progress must always mean primarily the increase of knowledge; the editor urged the increase of power
10 as its most characteristic feature, but the lady added at once that to her progress had always meant, and could only mean, increase in our appreciation of the humanity of others. The first two thoughts, harmonized and directed by the
15 third, may be taken to cover the whole field, and this volume to be merely a commentary upon them. What we have to consider is, when and how this idea of progress, as a general thing affecting mankind as a whole, first appeared in the world,
20 how far it has been realized in history, and how far it gives us any guidance and hope for the future. In the midst of a catastrophe which appears at first sight to be a deadly blow to the ideal, such an inquiry has a special interest and may have some
25 permanent value.

Words are the thought of ages crystallized, or rather embodied with a constantly growing soul. The word 'Progress', like the word 'Humanity', is one of the most significant. It is a Latin word, not
30 used in its current abstract sense until after the Roman incorporation of the Mediterranean world. It contains Greek thought summed up and applied by Roman minds. Many of the earlier Greek thinkers, Xenophanes and Empedocles as well as
35 Plato and Aristotle, had thought and spoken of a steady process in things, including man himself, from lower to higher forms; but the first writer who expounds the notion with sufficient breadth of view and sufficiently accurate and concrete
40 observation to provide a preliminary sketch, was the great Roman poet who attributed all the best that was in him to the Greeks and yet has given us a highly original picture of the upward tendency of the world and of human society upon it. He,
45 too, so far as one can discover, was the first to use the word 'progress' in the sense of our inquiry. The passage in Lucretius at the end of his fifth book on the Nature of Things is so true and brilliant and anticipates so many points in later thought
50 that it is worth quoting at some length, and the poet's close relation with Cicero, the typical Greco-Roman thinker, gives his ideas the more weight as an historical document.

He begins by describing a struggle for existence
55 in which the less well-adapted creatures died off, those who wanted either the power to protect themselves or the means of adapting themselves to the purposes of man. In this stage, however, man was a hardier creature than he afterwards
60 became. He lived like the beasts of the field and was ignorant of tillage or fire or clothes or houses. He had no laws or government or marriage, and though he did not fear the dark, he feared the real danger of fiercer beasts. Men often died a miserable
65 death, but not in multitudes on a single day as they do now by battle or shipwreck.

The next stage sees huts and skins and fire which softened their bodies, and marriage and the ties of family which softened their tempers. And
70 tribes began to make treaties of alliance with other tribes.

Speech arose from the need which all creatures feel to exercise their natural powers, just as the calf will butt before his horns protrude. Men began to
75 apply different sounds to denote different things, just as brute beasts will do to express different passions, as any one must have noticed in the cases of dogs and horses and birds. No one man set out to invent speech.

80 Fire was first learnt from lightning and the friction of trees, and cooking from the softening and ripening of things by the sun.

Then men of genius invented improved methods of life, the building of cities and private
85 property in lands and cattle. But gold gave power to the wealthy and destroyed the sense of contentment in simple happiness. It must always be so whenever men allow themselves to become the slaves of things which should be their
90 dependants and instruments.

They began to believe in and worship gods, because they saw in dreams shapes of preterhuman strength and beauty and deemed them immortal;

and as they noted the changes of the seasons and
all the wonders of the heavens, they placed their
gods there and feared them when they spoke in
the thunder. Metals were discovered through the
burning of the woods, which caused the ores to
run. Copper and brass came first and were rated
above gold and silver. And then the metals took
the place of hands, nails, teeth, and clubs, which
had been men's earliest arms and tools. Weaving
followed the discovery of the use of iron.

　　Sowing, planting, and grafting were learnt
from nature herself, and gradually the cultivation
of the soil was carried farther and farther up the
hills.

　　Men learnt to sing from the birds, and to blow
on pipes from the whistling of the zephyr through
the reeds: and those simple tunes gave as much
rustic jollity as our more elaborate tunes do now.

　　Then, in a summary passage at the end,
Lucretius enumerates all the chief discoveries
which men have made in the age-long process—
ships, agriculture, walled cities, laws, roads, clothes,
songs, pictures, statues, and all the pleasures of
life— and adds, 'these things practice and the
experience of the unresting mind have taught
mankind gradually as they have progressed from
point to point'.

21

Why did the author probably have three opinions put together in the first paragraph?

A) to include as many diverse perspectives as possible

B) to investigate any possible difference(s) between vocations or ways of life

C) because one of them served as a base on which to build toward to the next step of the discussion

D) because they are by nature among the best material that can be used for an introduction

22

In context, which of the following is the best interpretation of "whole field"?

A) philosophy

B) everyday life

C) defining a concept

D) a certain compromise

23

According to the passage, what is the most probable role of the three opinions mentioned in paragraph 1?

A) It provides an introduction to the main discussion of the concept, progress.

B) It provides the most significant argument to be commented upon.

C) It provides a foundation of scholarly enterprise to be expanded on later.

D) It provides a way of harmonizing and indicating a direction.

Test 5

24

According to the passage, what can be said about humanity?

A) It must have the same history as the word soul.

B) The clarity of its meaning has been improving for a long time.

C) Words such as this normally change their meanings constantly.

D) Its change in meaning might be related to it being used in the field of politics.

25

According to the passage, which of the following is most likely to be the first step in this application of these Roman minds in Question 23?

A) a correct and broad examination with hierarchical approaches

B) making a better use of rhythmic languages rather than prose even though they were to express the practical side of progress

C) taking full advantage of the concept of progress in a very contemporary perspective

D) tapping into the concept of the survival of the fittest

26

Which of following offers the best evidence for the answer to the previous question?

A) "Then men of genius invented improved methods of life, the building of cities and private property in lands and cattle." (Lines 83-85)

B) "He begins by describing a struggle for existence in which the less well-adapted creatures died off," (Lines 54-55)

C) "Fire was first learnt from lightning and the friction of trees," (Lines 80-81)

D) "which had been men's earliest arms and tools. Weaving followed the discovery of the use of iron." (Lines 101-103)

27

Which of the following is most likely the author's objective by saying "hardier" (Line 59), "but not in multitudes on a single day as they do now by battle or shipwreck" (Lines 65-66)?

A) to inform the reader of a sense of change in a certain direction

B) to directly reflect the extent at which humanity used to be uncivilized

C) to demonstrate one aspect of the more dangerous modern way of life

D) to stress how futile progress can be

E) to reveal the future direction of human progress

Test 5

28

Why did the author mention speech?

A) to link inevitable events in history such as treaties and wars

B) to demystify why humans are different from other species

C) to attribute certain phenomena

D) to expound a particular pathway

29

Why does the author most probably mention fire and cooking?

A) to show how humans have exploited nature in order to progress

B) to give an example of a direct case of cause and effect

C) to lead to a more significant stage of change in human history

D) as the possible beginning of environmental destruction

E) as a very plausible origin of war

30

Which of the following words most directly signifies the implied effect gold has on human beings?

A) "the wealthy" (Line 86)

B) "slaves" (Line 89)

C) "contentment" (Line 87)

D) "instruments" (Line 90)

31

According to the passage, why did people start to be religious?

A) because they were afraid of unexplainable dreams

B) because they were frightened by the changing seasons

C) because some figures in their dreams possessed what they did not have

D) because gods were very noisy when they spoke

32

According to the passage, which of the following might be the best interpretation of songs and statues?

A) They are the best representatives of the pleasures of life.

B) They might have provided something that humans needed as they moved through history.

C) People at the time moved around more frequently than they do at the present time.

D) They are probably the products of human esthetics.

Test 5

Questions 33-42 are based on the following passage.

Nothing is more certain than that each generation longs for a reassurance as to the value and charm of life, and is secretly afraid lest it lose its sense of the youth of the earth. This is doubtless
5 one reason why it so passionately cherishes its poets and artists who have been able to explore for themselves and to reveal to others the perpetual springs of life's self-renewal. And yet the average man cannot obtain this desired reassurance
10 through literature, nor yet through glimpses of earth and sky. It can come to him only through the chance embodiment of joy and youth which life itself may throw in his way. It is doubtless true that for the mass of men the message is never so
15 unchallenged and so invincible as when embodied in youth itself. One generation after another has depended upon its young to equip it with gaiety and enthusiasm, to persuade it that living is a pleasure, until men everywhere have anxiously
20 provided channels through which this wine of life might flow, and be preserved for their delight. The classical city promoted play with careful solicitude, building the theater and stadium as it built the market place and the temple. The Greeks held their
25 games so integral a part of religion and patriotism that they came to expect from their poets the highest utterances at the very moments when the sense of pleasure released the national life. In the medieval city the knights held their tourneys, the
30 guilds their pageants, the people their dances, and the church made festival for its most cherished saints with gay street processions, and presented a drama in which no less a theme than the history of creation became a matter of thrilling interest.
35 Only in the modern city have men concluded that it is no longer necessary for the municipality to provide for the insatiable desire for play. In so far as they have acted upon this conclusion, they have entered upon a most difficult and dangerous
40 experiment; and this at the very moment when the city has become distinctly industrial, and daily labor is continually more monotonous and subdivided. We forget how new the modern city is, and how short the span of time in which we have
45 assumed that we can eliminate public provision for recreation. A further difficulty lies in the fact that this industrialism has gathered together multitudes of eager young creatures from all quarters of the earth as a labor supply for the countless factories
50 and workshops, upon which the present industrial city is based. Never before in civilization have such numbers of young girls been suddenly released from the protection of the home and permitted to walk unattended upon city streets and to work
55 under alien roofs; for the first time they are being prized more for their labor power than for their innocence, their tender beauty, their ephemeral gaiety. Society cares more for the products they manufacture than for their immemorial
60 ability to reaffirm the charm of existence. Never before have such numbers of young boys earned money independently of the family life, and felt themselves free to spend it as they choose in the midst of vice deliberately disguised as pleasure.
65 This stupid experiment of organizing work and failing to organize play has, of course, brought about a fine revenge. The love of pleasure will not be denied, and when it has turned into all sorts of malignant and vicious appetites, then we, the
70 middle aged, grow quite distracted and resort to all sorts of restrictive measures. We even try to dam up the sweet fountain itself because we are affrighted by these neglected streams; but almost worse than the restrictive measures is our apparent
75 belief that the city itself has no obligation in the matter, an assumption upon which the modern city turns over to commercialism practically all the provisions for public recreation. Quite as one set of men has organized the young people into industrial
80 enterprises in order to profit from their toil, so another set of men and also of women, I am sorry to say, have entered the neglected field of recreation and have organized enterprises which make profit out of this invincible love of pleasure. In every city
85 arise so-called "places"—" gin-palaces," they are called in fiction; in Chicago we euphemistically say merely "places,"— in which alcohol is dispensed, not to allay thirst, but, ostensibly to stimulate gaiety, it is sold really in order to empty
90 pockets. Huge dance halls are opened to which hundreds of young people are attracted, many of whom stand wistfully outside a roped circle, for it requires five cents to procure within it for five

minutes the sense of allurement and intoxication
which is sold in lieu of innocent pleasure. These
coarse and illicit merrymakings remind one of the
unrestrained jollities of Restoration London, and
they are indeed their direct descendants, properly
commercialized, still confusing joy with lust, and
gaiety with debauchery.

33

What could be the best title of the passage?

A) The history of youth and the city
B) The changing effect of youth upon the city
C) The similarities between youth and the city
D) Youth in the city

34

Why did the author talk about poets and artists?

A) to show the importance of esthetic qualities
B) to emphasize the significance of youth
C) to lead into a different topic which later becomes more important
D) to establish a connection between different concepts, which the average person would be unable to recognize

35

Which choice does "it" (Line 5) refer to?

A) each generation
B) sense
C) youth
D) earth

Test 5

36

According to the passage, what can be said about earth and sky?

A) It would be impossible to feel young just by looking at them.

B) Anybody can sense the feeling of youth by getting a glimpse of them.

C) Seeing them might remind the observer of what his/her youth was like but probably only by accident.

D) They give most people a general sense of the natural beauty of youth.

37

According to the passage, which choice gives the best evidence for the role of theaters and stadiums when they were first built in cities?

A) "turned into all sorts of malignant and vicious appetites," (Lines 68-69)

B) "provided channels through which this wine of life might flow," (Lines 20-21)

C) "make profit out of this invincible love of pleasure." (Lines 83-84)

D) "ostensibly to stimulate gaiety," (Lines 88-89)

38

According to the author, what can be said about pleasure?

A) All the pleasure is malicious.

B) Most pleasure is a means to help old people remember what their youth was like.

C) Intoxication is the worst kind of pleasure.

D) There are basically two different kinds.

39

Which choice gives the best evidence for the answer to the previous question?

A) "The Greeks held their games so a part of religion and patriotism that they came to expect from their poets the highest utterances at the very moments" (Lines 24-27)

B) "when it has turned into all sorts of malignant and vicious appetites, then we, the middle aged, grow quite distracted and resort to all sorts of restrictive measures." (Lines 68-71)

C) "it requires five cents to procure within it for five minutes the sense of allurement and intoxication which is sold in lieu of innocent pleasure." (Lines 93-95)

D) "the sense of pleasure released the national life." (Lines 27-28)

40

According to the passage, what can be said about gaiety?

A) The young have more of it than the old.

B) It is absolutely irrelevant to young people.

C) It is more similar to joy than to lust.

D) It cannot be obtained from such places as stadiums.

Test 5

41

According to the passage, what is the connection between the city and the youth?

A) They used to be strongly related in every sense.

B) The city is a fountain of youth, and the fountain becomes more powerful as history progresses.

C) The city is responsible for maintaining the youth.

D) The city possesses many minor tracks to promote the beauty of the youth.

42

As used in line 22, "solicitude" most nearly means

A) concern

B) anxiety

C) hope

D) solitude

Test 5

Questions 43-52 are based on the following passage.

In a sense, the experience of the past may, unfortunately, provide a clue to the future. The last two great wars have shown an increasing emphasis on ideology or political faith as driving forces
5 behind warfare, rather than the considerations of coldly calculated diplomacy. Wars become more serious, and less gentlemanly; the enemy must be taken into account not merely as a man, but as a fanatic. To the normal group-loyalty of any good
10 soldier to his army, right or wrong, there is added the loyalty to the Ism or the Leader. Warfare thus goes back to the Wars of Faith. It is possible that techniques from the Christian-Mohammedan or from the Protestant-Catholic wars of the past
15 could be reexamined with a view to establishing those parts of their tested experience which may seem to be psychologically and militarily sound in our own time. How fast can converts be made from the other side? In what circumstances
20 should an enemy word of honor be treated as valid? How can heretics (today, read "subversive elements") be uprooted? Does the enemy faith have weak points which permit enemy beliefs to be turned against personnel at the appropriate
25 times? What unobjectionable forms should leaflets and broadcasts follow in mentioning subjects which are revered by the enemy but not by ourselves? The expansion of the Islamic Faith-and-Empire provides a great deal of procedural
30 information which cannot be neglected in our time. It has been said that men's faith should not be destroyed by violence, and that force alone is insufficient to change the minds of men. If this were true, it would mean that Germany can never
35 be de-Nazified, and that there is no hope that the democratic peoples captured by totalitarian powers can adjust themselves to their new overlords or, if adjusted, can be converted back to free principles. In reality warfare by Mohammed's captains and
40 successors demonstrated two principles of long-range psychological warfare which are still valid today:

A people can be converted from one faith to the other if given the choice between conversion
45 and extermination, stubborn individuals being rooted out. To effect the initial conversion, participation in the public ceremonies and formal language of the new faith must be required. Sustained counterintelligence must remain on the
50 alert against backsliders, but formal acceptance will become genuine acceptance if all public media of expression are denied the vanquished faith.

If immediate wholesale conversion would require military operations that were too extensive
55 or severe, the same result can be effected by toleration of the objectionable faith, combined with the issuance of genuine privileges to the new, preferred faith. The conquered people are left in the private, humble enjoyment of their old
60 beliefs and folkways; but all participation in public life, whether political, cultural or economic, is conditioned on acceptance of the new faith. In this manner, all up-rising members of the society will move in a few generations over to the new
65 faith in the process of becoming rich, powerful, or learned; what is left of the old faith will be a gutter superstition, possessing neither power nor majesty.

These two rules worked once in the rise of Islam. They were applied again by Nazi overlords
70 during World War II, the former in Poland, the Ukraine and Byelorussia, the latter in Holland, Belgium, Norway and other Western countries. The rules will probably be seen in action again. The former process is difficult and bloody, but quick;
75 the latter is as sure as a steam-roller. If Christians, or democrats, or progressives— whatever free men may be called— are put in a position of underprivilege and shame for their beliefs, and if the door is left open to voluntary conversion, so
80 that anyone who wants to can come over to the winning side, the winning side will sooner or later convert almost everyone who is capable of making trouble. (In the language of Vilfredo Pareto, this would probably be termed "capture of the rising
85 elite"; in the language of present-day Marxists, this would be described as "utilization of potential leadership cadres from historically superseded classes"; in the language of practical politics, it means "cut in the smart boys from the opposition,
90 so that they can't set up a racket of their own.")

Test 5

43

What could be the best title of the passage?

A) Why certain types of psychological warfare fail

B) Different types of psychological warfare

C) A focus on psychological warfare

D) The operation of a certain endeavor related to war

44

According to the passage, which of the following could be the driving force in the conduct of a war?

A) a winning diplomatic strategy

B) something practical

C) a combination of something ideological and something practical

D) an ideological approach

45

Which choice gives the best evidence for the answer to the previous question?

A) Lines 53-56 ("If immediate…faith,")

B) Lines 85-89 ("in the language…classes.")

C) Lines 3-5 ("emphasis…behind warfare.")

D) Lines 37-38 ("if…free principles.")

46

According to the passage, what would it be that needs to be done if simple persuasion proved ineffective?

A) stand the enemy's faith

B) grant significant and practical privileges to followers of the victor's new, preferred faith

C) end the war on terms that put restrictions on the enemy

D) make a greater effort to persuade the enemy

47

Which choice gives the best evidence for the answer to the previous question?

A) Lines 58-61 ("The conquered…in public life")

B) Lines 53-56 ("If immediate…faith,")

C) Lines 56-58 ("combined…preferred faith.")

D) Lines 73-75 ("The former…steam-roller.")

48

As used in line 53, "wholesale" most nearly means

A) economic

B) expansive

C) sustained

D) effective

133

Test 5

49

According to the passage, which of the following is true of a new faith after a war?

A) Every conquered person must either follow it or suffer cherishing the old faith.

B) Even when clinging to their prewar faith, the conquered people cannot be totally free from the influence of the new faith.

C) There are two rules in effect that help control a prewar faith.

D) What happened in Norway was a good example of what happens when a new faith is reluctantly embraced.

50

Which choice gives the best evidence for the answer to the previous question?

A) "The rules will probably be seen in action again." (Line 73)

B) "The conquered people are left in the private, humble enjoyment of their old beliefs and folkways;" (Lines 58-60)

C) "The former process is difficult and bloody, but quick; the latter is as sure as a steam-roller." (Lines 73-75)

D) "But all participation in public life, whether political, cultural or economic, is conditioned on acceptance of the new faith." (Lines 60-62)

51

As used in in line 82, "is capable of making trouble" most nearly means

A) can cause a revolution after the war is over

B) can change their minds

C) can never be converted

D) cannot endure further suffering as a conquered people

52

According to the passage, which of the following is most probably what the author means by "a racket of their own" (Line 90)?

A) a new faith that is compatible with the victor's

B) a new political activity which the victor will probably not accept

C) a faith that is unacceptable because it is too radical

D) social behavior that is unacceptable because it directly contradicts the victor's vision for a new society

STOP

TEST 6

1 2 3 4 5 6

Test 6

Reading | 65 minutes, 50 questions

DIRECTIONS

Each passage below is followed by a number of questions. After reading each passage, choose the best answer to each question based on what is stated or implied in the passage.

Questions 1-10 are based on the following passage.

"Sense with keenest edge unused Yet unsteel'd by scathing fire: Lovely feet as yet unbruised On the ways of dark desire!" These words written by a poet to his young son express the longing which
[5] has at times seized all of us, to guard youth from the mass of difficulties which may be traced to the obscure manifestation of that fundamental susceptibility of which we are all slow to speak and concerning which we evade public responsibility,
[10] although it brings its scores of victims into the police courts every morning. At the very outset we must bear in mind that the senses of youth are singularly acute, and ready to respond to every vivid appeal. We know that nature herself has
[15] sharpened the senses for her own purposes, and is deliberately establishing a connection between them and the newly awakened susceptibility of sex; for it is only through the outward senses that the selection of an individual mate is made and
[20] the instinct utilized for nature's purposes. It would seem, however, that nature was determined that the force and constancy of the instinct must make up for its lack of precision, and that she was totally unconcerned that this instinct ruthlessly seized the
[25] youth at the moment when he was least prepared to cope with it; not only because his powers of self-control and discrimination are unequal to the task, but because his senses are helplessly wide open to the world. These early manifestations of the
[30] sex susceptibility are for the most part vague and formless, and are absolutely without definition to the youth himself. Sometimes months and years elapse before the individual mate is selected and determined upon, and during the time when the
[35] differentiation is not complete— and it often is not— there is of necessity a great deal of groping and waste. This period of groping is complicated by the fact that the youth's power for appreciating is far ahead of his ability for expression. "The inner
[40] traffic fairly obstructs the outer current," and it is nothing short of cruelty to over-stimulate his senses as does the modern city. This period is difficult everywhere, but it seems at times as if a great city almost deliberately increased its perils. The newly
[45] awakened senses are appealed to by all that is gaudy and sensual, by the flippant street music, the highly colored theater posters, the trashy love stories, the feathered hats, the cheap heroics of the revolvers displayed in the pawn-shop windows. This
[50] fundamental susceptibility is thus evoked without a corresponding stir of the higher imagination, and the result is as dangerous as possible. We are told upon good authority that "If the imagination is retarded, while the senses remain awake, we
[55] have a state of esthetic insensibility,"— in other words, the senses become sodden and cannot be lifted from the ground. It is this state of "esthetic insensibility" into which we allow the youth to fall which is so distressing and so unjustifiable.
[60] Sex impulse then becomes merely a dumb and powerful instinct without in the least awakening the imagination or the heart, nor does it overflow into neighboring fields of consciousness. Every city contains hundreds of degenerates who have been
[65] over-mastered and borne down by it; they fill the

casual lodging houses and the infirmaries. In many instances it has pushed men of ability and promise to the bottom of the social scale. Warner, in his American Charities, designates it as one of the
70 steady forces making for failure and poverty, and contends that "the inherent uncleanness of their minds prevents many men from rising above the rank of day laborers and finally incapacitates them even for that position." He also suggests that the
75 modern man has a stronger imagination than the man of a few hundred years ago and that sensuality destroys him the more rapidly. It is difficult to state how much evil and distress might be averted if the imagination were utilized in its higher capacities
80 through the historic paths.

1

What could be the best title of the passage?

A) The inevitable entanglement of youth and the city

B) How city influences youth

C) The numerous obstacles in the city

D) Why it is so difficult to find a future spouse in the city

2

Which choice would most likely be the author's attitude toward natural disasters such as an earthquake, if s/he maintained the same attitude s/he has about youth?

A) S/he would immediately restore all losses caused by them.

B) S/he would individually hold responsible every individual affected by them.

C) S/he would argue for collective responsibility to deal with the necessary reconstruction.

D) Only natural disasters that occur in the city are of any consequence.

3

According to the passage, when the time comes to choose a mate, what is the solution to the problems caused by a lack of maturity?

A) sensuality

B) imagination

C) youth itself

D) a careful selection process

137

Test 6

4

Which choice gives the best evidence for the answer to the previous question?

A) "If the imagination is…a state of esthetic insensibility," (Lines 53-55)

B) "It is this state of "esthetic insensibility" …so unjustifiable." (Lines 57-59)

C) "Every city contains hundreds of…the infirmaries" (Lines 63-66)

D) "Sometimes months and years elapse…a great deal of groping and waste." (Lines 32-37)

5

The author sees the "fundamental susceptibility" mentioned in line 7-8 as

A) fundamentally malignant because it lacks imagination

B) something that could work better under certain conditions

C) absolutely indispensable

D) unconditionally risky no matter where it comes from

6

According to the passage, why would finding a spouse be more problematic than not finding one?

A) because males have difficulty expressing their needs

B) because qualifications do not always match expectations

C) because the inner conflict between the two opposite genders obstructs the surroundings

D) partly because some of their surroundings tends to produce more problems than they did before

7

Which choice gives the best evidence for the answer to the previous question?

A) "The inner traffic fairly obstructs the outer current," (Lines 39-40)

B) "it is nothing short of cruelty to over-stimulate his senses as does the modern city." (Lines 40-42)

C) "This fundamental susceptibility is thus evoked without a corresponding stir of the higher imagination," (Lines 49-51)

D) "This period is difficult everywhere, but it seems at times as if a great city almost deliberately increased its perils." (Lines 42-44)

New SAT Reading Prep

Test 6

8

Why did the author mention "casual lodging" (Line 66)?

A) to stress how inexpensive accommodations are in the city

B) to show how common a certain phenomenon is

C) to illustrate why a certain type of accommodation is more popular than other types

D) to suggest that youngsters regard lodgings as something very easy to get

9

As used in line 56, "sodden" most nearly means

A) invigorated

B) darkened

C) moisturized

D) dull

10

According to the passage, what is true of esthetic insensibility?

A) The fundamental susceptibility will always lead to it.

B) It can be mostly found on the ground.

C) One needs some sort of mental power to snap out of it.

D) It comes from a lack of artistic training.

Test 6

Questions 11-20 are based on the following passage.

This is a day of national consecration, and I am certain that on this day my fellow Americans expect that on my induction into the Presidency I will address them with a candor and a decision
[5] which the present situation of our people impels. This is preeminently the time to speak the truth, the whole truth, frankly and boldly. Nor need we shrink from honestly facing conditions in our country today. This great Nation will endure
[10] as it has endured, will revive and will prosper. So, first of all, let me assert my firm belief that the only thing we have to fear is fear itself— nameless, unreasoning, unjustified terror which paralyzes needed efforts to convert retreat into
[15] advance. In every dark hour of our national life a leadership of frankness and of vigor has met with that understanding and support of the people themselves which is essential to victory. And I am convinced that you will again give that support
[20] to leadership in these critical days. In such a spirit on my part and on yours we face our common difficulties. They concern, thank God, only material things. Values have shrunk to fantastic levels; taxes have risen; our ability to pay has
[25] fallen; government of all kinds is faced by serious curtailment of income; the means of exchange are frozen in the currents of trade; the withered leaves of industrial enterprise lie on every side; farmers find no markets for their produce; and
[30] the savings of many years in thousands of families are gone. More important, a host of unemployed citizens face the grim problem of existence, and an equally great number toil with little return. Only a foolish optimist can deny the dark realities of
[35] the moment. And yet our distress comes from no failure of substance. We are stricken by no plague of locusts. Compared with the perils which our forefathers conquered because they believed and were not afraid, we have still much to be thankful
[40] for. Nature still offers her bounty and human efforts have multiplied it. Plenty is at our doorstep, but a generous use of it languishes in the very sight of the supply.

Primarily this is because the rulers of the
[45] exchange of mankind's goods have failed, through their own stubbornness and their own incompetence, have admitted their failure and have abdicated. Practices of the unscrupulous money changers stand indicted in the court of
[50] public opinion, rejected by the hearts and minds of men. True they have tried, but their efforts have been cast in the pattern of an outworn tradition. Faced by failure of credit they have proposed only the lending of more money. Stripped of the lure of
[55] profit by which to induce our people to follow their false leadership, they have resorted to exhortations, pleading tearfully for restored confidence. They only know the rules of a generation of self-seekers. They have no vision, and when there is no vision
[60] the people perish. Yes, the money changers have fled from their high seats in the temple of our civilization. We may now restore that temple to the ancient truths. The measure of that restoration lies in the extent to which we apply social values
[65] more noble than mere monetary profit. Happiness lies not in the mere possession of money; it lies in the joy of achievement, in the thrill of creative effort. The joy, the moral stimulation of work no longer must be forgotten in the mad chase of
[70] evanescent profits. These dark days, my friends, will be worth all they cost us if they teach us that our true destiny is not to be ministered unto but to minister to ourselves—to our fellow men. Recognition of that falsity of material wealth as
[75] the standard of success goes hand in hand with the abandonment of the false belief that public office and high political position are to be valued only by the standards of pride of place and personal profit; and there must be an end to a conduct
[80] in banking and in business which too often has given to a sacred trust the likeness of callous and selfish wrongdoing. Small wonder that confidence languishes, for it thrives only on honesty, on honor, on the sacredness of obligations, on faithful
[85] protection, and on unselfish performance; without them it cannot live.

Test 6

11

What is the main topic of the passage?

A) America would be in danger without immediate and productive measures.

B) America can make a comeback as a world superpower.

C) There is a way for the nation to get back on course.

D) Money changers have created most of the major problems in the world.

12

According to the passage, who are most likely the rulers of the exchange of mankind's goods?

A) incompetent economists

B) immoral business people

C) corrupt politicians

D) whoever is responsible for the current ordeal

13

In context, what is the most probable reason for which what nature's offer weakens before it is actually used?

A) the way nature runs its course

B) historical inevitability

C) human interference

D) conflicts among international rivals

14

According to the passage, what could happen to people without vision?

A) They could physically die.

B) Their nation could disappear.

C) They could vanish into historical oblivion.

D) Money changers could abandon them.

15

As used in line 48, "abdicated" most nearly means

A) forgot

B) gave up

C) lessened

D) came back

16

As used in line 48, "unscrupulous" most nearly means

A) insufficient

B) incapable

C) bungling

D) unprincipled

Test 6

17

In the beginning of the passage, which of the following is most likely the reason that the author mentions the importance of candor?

A) because in general, it is the most important trait politicians must possess along with the sense of morality

B) because without it, it is practically impossible to comprehend what is happening in world economy

C) because the current economic situations in the U.S. is too dire to do anything about

D) because the status quo in a nation needs it to be looked at as it is

18

Which of the following is the major contrast the author employs throughout the passage?

A) the economy and politics

B) the U.S. and the world

C) money and spirit

D) idea and philosophy

19

Which of the following is the author's general attitude?

A) very pessimistic

B) carefully optimistic

C) reluctantly compromising

D) hopeful but with some fear

20

What is most likely the reason the author mentions locusts?

A) to directly criticize evil money changers

B) to lead the audience to a more important concept

C) to portray the magnitude of the natural disasters

D) to compare a biological crisis with an economic crises

Questions 21-30 are based on the following passage.

It is improbable that more nonsense has been written about aesthetics than about anything else: the literature of the subject is not large enough for that. It is certain, however, that about no subject
5 with which I am acquainted has so little been said that is at all to the purpose. The explanation is discoverable. He who would elaborate a plausible theory of aesthetics must possess two qualities—artistic sensibility and a turn for clear thinking.
10 Without sensibility a man can have no aesthetic experience, and, obviously, theories not based on broad and deep aesthetic experience are worthless. Only those for whom art is a constant source of passionate emotion can possess the data from
15 which profitable theories may be deduced; but to deduce profitable theories even from accurate data involves a certain amount of brain-work, and, unfortunately, robust intellects and delicate sensibilities are not inseparable. As often as not, the
20 hardest thinkers have had no aesthetic experience whatever. I have a friend blessed with an intellect as keen as a drill, who, though he takes an interest in aesthetics, has never during a life of almost forty years been guilty of an aesthetic emotion.
25 So, having no faculty for distinguishing a work of art from a handsaw, he is apt to rear up a pyramid of irrefragable argument on the hypothesis that a handsaw is a work of art. This defect robs his perspicuous and subtle reasoning of much of its
30 value; for it has ever been a maxim that faultless logic can win but little credit for conclusions that are based on premises notoriously false. Every cloud, however, has its silver lining, and this insensibility, though unlucky in that it makes my
35 friend incapable of choosing a sound basis for his argument, mercifully blinds him to the absurdity of his conclusions while leaving him in full enjoyment of his masterly dialectic. People who set out from the hypothesis that Sir Edwin Landseer was the
40 finest painter that ever lived will feel no uneasiness about an aesthetic which proves that Giotto was the worst. So, my friend, when he arrives very logically at the conclusion that a work of art should be small or round or smooth, or that to appreciate
45 fully a picture you should pace smartly before it or set it spinning like a top, cannot guess why I ask him whether he has lately been to Cambridge, a place he sometimes visits. On the other hand, people who respond immediately and surely to
50 works of art, though, in my judgment, more enviable than men of massive intellect but slight sensibility, are often quite as incapable of talking sense about aesthetics. Their heads are not always very clear. They possess the data on which any
55 system must be based; but, generally, they want the power that draws correct inferences from true data. Having received aesthetic emotions from works of art, they are in a position to seek out the quality common to all that have moved them, but, in fact,
60 they do nothing of the sort. I do not blame them. Why should they bother to examine their feelings when for them to feel is enough? Why should they stop to think when they are not very good at thinking? Why should they hunt for a common
65 quality in all objects that move them in a particular way when they can linger over the many delicious and peculiar charms of each as it comes? So, if they write criticism and call it aesthetics, if they imagine that they are talking about Art when they are
70 talking about particular works of art or even about the technique of painting, if, loving particular works they find tedious the consideration of art in general, perhaps they have chosen the better part.

Test 6

21

What would be the best title of the passage?

A) Art and sensibility

B) An esthetic hypothesis

C) Art and criticism

D) How art criticism is produced

22

Which of the following is not a prerequisite for creating a reasonable esthetic theory?

A) esthetic understandability

B) a certain level of intelligence

C) the capacity to view art as a resource of some kind

D) clearly artistic thinking

23

According to the passage, which of the following is a problem with the prerequisite mentioned in the previous question?

A) the incompatibility of relevant preconditions

B) the extreme difficulty involved in establishing a particular quality

C) the naiveté of the public

D) the low probability of artistic experiences

24

What is true of the author's very smart friend mentioned in the passage?

A) He has never been convicted of any emotional crime.

B) He is far too intelligent to see anything beautiful.

C) His brain might somehow be preventing him from experiencing esthetic emotion.

D) He is not cut out for appreciating art.

25

Which of the following is the mistake the author's friend makes as shown by the answer to the previous question?

A) He considers practical things as esthetic.

B) He confuses construction tools with those used for creating art.

C) He does not have the ability to speculate on the difference between tools and works of art.

D) He is unable to apply his or her intelligence to artistic contemplation.

26

Which of the following gives the best evidence for the answer to the previous question?

A) "my friend, when he arrives very logically at the conclusion that a work of art should be small or round or smooth," (Lines 42-44)

B) "he is apt to rear up a pyramid of irrefragable argument on the hypothesis that a handsaw is a work of art." (Lines 26-28)

C) "Sir Edwin Landseer was the finest painter that ever lived" (Lines 39-40)

D) "to appreciate fully a picture you should pace smartly before it or set it spinning like a top," (Lines 44-46)

27

Which of the following is the main dilemma clearly expressed in the passage?

A) Two essential qualities are unfortunately incompatible.

B) Many people are not intelligent or sensible enough to be properly artistic.

C) It is extremely difficult to distinguish between something artistic and a criticism.

D) Some people do not really care about what is truly esthetic.

28

Which of the following gives the best evidence for the answer to the previous question?

A) "they find tedious the consideration of art in general, perhaps they have chosen the better part." (Lines 72-73)

B) "more enviable than men of massive intellect but slight sensibility, are often quite as incapable of talking sense about aesthetics." (Lines 50-53)

C) "mercifully blinds him to the absurdity of his conclusions while leaving him in full enjoyment of his masterly dialectic." (Lines 36-38)

D) "unfortunately, robust intellects and delicate sensibilities are not inseparable." (Lines 18-19)

29

What is the most probable role of the questions in the later part of the passage?

A) to clarify why the main dilemma is in fact a dilemma

B) to lead to another perspective of the same argument

C) to rhetorically allude to a novel problem

D) to allow the author to retreat from his/her original position in order to make an apparent compromise

30

What does the author probably mean by "the better part" at the end of the passage?

A) what those with extreme intelligence can do

B) what those with artistic sensibility can do

C) what those with low intelligence can do

D) what those lacking in something can do

Questions 31-40 are based on the following passage.

In the last fifty years there has been much very fine and interesting speculation on the part of scientific men upon the age and origin of our earth. Here we cannot pretend to give even
[5] a summary of such speculations because they involve the most subtle mathematical and physical considerations. The truth is that the physical and astronomical sciences are still too undeveloped as yet to make anything of the sort more than an
[10] illustrative guesswork. The general tendency has been to make the estimated age of our globe longer and longer. It now seems probable that the earth has had an independent existence as a spinning planet flying round and round the sun for a longer
[15] period than 2,000,000,000 years. It may have been much longer than that. This is a length of time that absolutely overpowers the imagination. Before that vast period of separate existence, the sun and earth and the other planets that circulate round the
[20] sun may have been a great swirl of diffused matter in space. The telescope reveals to us in various parts of the heavens luminous spiral clouds of matter, the spiral nebulæ, which appear to be in rotation about a centre. It is supposed by many astronomers
[25] that the sun and its planets were once such a spiral, and that their matter has undergone concentration into its present form. Through majestic æons that concentration went on until in that vast remoteness of the past for which we have given figures, the
[30] world and its moon were distinguishable. They were spinning then much faster than they are spinning now; they were at a lesser distance from the sun; they travelled round it very much faster, and they were probably incandescent or molten at
[35] the surface. The sun itself was a much greater blaze in the heavens. If we could go back through that infinitude of time and see the earth in this earlier stage of its history, we should behold a scene more like the interior of a blast furnace or the surface
[40] of a lava flow before it cools and cakes over than any other contemporary scene. No water would be visible because all the water there was would still be superheated steam in a stormy atmosphere of sulphurous and metallic vapours. Beneath this
[45] would swirl and boil an ocean of molten rock substance. Across a sky of fiery clouds the glare of the hurrying sun and moon would sweep swiftly like hot breaths of flame. Slowly by degrees as one million of years followed another, this fiery scene
[50] would lose its eruptive incandescence. The vapours in the sky would rain down and become less dense overhead; great slaggy cakes of solidifying rock would appear upon the surface of the molten sea, and sink under it, to be replaced by other
[55] floating masses. The sun and moon growing now each more distant and each smaller, would rush with diminishing swiftness across the heavens. The moon now, because of its smaller size, would be already cooled far below incandescence, and
[60] would be alternately obstructing and reflecting the sunlight in a series of eclipses and full moons. And so with a tremendous slowness through the vastness of time, the earth would grow more and more like the earth on which we live, until at last
[65] an age would come when, in the cooling air, steam would begin to condense into clouds, and the first rain would fall hissing upon the first rocks below. For endless millenia the greater part of the earth's water would still be vaporized in the atmosphere,
[70] but there would now be hot streams running over the crystallizing rocks below and pools and lakes into which these streams would be carrying detritus and depositing sediment. At last a condition of things must have been attained in which a man
[75] might have stood up on earth and looked about him and lived. If we could have visited the earth at that time we should have stood on great lava-like masses of rock without a trace of soil or touch of living vegetation, under a storm-rent sky. Hot
[80] and violent winds, exceeding the fiercest tornado that ever blows, and downpours of rain such as our milder, slower earth to-day knows nothing of, might have assailed us. The water of the downpour would have rushed by us, muddy with the spoils of
[85] the rocks, coming together into torrents, cutting deep gorges and canyons as they hurried past to deposit their sediment in the earliest seas. Through the clouds we should have glimpsed a great sun moving visibly across the sky, and in its wake
[90] and in the wake of the moon would have come a diurnal tide of earthquake and upheaval. And the moon, which nowadays keeps one constant face to earth, would then have been rotating visibly and

Test 6

showing the side it now hides so inexorably. The
95 earth aged. One million years followed another,
and the day lengthened, the sun grew more distant
and milder, the moon's pace in the sky slackened;
the intensity of rain and storm diminished and the
water in the first seas increased and ran together
100 into the ocean garment our planet henceforth
wore. But there was no life as yet upon the earth;
the seas were lifeless, and the rocks were barren.

31

What could be the best title of the passage?

A) The Earth as a heavenly body
B) The Earth in connection with other heavenly bodies
C) The Earth in the solar system
D) The Earth in time.

32

According to the passage, the lack of which of the following is the cause of our human ignorance about the age of the Earth?

A) speculation
B) capable scientists
C) proper means of investigation
D) science

33

Which choice in Question 32 can most probably work as a reason that is very closely related to why the author says the earth might be much older than 2,000,000,000 years?

Test 6

34

What does the author mean by "overpowers the imagination" (Line 17)?

A) The concept of speculating on the age of the earth is unimaginable.

B) 2,000,000,000 years is beyond a human's ability to conceptualize.

C) 2,000,000,000 years is an amount too powerful to imagine.

D) The age of the Earth is not something to be imagined.

35

According to the passage, why did the author say "an illustrative guesswork" (Lines 9-10)?

A) to stress the nature of science

B) to claim that science cannot be depended on

C) to suggest the inherent limitations from which science suffers

D) to make sure the reader understands the immaturity of science

36

Which of the following is probably the reason why the author talks about what the telescope reveals?

A) to show the source of interpretation

B) to provide a source of a possible misinterpretation

C) to introduce a different subject matter

D) to allude to the very beginning of the previously mentioned diffusion

37

As used in line 25, "spiral" most nearly means

A) diffusion

B) rotation

C) sphere

D) concentration

38

Which choice gives the best evidence for the answer to the previous question?

A) "The sun and earth and the other planets that circulate round the sun may have been a great swirl of diffused matter in space." (Lines 18-21)

B) "that their matter has undergone concentration into its present form." (Lines 26-27)

C) "luminous spiral clouds of matter, the spiral nebulæ, which appear to be in rotation about a centre." (Lines 22-24)

D) "concentration went on until in that vast remoteness of the past for which we have given figures," (Lines 28-29)

39

As used in line 50, "incandescence" most nearly means

A) fire

B) temperature

C) bright light

D) emission of light

Test 6

40

According to the passage, the discussion of which will most logically follow?

A) the development of rocks
B) the history of weather on Earth
C) life
D) the continuing cooling process of the Earth

Test 6

Questions 41-50 are based on the following passage.

   The first and most obvious light in which the sea presents itself from the political and social point of view is that of a great highway; or better, perhaps, of a wide common, over which men may
5 pass in all directions, but on which some well-worn paths show that controlling reasons have led them to choose certain lines of travel rather than others. These lines of travel are called trade routes; and the reasons which have determined
10 them are to be sought in the history of the world. Notwithstanding all the familiar and unfamiliar dangers of the sea, both travel and traffic by water have always been easier and cheaper than by land. The commercial greatness of Holland was due
15 not only to her shipping at sea, but also to the numerous tranquil water-ways which gave such cheap and easy access to her own interior and to that of Germany. This advantage of carriage by water over that by land was yet more marked in
20 a period when roads were few and very bad, wars frequent and society unsettled, as was the case two hundred years ago. Sea traffic then went in peril of robbers, but was nevertheless safer and quicker than that by land. A Dutch writer of that time,
25 estimating the chances of his country in a war with England, notices among other things that the water-ways of England failed to penetrate the country sufficiently; therefore, the roads being bad, goods from one part of the kingdom to the other
30 must go by sea, and be exposed to capture by the way. As regards purely internal trade, this danger has generally disappeared at the present day. In most civilized countries, now, the destruction or disappearance of the coasting trade would only be
35 an inconvenience, although water transit is still the cheaper. Nevertheless, as late as the wars of the French Republic and the First Empire, those who are familiar with the history of the period, and the light naval literature that has grown up
40 around it, know how constant is the mention of convoys stealing from point to point along the French coast, although the sea swarmed with English cruisers and there were good inland roads. Under modern conditions, however, home trade is
45 but a part of the business of a country bordering on the sea. Foreign necessaries or luxuries must be brought to its ports, either in its own or in foreign ships, which will return, bearing in exchange the products of the country, whether they be the fruits
50 of the earth or the works of men's hands; and it is the wish of every nation that this shipping business should be done by its own vessels. The ships that thus sail to and fro must have secure ports to which to return, and must, as far as possible, be followed
55 by the protection of their country throughout the voyage. This protection in time of war must be extended by armed shipping. The necessity of a navy, in the restricted sense of the word, springs, therefore, from the existence of a peaceful
60 shipping, and disappears with it, except in the case of a nation which has aggressive tendencies, and keeps up a navy merely as a branch of the military establishment. As the United States has at present no aggressive purposes, and as its merchant service
65 has disappeared, the dwindling of the armed fleet and general lack of interest in it are strictly logical consequences.

Test 6

41

What would be the best title of the passage?

A) The sea and its military possibilities

B) The importance of the sea in European history

C) The influence of sea power upon history

D) A historic interpretation of sea power in various parts of the world

42

According to the passage which of the following can be most directly inferred about maritime trade routes?

A) They were established because they were politically easier to control than other sea routes.

B) They were viewed as the greatest highways of commerce.

C) For some practical reasons they were more frequently taken advantage of than other paths.

D) They were the main cause of war.

43

According to the passage, which of the following can be inferred about the claim made by a Dutch writer?

A) His country had a greater chance of going to war with England than with other countries.

B) England needed more rivers and lakes to avoid war with his country.

C) His country's chances of victory in a war with England might have come from certain aspects of England's geography.

D) His country had to attack England's shipping on the high seas.

44

Which of the following is the most direct evidence for the answer to the previous question?

A) "generally disappeared at the present day." (Line 32)

B) "failed to penetrate the country sufficiently" (Lines 27-28)

C) "nevertheless safer and quicker than that by land." (Lines 23-24)

D) "inconvenience," (Line 35)

Test 6

45

Which of the following, if proved, would work as the most direct criticism toward the author's argument?

A) European countries only had peaceful motives for maintaining naval forces which were solely for self-defense.

B) There were so many reasons why countries went to war; needing to control sea routes was just one reason.

C) The U.S. has a history of using its naval forces for more than just the protection of its peaceful shipping.

D) The origin of war can easily be attributed to how ocean highways came into being.

46

Which of the following is the most direct evidence for the answer to the previous question?

A) "from the political and social point of view is that of a great highway;" (Lines 2-3)

B) "the United States has at present no aggressive purposes," (Lines 63-64)

C) "disappears with it" (Line 60)

D) "wars frequent and society unsettled" (Lines 20-21)

47

Which of the following can best be inferred from the claim the author is making about the navy?

A) It was the first form of military endeavor in the history of armed forces.

B) It probably came into existence not as part of a war effort.

C) Historically, most countries used it to protect their peaceful shipping.

D) The U.S. has the largest navy in the world.

48

According to the passage, which of the following cannot be true?

A) Almost every nation had a navy which was traditionally used for the protection of peaceful shipping.

B) Some sea routes were harder to use than others.

C) At present, in some cases, domestic trade routes are not very important.

D) It was inevitable that the American navy would not expand over the course of the country's history.

49

Which of the following is the most direct evidence for the answer to the previous question?

A) Lines 14-18 ("The commercial…Germany.")

B) Lines 57-60 ("The necessity…shipping,")

C) Lines 53-56 ("The ships…voyage.")

D) Lines 22-24 ("Sea traffic…by land.")

New SAT Reading Prep 152

Test 6

50

What can be said about land and water transit?

A) One was always cheaper than the other.

B) One was always better than the other.

C) One was always more desired than the other.

D) At a certain point in history one was more available than the other.

STOP

The Redesigned SAT Practice Tests

Strategy

Answer Keys & Explanations

The most efficient SAT taking STRATEGY

In fact, the best strategy is no strategy. Needing no strategy because the passage you are dealing with is so easy to understand is the best situation ever, so the strategy introduced here is the best alternative.

First of all, there are four simple, different ways of telling the answer from the rest of answer choices.

1. POSITIVE VS. NEGATIVE

A significant number of answer choices can be classified either as distinctively POSITIVE or NEGATIVE. No matter how difficult any answer choice might be, If it is either POSITIVE or NEGATIVE, it is relatively easy to see if that answer choice is the answer or nor. Let's take a look at the following example.

> 43. What is the author's attitude toward space travel?
> (A) Enthusiastic
> (B) Ambitious
> (C) Hopeful
> (D) Cautious

If in context, the author's attitude toward space travel is positive, we need to know exactly in what way the author is positive toward that, but if it is negative, the only possible answer is (D).

2. WRONG PERSPECTIVE

No matter how difficult any choice is to understand, if only one or two of the choices have the relevant perspective to the question it would be not that difficult. An example for this.

> 27. Why did the author oppose further investment in medical care?
> (A) Because it would be a huge waste in time and money.
> (B) Because it would create more XYZ problems than now
> (C) Because it would be such a mistake as helping the enemy nations
> (D) Because it would need more experts than society can offer.

New SAT Reading Prep

No matter what XYZ might mean if the argument is about financial problems the answer has to be (A).

3. CLOSER PARAPHRASING

If two or more answer choices look as if they mean the same, whichever is more closely paraphrased is the answer, and the other choice(s) must be wrongly inferred.

    56. Which of the following would be correct understanding of newly constructed museum downtown?
        (A) displaying a wide variety of visual exhibits
        (B) being represented as a major art museum
        (C) maintaining a position as a foremost art experiment
        (D) being characterized as a good place for many artworks

Let's say the exact expression used in the passage is "the greatest number of paintings are displayed". If we casually look at the four choices, all of them look possible to be the answer. However, if we look at the following translations, the answer would be obvious.

    (A) the greatest number of paintings -?-> a wide variety of visual exhibits
    (B) the greatest number of paintings -?-> a major art museum
    (C) the greatest number of paintings -?-> a foremost art experiment
    (D) the greatest number of paintings -?-> a good place for many artworks
    The question is very simple; can they all be paraphrased as intended as above?

(A) the greatest number might and might not be a wide variety because only a few kinds of paintings but a lot of them are possible: Wrong choice.
(B) Of course if any museum possesses the greatest number of paintings, it may well be a major art museum, but it doesn't have to be, because all those paintings are in very low quality. All we know is the number: a typical case of WRONG INFERENCE (to be explained later).
(C). if a museum possesses the greatest number of paintings, there is a fairly good chance that the museum is a very progressive and experimental place, but it is only a possibility, no matter how strong it is: a typical case of WRONG INFERENCE (to be explained later).
(D) Even though 'many' cannot be translated as the greatest number of, the other way around is always true. So we can say (D) is more closely paraphrased than (A).

4. INCLUSIVENESS

If an answer choice is inclusive of another, then at all times the inclusive choice is the answer.

18. What is the author mainly talking about as the reason for his return?

    (A) an animal
    (B) a cat
    (C) a dog
    (D) some big animal

No matter how difficult the entire passage is, if the answer choices are like the above, the answer is obviously (A) because any of the other three choices is the answer, automatically (A) is still the answer. Since there can't be two answers, the answer is (A), even though we don't have the passage.

We can easily say that either a cat or a dog, or even some big animal is probably mentioned in the passage, but that is not the reason for the author's return, it was "a sheep" that made him come home. However, without knowing all this, just by looking at the four choices, we should be able to tell the answer must be (A).

The second part of our Strategy is focused on the wrong choices; there is only one correct choice, but three WRONG choices, so in a way wrong choices are more important. The wrong choices display interesting traits as follows

    1. TOO NARROW or TOO BROAD to be the answer
    2. wrong COMPARISON and CONTRAST to be the answer
    3. wrong CAUSE and EFFECT to be the answer
    4. WRONG INFERENCE

In fact, 1, 2, 3 are, broadly speaking, part of WRONG INFERENCE, but those three are distinctively different, so they are separated from WRONG INFERENCE. These four traits or types need no examples for further explanation because they as self-explanatory as they sound. Thus, when you read explanations using those four concepts, you will just know what is happening.

New SAT Reading Prep

TEST 1

Answer Keys & Explanations

Test 1

There is some confusion in the use of the terms "nutrient," "plant food," etc., as applied to the nutrition and growth of plants. Strictly speaking, these terms ought probably to be limited in their
5   application to the organized compounds within the plant which it uses as sources of energy and of metabolizable material for the development of new cells and organs during its growth.

   Botanists quite commonly use the terms in this
10 way. But students of the problems involved in the relation of soil elements to the growth of plants, including such practical questions as are involved in the maintenance of soil productivity and the use of commercial fertilizers for the growing of
15 economic plants, or crops, are accustomed to use the terms "plant foods," or "mineral nutrients," to designate the chemical elements and simple gaseous compounds which are supplied to the plant as the raw material from which its food and
20 tissue-building materials are synthetized. Common usage limits these terms to the soil elements; but there is no logical reason for segregating the raw materials derived from the soil from those derived from the atmosphere.

25   The essential difference between these raw materials for plant syntheses and the organic compounds which are produced within the plants and used by them, and by animals, as food, is that the former are inorganic and can furnish only
30 materials but no energy to the organism; while the latter are organic and supply both materials and potential energy. It would probably be the best practice to confine the use of the word "food" to materials of the latter type, and several attempts
35 have been made to limit its use in this way and to apply some such term as "intake" to the simple raw materials which are taken into the organism and utilized by it in its synthetic processes. But the custom of using the words "food," or "nutrient," to
40 represent anything that is taken into the organism and in any way utilized by it for its nourishment has been followed so long and the newer terms are themselves so subject to criticism that they have not yet generally supplanted the loosely used word
45 "food."

   If such use is permitted, however, it is necessary to recognize that only the green parts of green plants can use this inorganic "food," and that the colorless plants must have organic food.

50   To avoid this confusion, the suggestion has recently been made that all of the intake of plants and animals shall be considered as food, but that those forms which supply both materials and potential energy to the organism shall be
55 designated as synergic foods, while those which contain no potential energy shall be known as anergic foods. On this basis, practically all of the food of animals, excepting the mineral salts and water, and all of the organic compounds which
60 are synthetized by plants and later used by them for further metabolic changes, are synergic foods; while practically all of the intake of green plants is anergic food.

   It is with the latter type of food materials
65 that this chapter is to deal; while the following and all subsequent chapters deal with the organic compounds which are synthetized by plants and contain potential energy and are, therefore, capable of use as synergic food by either the plants
70 themselves or by animals. It will be understood, therefore, that in this chapter the word "food" is used to mean the anergic food materials which are taken into and used by green plants as the raw materials for the synthesis of organic compounds,
75 with the aid of solar energy, or that of previously produced synergic foods. In all later chapters, the term "food" will be used to mean the organic compounds which serve as the synergic food for the green parts of green plants and as the sole
80 supply of nutrient material for the colorless parts of green plants and for parasitic or saprophytic forms.

Test 1

1

What would be the best title of the passage?

A) The differences between green plants and their colorless counterparts

B) The ways food is utilized within different kinds of plants

C) How a certain definition affects some interpretation

D) Possible differences between organic and inorganic food

The best answer is (C).
This passage talks about how a certain definition ("as applied to the nutrition and growth of plants") affects ("If such use is permitted,…it is necessary to recognize that only the green parts of green plants can use this inorganic "food," and that the colorless plants must have organic food.") some interpretation ("…shall be considered as food,")

(A); Green plants and colorless plants are mentioned but to show how different terms are used ("however, it is necessary to recognize that only the green parts of green plants can use this inorganic "food," and that the colorless plants must have organic food") for different kinds of plants. (B); Because of (A), the answer, (B) is mentioned. (D); The author concentrates only on one perspective that is nutrients, food, not possible differences)

2

Which of the following is the primary conflict described in the passage?

A) conflicting ways food can be observed

B) complications involved in looking at a certain phenomenon

C) problems distinguishing what is green and what is not

D) problems distinguishing what is organic and what is inorganic

The best answer is (B).
Actually, (B) here is like an extension of (C) in the previous question. Depending on how we use the term "food"("loosely used word 'food.'") (certain phenomenon), "it is necessary to recognize that only the green parts of green plants can use this inorganic "food," and that the colorless plants must have organic food." "subject to criticism."(complication)

(A); There are only two ways: strict and loose
(C), (D); What needs to be distinguished is what food is, and what food is not)

3

Which of the following gives the most direct evidence for the answer to the previous question?

A) Lines 28-32 ("and used…energy.")

B) Lines 32-35 ("It would…this way")

C) Lines 51-55 ("that all…foods,")

D) Lines 56-63 ("contain…food")

The best answer is (C).
Refer to the explanation for the previous question.

4

According to the passage, what is the difference between organic crude material and inorganic counterpart?

A) one provides integral substances

B) the way energy is taken advantage of

C) the variety of functions they serve in plant

D) the fact that energy is produced to secure the production of one of the two

Test 1

The best answer is (C).
"the former are inorganic and can furnish only materials (function 1) but no energy to the organism; while the latter are organic and supply both materials and potential energy (function 2)"

(A), (B), (D); The explanation for (C) tells pretty much everything about why these are wrong.

5

Which of the following gives the most direct evidence for the answer to the previous question?

A) Lines 28-32 ("and used…energy.")
B) Lines 32-35 ("It would…this way")
C) Lines 51-55 ("that all…foods,")
D) Lines 56-63 ("contain…food")

The best answer is (B).
Refer to the explanation for the previous question.

6

Which of the following does such use refer to?

A) "loosely using the word 'food'." (Lines 44-45)
B) "criticism" (Line 43)
C) "the custom of using the words 'food,' or 'nutrient,'" (Lines 38-39)
D) using "the newer terms" (Line 42)

The best answer is (A).
(A) is directly above such use, it is the only possibility in context.

7

Which of the following is most consistent with the author's attitude?

A) Only the green parts of green plants can use this inorganic "food."
B) Colorless plants must have organic food.
C) Traditional use of such terms as "food" must be respected.
D) However terms such as food and intake are used, they must be used with caution.

The best answer is (D).
In the 3rd paragraph, the author talks about a suggestion to avoid a confusion, and the suggestion is to make a compromise ("…all of the intake of plants and animals shall be considered as food,… those forms…shall be designated as synergic foods, while those…shall be known as anergic foods. On this basis, practically all of the food of animals, excepting the mineral salts and water,…are synergic foods; while practically all of the intake of green plants is anergic food.").
The author is being very careful. The author is also very cautious about the possible objection. ("But the custom of using the words "food," or "nutrient," to represent anything that is taken into the organism and in any way utilized by it for its nourishment has been followed so long and the newer terms are themselves so subject to criticism that they have not yet generally supplanted the loosely used word "food.")

(A), (C); The author is making a compromise, going in between two ideas.
(B); The author wouldn't agree that colorless plants need organic food ("If such use is permitted, however, it is necessary to recognize that only the green parts of green plants can use this inorganic "food," and that the colorless plants must have organic food.")

Test 1

8

Which of the following gives the most direct evidence for the answer to the previous question?

A) "so long" (Line 41) and "criticism" (Line 43)
B) "custom" (Line 39) and "nourishment" (Line 41)
C) "must" and "organic" (Line 49)
D) "best practice" (Lines 32-33) and "limit" (Line 35)

The best answer is (A).
Refer to the explanation for the answer to the previous question.

9

Which of the following is a suggested solution to the main problem of the passage?

A) introducing a novel concept of food to designate new kinds of food
B) redefining the connection between "intake" and "food"
C) classifying a pivotal concept in a novel fashion.
D) making a compromise between traditional and modern ways of defining biological terms

The best answer is (C).
This is more of an extension of Question 7 in that "avoiding a confusion" is a way of solving a problem. In order to "avoid this confusion" (4th paragraph) two novel concepts ("synergic", "anergic") have been introduced (a novel fashion). The pivotal concept would be "food."

(A); Neither synergic nor anergic refers to new kinds of food.
(B); The author is making a compromise about how to define "food", not talking about the connection between "intake" and "food": a case of WRONG PERSPECTIVE.
(D); In order to make a compromise, the author used a suggestion involving such new concepts as "synergic" and "anergic", which have nothing to do with traditional or modern ways of making biological definitions.

10

What is the role of the last paragraph compared to the passage as a whole?

A) reiteration
B) conclusion
C) changing the main direction
D) additional information

The best answer is (D).
Up until the last paragraph, the author had been talking about how to define "food", but in the last paragraph, s/he showed some interest in one of the two kinds of "food", the classification of which was possible only after the author defined what "food" was. Thus, the whole passage is a definition of "food" and (classification) a specific kind of "food"("anergic"). Thus the detailed explanation of "anergic food" can be additional to classifying "food" as "synergic" and "anergic".

(C); Since both "synergic" and "anergic" came from the process of defining "food", specifically taking about "anergic food" cannot understood as changing the main direction of the passage.

Test 1

Spain, as everyone knows, was the country behind the discovery of America. Few people know, however, what an important part the beautiful city of Granada played in that famous event. It was in October, 1492, that Columbus first set foot on the New World and claimed it for Spain. In January of that same year another territory had been added to that same crown; for the brave soldier-sovereigns, Ferdinand and Isabella, had conquered the Moorish kingdom of Granada in the south and made it part of their own country. Nearly eight hundred years before, the dark-skinned Moors had come over from Africa and invaded the European peninsula which lies closest to the Straits of Gibraltar, and the people of that peninsula had been battling fiercely ever since to drive them back to where they came from. True, the Moor had brought Arabian art and learning with him, but he had brought also the Mohammedan religion, and that was intolerable not only to the Spaniards but to all Europeans. No Christian country could brook the thought of this Asiatic creed flourishing on her soil, so Spain soon set to work to get rid of it. This war between the two religions began in the north near the Bay of Biscay whither the Christians were finally pushed by the invaders. Each century saw the Moors driven a little farther south toward the Mediterranean, until Granada, where the lovely Sierra Nevadas rise, was the last stronghold left them. Small wonder, then, that when Granada was finally taken the Spanish nation was supremely happy. Small wonder that they held a magnificent fete in their newly-won city in the "Snowy Mountains." The vanquished Moorish king rode down from his mountain citadel and handed its keys to Ferdinand and Isabella. Bells pealed, banners waved, and the people cheered wildly as their victorious sovereigns rode by. And yet, so we are told by a writer who was present, in the midst of all this rejoicing one man stood aside, sad and solitary. While all the others felt that their uttermost desire had been granted in acquiring the Moorish kingdom, he knew that he could present them with a far greater territory than Granada if only they would give him the chance. What were these olive and orange groves beside the tropic fertility of the shores he longed to reach, and which he would have reached long ere this, he told himself regretfully, if only they had helped him! What was the Christianizing of the few Moors who remained in Spain compared with the Christianizing of all the undiscovered heathen across the Atlantic! And so on that eventful January 2, 1492, when a whole city was delirious with joy,

"There was crying in Granada when the sun was going down, Some calling on the Trinity some calling on Mahoun. Here passed away the Koran therein the Cross was borne. And here was heard the Christian bell and there the Moorish horn."

Mahoun = Mohammad / Muhammad / Muhammed

Test 1

11

The point of the passage could have been a lot clearer should which of the following be known?

A) the main reason why Columbus suffered
B) the primary conflict between moors and Europeans
C) why the people of Granada were exhilarated
D) the exact role the city of Granada played in the discovery of the new world

The best answer is (D).

(A); Based on "if only they would give him the chance" he wasn't given the chance to set sail to discover the new world.
(B); Based on "the Mohammedan religion, and that was intolerable not only to the Spaniards but to all Europeans", it was religion.
(C); Based on "when Granada was finally taken the Spanish nation was supremely happy", it can be known that Christians defeated the moors at the city of Granada.

12

According to the passage, why was Spanish royalty probably reluctant to go with Columbus's plan?

A) because it was preposterous
B) because the royal government was faced with other more urgent matters
C) because he asked too much as a reward for the possible success of his plan
D) because he was a foreigner

The best answer is (B).
We know they, the Spanish royalty had not yet helped Columbus ("if only they had helped him!"), and Spain finally won the war ("The vanquished Moorish king") so, while considering Columbus's plan, Spanish royalty had to fight a war with the Moors. This war was probably the other more urgent matter they had to attend to.

(A), (C), (D); None of these can mean war with the Moors, and in the passage nothing other than war is implied as an obstacle to the approval of Columbus's plan by Spanish royalty.

13

As used in line 22, "brook" most nearly means

A) embrace
B) resent
C) picture
D) bear

The best answer is (D).
We need to find something that matches with "the thought of this Asiatic creed flourishing on her soil" in the minds of the Spanish people, who are all Christians. The best possible response is some other religion that Christians would be unable to tolerate. So the answer is obvious unless the passage implies something else and that is not the case here.

14

As used in line 38, "sovereigns" most nearly means

A) independent people
B) absolution
C) queens
D) rulers

The best answer is (D).
We need to find something that matches with "cheered", "victorious", "rode by" so we are looking for more than one person who ("rode by") who the public could cheer ("cheered") and who had led the people to victory in war ("victorious"), so it

will be members of royalty, and/or military leaders.

(A); a case of WRONG PERSPECTIVE
(B); Absurd
(C); a case of TOO NARROW

15

According to the passage, why was the one man sad as explained?

A) because he was not satisfied with the victory mentioned.

B) because he was anxious about the possible outcomes of the victory mentioned.

C) because he thought some people were near-sighted.

D) because he could easily find the new world.

The best answer is (C).
According to the passage, Columbus was "sad" because he wasn't given the chance to set sail and eventually to discover the new world. If he had been allowed to set sail, he could have given his royal patrons something bigger than Granada ("a far greater territory than Granada", "beside the tropic fertility of the shores he longed to reach", "the Christianizing of all the undiscovered heathen across the Atlantic!"), so the people rejoicing over the small victory can be said to be missing the bigger picture; they are near-sighted.

(A); It is not the victory itself with which he had problems.
(B); He was not anxious about the victorious outcome of the war, but rather his future discoveries.
(D); The amount of effort required to discover the new world cannot be known from the passage alone.

16

Which choice best explains the answer to the previous question?

A) He could have given the people of Spain much more than the victory mentioned in the passage.

B) He has given the people of Granada something to go on with.

C) His plan could have been more religiously satisfying.

D) The people of Granada could have benefited more than from the victory mentioned in the passage.

The best answer is (A).
Refer to the explanation for the answer to the previous question.

17

Which choice gives the best evidence for the answer to the previous question?

A) "compared with the Christianizing of all the undiscovered heathen across the Atlantic!" (Lines 51-53)

B) "beside the tropic fertility of the shores he longed to reach, and which he would have reached long ere this" (Lines 47-49)

C) "a far greater territory than Granada" (Lines 44-45)

D) "And so on that eventful January 2, 1492, when a whole city was delirious with joy," (Lines 53-54)

The best answer is (D).

(A), (B), (C); All of these are the cases of TOO NARROW.

Test 1

18

What could be the best topic of the passage?

A) Why Columbus was upset about the victory of Granada

B) Columbus's responses to Christianity and Islam

C) The religious conflict in Granada and its impact on Columbus

D) How a specific historical event at a historical location might have affected an important historical figure

The best answer is (D).
historical event= the victory at Granada,
an important historical figure= Columbus,
a historical location= Granada,
How, affected = giving him the chance to set sail. Since the war had been won, it is very possible that Columbus would or might be given an opportunity by Spanish royalty.

(A); He wasn't upset about the victory itself. He was "sad" about the fact that people didn't see the bigger picture. Refer to Question 15.
(B), (C); Columbus's only interest was in sailing for discovery, not any religion or religious conflict.

19

According to the passage, what can be said about the invasion of Granada by the Moors?

A) It only created a severe religious conflict.

B) It made a cultural contribution to Christians.

C) It was a source of Columbus's ambition to set sail on a journey to the new world.

D) Directly because of it, Columbus had a hard time getting his plans implemented.

The best answer is (B).
Even though it was a form of invasion, the invasion did result in cultural contributions ("the Moor had brought Arabian art and learning with him,")

(A); Since the invasion also had positive effects, the statement is wrong: a case of TOO NARROW.
(C); The only possible source for Columbus's ambition is the riches and religious effect that his discovery could bring ("a far greater territory than Granada", "beside the tropic fertility of the shores he longed to reach", "the Christianizing of all the undiscovered heathen across the Atlantic!"), not the Moorish invasion.
(D); This is tricky. Depending on how we look at this, this choice might sound correct, but the real and direct cause of his trouble is not the invasion itself, but the reluctant Spanish royalty.

20

Which of the following gives the best interpretation of the last sentence of the passage?

A) The religious conversion of the moors had failed.

B) The religious conflict had not totally disappeared.

C) There were some Moors still residing in the area even after the victory.

D) It was impossible for the Christians to accept other religions.

The best answer is (C).
There were obviously Christians ("Some calling on the Trinity") but also some Moors ("some calling on Mahoun.")

(A); It cannot be said that the conversion had failed, nor that it had been successful ("the Christianizing of the few Moors who remained in Spain"); in other words, the conversion was in progress.
(B); There were still some Moors who followed a different religion, but it is not clear whether or not there was any religious conflict.
(D); This is true, but cannot be known or inferred from the last sentence.

The story of our world is a story that is still very imperfectly known. A couple of hundred years ago men possessed the history of little more than the last three thousand years. What happened before that time was a matter of legend and speculation. Over a large part of the civilized world it was believed and taught that the world had been created suddenly in 4004 B.C., though authorities differed as to whether this had occurred in the spring or autumn of that year. This fantastically precise misconception was based upon a too literal interpretation of the Hebrew Bible, and upon rather arbitrary theological assumptions connected therewith. Such ideas have long since been abandoned by religious teachers, and it is universally recognized that the universe in which we live has to all appearances existed for an enormous period of time and possibly for endless time. Of course there may be deception in these appearances, as a room may be made to seem endless by putting mirrors facing each other at either end. But that the universe in which we live has existed only for six or seven thousand years may be regarded as an altogether exploded idea. The earth, as everybody knows nowadays, is a spheroid, a sphere slightly compressed, orange fashion, with a diameter of nearly 8,000 miles. Its spherical shape has been known at least to a limited number of intelligent people for nearly 2,500 years, but before that time it was supposed to be flat, and various ideas which now seem fantastic were entertained about its relations to the sky and the stars and planets. We know now that it rotates upon its axis (which is about 24 miles shorter than its equatorial diameter) every twenty-four hours, and that this is the cause of the alternations of day and night, that it circles about the sun in a slightly distorted and slowly variable oval path in a year. Its distance from the sun varies between ninety-one and a half millions at its nearest and ninety-four and a half million miles. About the earth circles a smaller sphere, the moon, at an average distance of 239,000 miles. Earth and moon are not the only bodies to travel round the sun. There are also the planets, Mercury and Venus, at distances of thirty-six and sixty-seven millions of miles; and beyond the circle of the earth and disregarding a belt of numerous smaller bodies, the planetoids, there are Mars, Jupiter, Saturn, Uranus and Neptune at mean distances of 141, 483, 886, 1,782, and 1,793 millions of miles respectively.

These figures in millions of miles are very difficult for the mind to grasp. It may help the reader's imagination if we reduce the sun and planets to a smaller, more conceivable scale. If, then, we represent our earth as a little ball of one inch diameter, the sun would be a big globe nine feet across and 323 yards away, that is about a fifth of a mile, four or five minutes' walking. The moon would be a small pea two feet and a half from the world. Between earth and sun there would be the two inner planets, Mercury and Venus, at distances of one hundred and twenty-five and two hundred and fifty yards from the sun. All round and about these bodies there would be emptiness until you came to Mars, a hundred and seventy-five feet beyond the earth; Jupiter nearly a mile away, a foot in diameter; Saturn, a little smaller, two miles off; Uranus four miles off and Neptune six miles off.

Then nothingness and nothingness except for small particles and drifting scraps of attenuated vapour for thousands of miles. The nearest star to earth on this scale would be 40,000 miles away. These figures will serve perhaps to give one some conception of the immense emptiness of space in which the drama of life goes on. For in all this enormous vacancy of space we know certainly of life only upon the surface of our earth. It does not penetrate much more than three miles down into the 4,000 miles that separate us from the centre of our globe, and it does not reach more than five miles above its surface. Apparently all the limitlessness of space is otherwise empty and dead. The deepest ocean dredgings go down to five miles. The highest recorded flight of an aeroplane is little more than four miles. Men have reached to seven miles up in balloons, but at a cost of great suffering. No bird can fly so high as five miles, and small birds and insects which have been carried up by aeroplanes drop off insensible far below that level.

Test 1

21

What could be the best title of the passage?

A) The earth in many perspectives

B) The world in space

C) The earth as a place for the living

D) The world in its heavenly habitat

The best answer is (B).
The evidence for this can be found throughout the passage.
"…it was supposed to be flat, and various ideas which…about its relations to the sky and the stars and planets…it rotates upon its axis (which is about 24 miles shorter than its equatorial diameter) every twenty-four hours, and that…that it circles about the sun in a slightly distorted and slowly variable oval path in a year."
"About the earth circles a smaller sphere, the moon, at an average distance of 239,000 miles… There are also the planets, Mercury and Venus, at distances of thirty-six and sixty-seven millions of miles; and beyond the circle of the earth and disregarding a belt of numerous smaller bodies, the planetoids, there are Mars, Jupiter, Saturn, Uranus and Neptune at mean distances of…. "
"Then nothingness and nothingness except for small particles and drifting scraps of attenuated vapour for thousands of miles. The nearest star to earth on this scale would be 40,000 miles away."

(A); There is only one spatial perspective.
(C); The earth as a heavenly body is a completely different perspective from the earth as a place for humans and other life forms.
(D); According to the passage, no place other than the earth is known to harbor life forms; the expression, the heavenly habitat is absurd.

22

As used in line 31, "fantastic" most nearly means

A) splendid

B) fantasized

C) wrong

D) fabulous

The answer is (C).
The author says, "we know now…", which means previous "various ideas" were wrong.

(A), (B), (D); None of these can mean wrong.

23

According to the passage, what kind of role is played by mirrors in a room?

A) imagination

B) caution

C) foreboding

D) diversion

The answer is (B).
The author says "there may be deception in these appearances" and this is similar to "a room" that "may be made to seem endless by putting mirrors facing each other at either end." Thus, mirrors are used as a cautionary device for the possible deception.

(A); Analogy is not imagination.
(C); This analogy is not used as a tool of foreboding. In other words, the deception above was only a possibility; as it turns out it was not deception, so this analogy doesn't work as a device of foreboding.
(D); The author uses this analogy as a cautionary device to show that s/he is aware of the possibility; thus, s/he is not trying to confuse the reader.

Test 1

24

Why does the author say "precise" when s/he talks about a certain misconception?

A) to reveal previously hidden elements

B) to stress the degree of misconception

C) to emphasize a certain accuracy

D) to allude to an irony suggested by the situation in general

The best answer is (B).
The author says, "fantastically precise misconception", which can easily be interpreted as very (=precisely) wrong (=fantastic) misconception.

(A); A simple expression for a certain degree or magnitude cannot be a hidden element since it cannot change the course of the passage in that direction.
(C); This choice totally misrepresents the negativity of "precise".
(D); By using the expression "precise misconception" the author is employing the literary technique of sarcasm, not irony.

25

Which choice gives the best evidence for the cause of a "shorter" (Line 34) axis as explained in the passage?

A) "flat" (Line 31)

B) "compressed" (Line 26)

C) "enormous" (Line 77)

D) "alternations" (Line 36)

The best answer is (B).
compressed (cause) → shorter (effect)

(A), (C), (D), None of these bear any relation to "shorter" such as that of cause and effect in (B).

26

According to the passage, which choice is the best approximation of the number of heavenly bodies in the solar system?

A) nine

B) just a few

C) a lot more than a dozen

D) countless

The answer is (C).
This is a rather simple question. "a belt of numerous smaller bodies,"+"the earth"+"the moon"+"Mars, Jupiter, Saturn, Uranus and Neptune"= a lot more than seven and more than twelve.

27

Which choice gives the best evidence for the answer to the previous question?

A) "Mars, Jupiter, Saturn, Uranus and Neptune" (Line 49)

B) "a belt of numerous smaller bodies" (Lines 47-48)

C) "not the only bodies to travel round the sun." (Lines 43-44)

D) "at mean distances of 141, 483, 886, 1,782, and 1,793 millions of miles respectively." (Lines 51-52)

The best answer is (B).
Refer to the explanation for the answer to the previous question.

New SAT Reading Prep

Test 1

28

What is the author trying to do in the second paragraph?

A) put the reader in perspective

B) help the reader see precisely what is happening outside the earth

C) explain in detail what is happening around the sun

D) provide clues to what might happen if anything goes wrong

The best answer is (A).
The author says, "These figures in millions of miles are very difficult for the mind to grasp," and tries to remedy this situation by using "nine feet across and 323 yards away,": different unit, different dimension: different dimension, different perspective.

29

Which choice gives the best evidence for the answer to the previous question?

A) "These figures in millions of miles are very difficult for the mind to grasp." (Lines 52-53)

B) "It may help the reader's imagination if we reduce the sun and planets to a smaller, more conceivable scale." (Lines 53-55)

C) "For in all this enormous vacancy of space we know certainly of life only upon the surface of our earth." (Lines 76-78)

D) "Apparently all the limitlessness of space is otherwise empty and dead." (Lines 82-84)

The best answer is (A).
Refer to the explanation for the answer to the previous question.

30

According to the passage, what is the probable reason why the author mentioned ocean dredgings and aeroplane?

A) to show a contrast between limitlessness and limitations

B) to provide a few pieces of evidence for the previous argument

C) to supply some of the possible causes of the previous claim

D) to argue for examinable consequences of a previously mentioned hypothesis

The best answer is (B).
"The deepest ocean dredgings go down to five miles. The highest recorded flight of an aeroplane is little more than four miles", which means the deepest point on earth is not more than 5 miles below sea level, and the highest point is just 4 miles above sea level. Life can exist only within this very small range; beyond this there is nothing but emptiness; the author uses these two limits as evidence for "Apparently all the limitlessness of space is otherwise empty and dead."

Test 1

We may all agree about aesthetics, and yet differ about particular works of art. We may differ as to the presence or absence of the quality x. My immediate object will be to show that significant form is the only quality common and peculiar to all the works of visual art that move me; and I will ask those whose aesthetic experience does not tally with mine to see whether this quality is not also, in their judgment, common to all works that move them, and whether they can discover any other quality of which the same can be said. Also at this point a query arises, irrelevant indeed, but hardly to be suppressed: "Why are we so profoundly moved by forms related in a particular way?" The question is extremely interesting, but irrelevant to aesthetics. In pure aesthetics we have only to consider our emotion and its object: for the purposes of aesthetics we have no right, neither is there any necessity, to pry behind the object into the state of mind of him who made it. Later, I shall attempt to answer the question; for by so doing I may be able to develop my theory of the relation of art to life. I shall not, however, be under the delusion that I am rounding off my theory of aesthetics. For a discussion of aesthetics, it need be agreed only that forms arranged and combined according to certain unknown and mysterious laws do move us in a particular way, and that it is the business of an artist so to combine and arrange them that they shall move us. These moving combinations and arrangements I have called, for the sake of convenience and for a reason that will appear later, "Significant Form." A third interruption has to be met. "Are you forgetting about colour?" someone inquires. Certainly not; my term "significant form" included combinations of lines and of colours. The distinction between form and colour is an unreal one; you cannot conceive a colourless line or a colourless space; neither can you conceive a formless relation of colours. In a black and white drawing the spaces are all white and all are bounded by black lines; in most oil paintings the spaces are multi-coloured and so are the boundaries; you cannot imagine a boundary line without any content, or a content without a boundary line. Therefore, when I speak of significant form, I mean a combination of lines and colours (counting white and black as colours) that moves me aesthetically. Some people may be surprised at my not having called this "beauty." Of course, to those who define beauty as "combinations of lines and colours that provoke aesthetic emotion," I willingly concede the right of substituting their word for mine. But most of us, however strict we may be, are apt to apply the epithet "beautiful" to objects that do not provoke that peculiar emotion produced by works of art. Everyone, I suspect, has called a butterfly or a flower beautiful. Does anyone feel the same kind of emotion for a butterfly or a flower that he feels for a cathedral or a picture? Surely, it is not what I call an aesthetic emotion that most of us feel, generally, for natural beauty. I shall suggest, later, that some people may, occasionally, see in nature what we see in art, and feel for her an aesthetic emotion; but I am satisfied that, as a rule, most people feel a very different kind of emotion for birds and flowers and the wings of butterflies from that which they feel for pictures, pots, temples and statues. Why these beautiful things do not move us as works of art move is another, and not an aesthetic, question. For our immediate purpose we have to discover only what quality is common to objects that do move us as works of art. In the last part of this chapter, when I try to answer the question— "Why are we so profoundly moved by some combinations of lines and colours?" I shall hope to offer an acceptable explanation of why we are less profoundly moved by others.

Test 1

31

What would be the best title of the passage?

A) The immediate and distant object

B) Esthetics in works of art

C) What significant form does in esthetics

D) The difference between esthetics and works of art.

The best answer is (B).
First of all, the two key concepts in the very first sentence are esthetics and works of art. Therefore, even if these two are not part of the theme of the passage, they must be somehow related. Thus, the second sentence is very important. Contextually, quality x is a random example of the reasons why people have different opinions about a particular work of art. In other words, the second sentence works as a way of specifying or elaborating on the first. In further words, the first sentence appears closely related to the main theme. Therefore, you should be looking for any answer choice that deals with esthetics and works of art, but unfortunately there are two choices like that, (B) and (D). However, by carefully comparing (B) and (D), you can easily tell the answer has to be (B), because conceptually (B) can include (D). (The strategy of INCLUSIVENESS) But all we have done so far is show how to pick the answer; we still don't know why the others cannot be the answer.

(A); Even if the object here means work of art, the concept of esthetics is missing. (Wrong Perspective)
(C); It says in the passage that "significant form is the only quality…" In other words, even though this significant quality is part of esthetics, it alone cannot mean esthetics as a whole.
(D); The concept of "difference" is the problem. From the first two sentences, the difference that matters in this passage is that of people's opinion about or response to a particular work of art, not the difference between esthetics and works of art. (Wrong Perspective)

32

Which of the following is most likely the author's intention for writing this passage?

A) to attempt to explain how an individual artwork is perceived within the boundary of esthetics

B) to show the superiority of esthetics to the way each artwork differently moves different people

C) to compare and contrast the concept of esthetics and the physical objects of art

D) to defy the traditional perception of esthetics and art

The best answer is (A).
As shown in Question 31, the passage is about Esthetics in or and works of art. In dealing with these two main concepts, the author began by talking about "significant form"; it is "the only quality common" "to all works of visual art". Thus, it is the quality x which is never absent. The author also uses the word move, which can be interpreted as inspire, or make…feel something, and so on. The answer choices that contain this idea are (A) (how/perceived), (B) (moves), and (D) (perception). So, that does not help much.

(D); In order to defy anything traditional, the passage needs to involve a certain time factor: traditional, modern, yesterday, and/or the past. The passage is focused on "common and peculiar" quality, and "certain unknown and mysterious law" as well as "combinations of lines and of colours", and "distinction between form and colour", none of which has anything to do with time. (B); There is no concept or expressions that can be translated as superiority of esthetics. In other words, the reason (D) cannot be the answer is exactly the same as why (B) cannot be the answer. So in this case, eliminating the wrong answers is easier than identifying the correct answer. But where is the part of the passage that tells you that the passage is within the boundary of esthetics? It is actually very easy. Since the passage is about esthetics in works of art, the author never leaves the realm of esthetics. So, unless you can find any evidence to prove otherwise, you don't need to find any proof for this.

33

Which of the following is the most essential contrast throughout the passage?

A) some commonality and corresponding particularity
B) esthetics and art
C) specialists and generalists
D) depth and superficiality

The best answer is (A).
Based on how we eliminated 32-(B), we know the main concept, significant form, has "common and peculiar" qualities. The main difficulty with this question is that a single concept, significant form, possesses two contrasting perspectives within itself: common and peculiar. Peculiar here means particular or specific to a particular work of art, which means every art work has significant form, but every significant form is different. Thus we can say that something common, which is to say the same in every piece of art work, is different each time. This is a contrast. The rest of the answer choices are simple eye-catchers that use common sense, especially (C) and (D).

34

According to the author, which of the following might be the best definition of art?

A) Something that has something in common with other things, but in a different way with a different consequence
B) Something that is too abstract to define in simple words or expressions
C) An enterprise for which there should be two approaches: immediate and distant
D) Something that creates double standard

The explanation for the previous question will work just fine for this question. It can easily be seen that in fact this question is nothing more than an extension of the previous question.

35

What is the most probable role of the author's "immediate object" in relation to the two immediately previous sentences?

A) To make an effective compromise
B) To create a slow diversion
C) To propose a reluctant solution
D) To suggest a hidden goal

The best answer is (D).
Stating that there is an "immediate object" has to mean that there is another more distant object. So in order for (D) to be the answer, that more distant object needs to be more important, and that more distant object can be referred to as 'hidden' Thus, we need to start eliminating wrong choices that are irrelevant to this more distant object.

(A), (B), (C) None of them has to do with the idea of "immediate" / distant.

36

Which of the following is the best assessment about "significant form"?

A) an inevitable compromise needed to deal with an old problem
B) a link by which to solve the previously mentioned problem
C) any combination of lines and colors
D) whatever is considered beautiful is composed

Test 1

of

The best answer is (B).
The problem here "differ about particular works of art" and solution is "only quality common and peculiar to all the works of visual art that move me". In other words, significant form is the only quality to link ("only quality common and peculiar to all the works of visual art"), since it creates a link among all works of visual art, the differences, which are problematic, can be taken care of, which is a solution.

(A); There is no old or new problem; there is only a problem, so naturally no compromise is possible.
(C); The author calls "These moving combinations and arrangements" "Significant Form." And these combinations are limited to those that "move" the viewer, so these are not just any combination.
(D); This choice is similar to (C) in that 'whatever' is similar to 'any'. Those combinations that move the viewer are not the same as whatever is beautiful. What "moves" us is not necessarily beautiful; the author never implied anything of that nature.

37

Which of the following is the closest in meaning to "tally with" as used in line 8?

A) record
B) count
C) **match**
D) respond to

The best answer is (C).
The author is talking about the artistic experiences of different people including himself or herself. Also, at the beginning of the passage the author says "We may differ as to the presence or absence of the quality x." Therefore, it is obvious that the author talking about the different artistic responses ("esthetics") of different people who have different artistic experiences.

38

According to the passage, what does "this quality" (Line 8) refer to?

A) **significant form**
B) esthetic experience
C) the fact that some people's esthetic experience does not tally with the author's
D) my immediate object

The answer is (A).
Because of the phrase "also, in their judgment, common to all works that move them" the answer must be something that is "common to all works that move them".

39

According to the passage, which of the following is the best inference about the author's long-term objective as compared with the immediate objective mentioned in the passage?

A) finding insignificant form
B) finding insignificant lines and colors
C) **appreciating different effects of the concept used as the author's immediate object**
D) illustrating the comparison and contrast related to commonality and diversity

The best answer is (C).
The author continually refers to the immediate object up until the last two sentences in which the author says "Why are we so profoundly moved by some combinations of lines and colours?" "I shall hope to offer an acceptable explanation of why we are less profoundly moved by others." So the contrast here is between "so profoundly moved" and "less profoundly moved", two very different effects.

(A), (B); Different levels of being moved by

different artworks cannot be called insignificant. (D); Different levels of being moved by different artworks cannot be interpreted as illustrating the comparison and contrast related to commonality and diversity. Simply no relevance here.

40

Which of the following gives the most direct evidence for the answer to the previous question?

A) "My immediate object will be to show…also, in their judgment," (Lines 3-4)

B) "In pure aesthetics…there any necessity," (Lines 16-19)

C) "Some people may…called this 'beauty.'" (Lines 49-51)

D) "For our immediate purpose…why we are less profoundly moved by others." (Lines 72-79)

The best answer is (D).
Refer to the previous question.

We observe today not a victory of party but a celebration of freedom—symbolizing an end as well as a beginning—signifying renewal as well as change. For I have sworn before you and Almighty God the same solemn oath our forebears prescribed nearly a century and three quarters ago.

The world is very different now. For man holds in his mortal hands the power to abolish all forms of human poverty and all forms of human life. And yet the same revolutionary beliefs for which our forebears fought are still at issue around the globe—the belief that the rights of man come not from the generosity of the state but from the hand of God.

We dare not forget today that we are the heirs of that first revolution. Let the word go forth from this time and place, to friend and foe alike, that the torch has been passed to a new generation of Americans—born in this century, tempered by war, disciplined by a hard and bitter peace, proud of our ancient heritage—and unwilling to witness or permit the slow undoing of those human rights to which this Nation has always been committed, and to which we are committed today at home and around the world.

Let every nation know, whether it wishes us well or ill, that we shall pay any price, bear any burden, meet any hardship, support any friend, oppose any foe to assure the survival and the success of liberty.

This much we pledge—and more.

To those old allies whose cultural and spiritual origins we share, we pledge the loyalty of faithful friends. United, there is little we cannot do in a host of cooperative ventures. Divided, there is little we can do—for we dare not meet a powerful challenge at odds and split asunder.

To those new states whom we welcome to the ranks of the free, we pledge our word that one form of colonial control shall not have passed away merely to be replaced by a far more iron tyranny. We shall not always expect to find them supporting our view. But we shall always hope to find them strongly supporting their own freedom—and to remember that, in the past, those who foolishly sought power by riding the back of the tiger ended up inside.

To those people in the huts and villages of half

… the globe struggling to break the bonds of mass
50 misery, we pledge our best efforts to help them
help themselves, for whatever period is required—
not because the Communists may be doing it, not
because we seek their votes, but because it is right.
If a free society cannot help the many who are
55 poor, it cannot save the few who are rich.

    To our sister republics south of our border,
we offer a special pledge—to convert our good
words into good deeds—in a new alliance for
progress—to assist free men and free governments
60 in casting off the chains of poverty. But this
peaceful revolution of hope cannot become the
prey of hostile powers. Let all our neighbors know
that we shall join with them to oppose aggression
or subversion anywhere in the Americas. And
65 let every other power know that this hemisphere
intends to remain the master of its own house.

    To that world assembly of sovereign states,
the United Nations, our last best hope in an age
where the instruments of war have far outpaced
70 the instruments of peace, we renew our pledge of
support—to prevent it from becoming merely a
forum for invective—to strengthen its shield of
the new and the weak—and to enlarge the area in
which its writ may run.

41

Why did the author talk about the power?

A) in order to show some possible dreadful consequences

B) because there is hope despite its negative aspects

C) in order to emphasize its ambiguity

D) because its negative aspects surpass its positive aspects

The best answer is (C).
Judging from "the power to abolish all forms of human poverty and all forms of human life", this power can do either great good or great evil, which indicates that it has a dual nature and this produces ambiguity.

(A); This only refers to the negative aspects, so it is a case of TOO NARROW.
(B); Refer to the explanation for (C). There is a good side and a bad side, and that's all. There is no indication that one side is stronger than the other, so it is a case of WRONG COMPARISON AND CONTRAST.
(D); Refer to the explanation for (C). There are just two sides; good and bad. There is no indication that one side is stronger than the other, so it is a case of WRONG COMPARISON AND CONTRAST.

42

Which of the following is the best interpretation of the second paragraph in connection with the first paragraph?

A) generalization

B) specification

C) cause and effect

D) comparison and contrast

Test 1

The best answer is (D).
At the beginning of the second paragraph, it says "The world is very different now" and the rest of the paragraph is about this difference.

(A), (B), (C); None of these can mean contrast.

43

Why did the author mention that first revolution?

A) to improve the strength of the present revolution

B) to stress the necessity of a certain kind of continuity

C) because the present revolution is not as powerful as the first one was.

D) because the author is ashamed of the current generation who are incapable of maintaining the revolution that began long ago.

The best answer is (B).
The sentence following the first revolution is "Let the word go forth from this time and place, to friend and foe alike, that the torch has been passed to a new generation of Americans."
So it is the job of the "heirs of the first revolution" to "let the word go forth from this time and place, to friend and foe alike, that the torch has been passed to a new generation of Americans." Phrases like "go forth" and "passed" imply some sort of continuation and the new generation of Americans must be part of this process: a certain kind of continuity.

(A); A continuation does not necessarily mean that anything will be strengthened or weakened.
(C); A continuation does not necessarily mean that anything will become more or less powerful.
(D); The same as (C).

44

What does "the word" (Line 16) refer to?

A) revolution

B) heirs

C) linguistic approach

D) revolutionary concept

The best answer is (A).
Refer to the explanation for the previous question.

45

Which of the following is most directly related with the concept of "torch" (Line 18)?

A) democracy

B) revolution

C) human rights

D) history

The best answer is (B).
Refer to the explanation for Question 43.

46

What's probably the most direct role of "bitter peace" (Line 20) in the passage as a whole?

A) to emphasize the difficulties involved in dealing with the present reality

B) to demonstrate the differences between it and war

C) to instill foreboding about a possibly dreadful future

D) to emphasize the need of revolution

The best answer is (A).
Based on "tempered by war, disciplined by a hard

Test 1

and bitter peace", "bitter peace" is something that can be compared with war; obviously war is negative and peace is positive, so there must be a problem with this peace that is currently possible; since the nation is at peace and "bitter" suggests serious difficulties, the answer is rather obvious, a typical case of simple PARAPHRASING.

(B); "War" and "bitter peace" both play a negative role.
(C); The author strongly suggests that the future will be whatever the audience, who are Americans, create. So the future is not necessarily negative.
(D); This is a tricky one because Americans might need to do something about the "bitter peace", but this is not a certainty and whatever they do, it need not be a revolution. It might be a revolution, but it doesn't have to be. A typical case of WRONG INFERENCE.

47

According to the passage, which of the following is most consistent with the author's argument?

A) America as a nation will not tolerate the weakening of human rights.

B) Wars can irreversibly change the nature of a certain group of people.

C) Challenge is part of America's tradition.

D) America will cherish human rights for decades to come.

The best answer is (C).
In the 3rd paragraph, it says "…we are the heirs of that first revolution…proud of our ancient heritage—and unwilling to witness or permit the slow undoing of those human rights to which this Nation has always been committed,"
In the 6th paragraph, the author says "Divided, there is little we can do—for we dare not meet a powerful challenge at odds and split asunder."

(A); In the 2nd paragraph, "And yet the same revolutionary beliefs for which our forebears fought are still at issue around the globe—the belief that the rights of man come not from the generosity of the state but from the hand of God." So we know that there is a problem with the rights of man.
(B); In the 3rd paragraph, it says "tempered by war", but it says nothing about the nature of this tempering; whether or not it is irreversible cannot be known.
(D); In the 4th paragraph, it says "oppose any foe to assure the survival and the success of liberty", so we know that America will cherish it, but there is not enough evidence to make predictions about the future.

48

Which of the following gives the best evidence to support the answer to the previous question?

A) 1st paragraph

B) 2nd paragraph

C) 3rd paragraph

D) 4th paragraph

The best answer is (C).
Refer to the explanation for the previous question.

49

What is the author's attitude toward freedom?

A) He will never make any compromise that jeopardizes it.

B) He cares more about getting it than about defending it.

C) He is rather pessimistic about it.

D) Poor people living in the countryside need more help defending it than rich people living in urban areas.

The best answer is (A).
In the 3rd paragraph, the author says "…unwilling

to witness or permit the slow undoing of those human rights to which this Nation has always been committed, and to which we are committed today at home and around the world."

(B); The same part of the passage as the explanation for (A) works here too; "slow undoing" means destroying freedom or human rights, so "unwilling to witness" means defending it. Thus the author doesn't care more about defending freedom or human rights than getting it, or the other way around; the author never compared getting freedom or human rights with defending them.
(C); In the last paragraph, the author says "our last best hope...renew our pledge of support—to prevent it from becoming merely a forum for invective—to strengthen its shield of..." so he is rather optimistic.
(D); In the 8th paragraph, the author says, "To those people in the huts and villages of half the globe..., we pledge our best efforts to help them help themselves,...—not because the Communists may be doing it, not because we seek their votes, but because it is right." "If a free society cannot help the many who are poor, it cannot save the few who are rich." So when it comes to defending rights and freedoms, the author does not distinguish among the various geographical areas or classes of people.

50

Which of the following gives the best evidence to support the answer to the previous question?

A) 3rd paragraph
B) 4th paragraph
C) 5th paragraph
D) 6th & 7th paragraph

The best answer is (A).
Refer to the explanation for the previous question.

TEST 2

Answer Keys & Explanations

Test 2

When in the Course of human events, it becomes necessary for one people to dissolve the political bands, which have connected them with another, and to assume among the powers of the
5 earth, the separate and equal station to which the Laws of Nature and of Nature's God entitle them, a decent respect to the opinions of mankind requires that they should declare the causes which impel them to the separation.
10 We hold these truths to be self-evident, that all men are created equal, that they are endowed by their Creator with certain unalienable Rights, that among these are Life, Liberty and the pursuit of Happiness.—That to secure these
15 rights, Governments are instituted among Men, deriving their just powers from the consent of the governed, —That whenever any Form of Government becomes destructive of these ends, it is the Right of the People to alter or to abolish
20 it, and to institute new Government, laying its foundation on such principles and organizing its powers in such form, as to them shall seem most likely to effect their Safety and Happiness. Prudence, indeed, will dictate that Governments
25 long established should not be changed for light and transient causes; and accordingly all experience hath shewn, that mankind are more disposed to suffer, while evils are sufferable, than to right themselves by abolishing the forms to which they
30 are accustomed. But when a long train of abuses and usurpations, pursuing invariably the same Object evinces a design to reduce them under absolute Despotism, it is their right, it is their duty, to throw off such Government, and to provide new
35 Guards for their future security. Such has been the patient sufferance of these Colonies; and such is now the necessity which constrains them to alter their former Systems of Government. The history of the present King of Great Britain is a history
40 of repeated injuries and usurpations, all having in direct object the establishment of an absolute Tyranny over these States. To prove this, let Facts be submitted to a candid world.
 He has refused his Assent to Laws, the most
45 wholesome and necessary for the public good.
 He has forbidden his Governors to pass Laws of immediate and pressing importance, unless suspended in their operation till his Assent should be obtained; and when so suspended, he has utterly
50 neglected to attend to them.
 He has refused to pass other Laws for the accommodation of large districts of people, unless those people would relinquish the right of Representation in the Legislature, a right
55 inestimable to them and formidable to tyrants only.
 He has called together legislative bodies at places unusual, uncomfortable, and distant from the depository of their public Records, for the sole
60 purpose of fatiguing them into compliance with his measures.

Test 2

1

Which of the following can be inferred about "separation" (Line 9) in the passage?

A) In order to achieve it, the laws of nature and of nature's God must be understood in advance.

B) In order for that to happen, why it must happen must also be revealed because whoever needs it requires others' agreement.

C) It cannot be accomplished by human enterprise alone.

D) The cause of it cannot be separated from that of occupying a land.

The best answer is (C).
The separation mentioned in the passage needs more than human endeavor. ("the Laws of Nature and of Nature's God entitle them")

(A); "entitle" cannot be understood as 'must be understood in advance'.
(B); The possible reasons for the separation are mentioned in the second paragraph ("that all men are created equal, that they are endowed by their Creator with certain unalienable Rights"), but the passage doesn't say why the reasons must be revealed ("should declare the causes which impel them to the separation"); the reasons must be revealed, but why they have to be revealed cannot be inferred from the passage.
(D); The causes of the separation are stated as explained in (B), but the causes of occupying a land ("equal station to which the Laws of Nature and of Nature's God entitle them,") are unknown, so the connection between known causes and unknown causes cannot be established.

2

Which of the following is the closest in meaning to "assume" as used in line 4?

A) speculate

B) contemplate

C) apprehend

D) take

The best answer is (D).
The clue is "power" which is something to 'take'. Also in context, after political disconnection ("dissolve the political bands which have connected them with another") and before the separation ("which impel them to the separation"), what people naturally need to do is to take or hold powers to occupy a land. ("the separate and equal station to which the Laws of Nature and of Nature's God entitle them,")

(A), (B), (C); None of these goes well with "powers" or the context explained for (D).

3

Which of the following cannot be implied from the first paragraph?

A) the reason for severing a relationship

B) the reason some new link can be forged

C) prerequisites for some link to be broken

D) the way in which politics and religion are connected

The best answer is (B).
The only thing that can be called 'link' here is the political connection ("the political bands which have connected them with another"), and the first paragraph only talks about disconnecting it ("dissolve"), not why it had been or could have been formed; the reason for the political connection between colonial America and Britain

Test 2

cannot be inferred from the first paragraph alone.

(A); The reason some relation can be broken ("dissolved") is clearly stated. ("that all men are created equal, that they are endowed by their Creator with certain unalienable Rights,")
(C); A prerequisite is a type of reason, so (C) is essentially the same as (A).
(D); Certain people need to be politically disconnected by claiming their territory ("separate and equal station") as theirs which was given by God ("to which the Laws of Nature and of Nature's God entitle them") not as in a subordinate state ("separate and equal"), which means America's independence from Britain. In other words, by claiming some 'religiously' given land as their own, Americans gain 'political' independence. This is how religion is connected with politics; their claim that the land was given to them by God justifies their political freedom from Britain.

4

Which of the following is most likely to be part of "truths" (Line 10)?

A) Sometimes people need to dissolve the political bands connecting them with others.

B) Due to their political differences, a group of people must sometimes separate itself from another.

C) Disconnecting two political groups necessitates that the cause of the disconnection be known.

D) Most political collaborations are undesirable.

The best answer is (C), and this is almost exactly stated in the passage. ("they should declare the causes which impel them to the separation.")

(A); These truths are placed in two different places (1st and 2nd paragraph), and (A) is related with the 1st. ("necessary for one people to dissolve the political bands which have connected them with another,") "People" as used in the passage refers to a national, but the same word in (A) means persons: a case of WRONG PERSPECTIVE.
(B); The same case of WRONG PERSPECTIVE.
(D); There is no evidence that the author believes most political unions are undesirable, no matter how bad the "political bands" might be.

5

According to the passage, what can be said about the equality of men?

A) It depends on a person's nationality.

B) It is a product of individuality.

C) It is directly related to America's Declaration of Independence.

D) Political separation is a prerequisite for both human and national equality.

The best answer is (C).
This is essentially an extension of Q 2, 3, and 4. The equality of men ("all men are created equal,") is part of the truth ("We hold these truths to be self-evident"), and these truths include the necessity of being disconnected when there are reasons for such a disconnection ("causes which impel them to the separation."), and the causes must be "that all men are created equal, that they are endowed by their Creator with certain unalienable Rights," Thus, if equality is damaged, the people whose equality has been damaged must disconnect themselves from those who have damaged that equality.

(A); Inequality is the stated reason for this political separation and there is no connection between a man's nationality and the equality of all men.
(B); Since nothing in the passage implies any connection between equality and individuality, (B) cannot be the answer.
(D); As explained in (A), since inequality is a reason for separation, (D) cannot be the answer.

Test 2

6

Which of the following is the best interpretation of the pursuit of happiness?

A) It is one of the scores of rights that cannot be taken away by a whim of the government.

B) Being one of the most integral rights it can never be taken away.

C) Its existence depends directly on the other two unalienable rights.

D) It is involved with the source of power necessary to justify a political disconnection.

The best answer is (D).
"it is the Right of the People to alter or to abolish it, and to institute new Government, laying its foundation on such principles and organizing its powers in such form, as to them shall seem most likely to effect their Safety and Happiness." Thus, what makes happiness possible is most likely the organizing of the powers of government in a manner that ensures its possibility.

(A); There are only "certain unalienable Rights". "Scores" suggests there are many, but "certain" suggests there are only a few.
(B); "certain unalienable Rights" can be very integral, but there is no indication that they are the most integral rights.
(C); No connection is stated or can be inferred between the three "unalienable Rights" mentioned.

7

Which of the following is a prerequisite for "Life" and "Liberty" (Line 13)?

A) pursuit of Happiness
B) a certain form of mutual understanding
C) agreement among the governed
D) manipulation of the people by the governors

The best answer is (B).
The author says a certain form of mutual understanding ("deriving their just powers from the consent of the governed") is needed to obtain life and liberty ("to secure these rights,")

(A); Pursuit of Happiness is one of the "unalienable rights" along with life and Liberty and to secure all three rights. "The consent of the governed" is needed as explained in (B).
(C); What is needed is "the consent of the governed" and this consent does not imply that the governed are all in agreement.
(D); "Consent" cannot be manipulated by the governors ("government"); manipulation has a strongly negative implication, but "consent" implies something positive.

8

Which of the following is consistent with the author's arguments?

A) Without the three fundamental rights, no government can be founded.

B) The people's right to fight against repressive governments is more important than liberty in general.

C) As a right, Life is as important as any other right.

D) The people have a right to change their government if that change will result in improvements in their lives.

The best answer is (D).
The people have a right to change their government ("to alter or to abolish it, and to institute new Government,") if that change results in improvements in their lives ("laying its foundation on such principles and organizing its powers in such form, as to them shall seem most likely to effect their Safety and Happiness."

(A); The three fundamental rights are important and must be protected, but that does not mean that

no government can be established without these three rights: a case of WRONG INFERENCE
(B); A lack of liberty can be a major reason for subverting the government, but that doesn't mean that people's right to do this is more important than the liberty itself, and the same is true the other way around.
(C); The author never compared the importance of the various rights.

9

Which of the following serves as direct evidence for the answer to the previous question?

A) Lines 1-9 ("When…separation.")
B) Lines 10-13 ("We hold…Liberty")
C) Lines 14-17 ("That to…the governed,")
D) Lines 19-22 ("it is…shall seem")

The best answer is (D).
Refer to the explanation for the answer to the previous question.

10

In context, what is the author trying to say by "Laws" (Line 44)?

A) English laws
B) international laws
C) common sense
D) politically advanced laws

The best answer is (C).
By saying "the most wholesome and necessary for the public good", the author implies that laws are not limited by any political boundaries, including national boundaries.

   Like every concrete political conception, Fascism is thought and action. It is action with an inherent doctrine which, arising out of a given system of historic forces, is inserted in it and works
5 on it from within. It has therefore a form co-related to the contingencies of time and place; but it has at the same time an ideal content which elevates it into a formula of truth in the higher region of the history of thought. There is no way of exercising
10 a spiritual influence on the things of the world by means of a human will-power commanding the wills of others, without first having a clear conception of the particular and transient reality on which the will-power must act, and without
15 also having a clear conception of the universal and permanent reality in which the particular and transient reality has its life and being. To know men we must have a knowledge of man; and to have a knowledge of man we must know the
20 reality of things and their laws. There can be no conception of a State which is not fundamentally a conception of Life. It is a philosophy or intuition, a system of ideas which evolves itself into a system of logical contraction, or which concentrates itself
25 in a vision or in a faith, but which is always, at least virtually, an organic conception of the world.
   Fascism would therefore not be understood in many of its manifestations (as, for example, in its organisations of the Party, its system of
30 education, its discipline) were it not considered in the light of its general view of life. A spiritualised view. To Fascism the world is not this material world which appears on the surface, in which man is an individual separated from all other
35 men, standing by himself and subject to a natural law which instinctively impels him to lead a life of momentary and egoistic pleasure. In Fascism man is an individual who is the nation and the country. He is this by a moral law which embraces
40 and binds together individuals and generations in an established tradition and mission, a moral law which suppresses the instinct to lead a life confined to a brief cycle of pleasure in order, instead, to replace it within the orbit of duty in a superior
45 conception of life, free from the limits of time and space a life in which the individual by self-abnegation and by the sacrifice of his particular interests, even by death, realises the entirely

spiritual existence in which his value as a man
50 consists.
    It is therefore a spiritual conception, itself
also a result of the general reaction of the Century
against the languid and materialistic positivism
of the Eighteenth Century. Anti-positivist, but
55 positive: neither sceptical nor agnostic, neither
pessimistic nor passively optimistic, as are in
general the doctrines (all of them negative) which
place the centre of life outside of man, who by
his free will can and should create his own world
60 for himself. Fascism wants a man to be active
and to be absorbed in action with all his energies;
it wants him to have a manly consciousness of
the difficulties that exist and to be ready to face
them. It conceives life as a struggle, thinking that
65 it is the duty of man to conquer that life which
is really worthy of him: creating in the first place
within himself the (physical, moral, intellectual)
instrument with which to build it. As for the
individual, so for the nation, so for mankind.
70 Hence the high value of culture in all its forms (art,
religion, science) and the supreme importance of
education. Hence also the essential value of labour,
with which man conquers nature and creates
the human world (economic, political, moral,
75 intellectual).
    This positive conception of life is evidently
an ethical conception. And it comprises the
whole reality as well as the human activity which
domineers it. No action is to be removed from the
80 moral sense; nothing is to be in the world that is
divested of the importance which belongs to it in
respect of moral aims. Life, therefore, as the Fascist
conceives it, is serious, austere, religious; entirely
balanced in a world sustained by the moral and
85 responsible forces of the spirit. The Fascist disdains
the "easy" life.
    Fascism is a religious conception in which
man is considered to be in the powerful grip
of a superior law, with an objective which will
90 transcends the particular individual and elevates
him into a fully conscious member of a spiritual
society. Anyone who has stopped short at the
mere consideration of opportunism in the
religious policy of the Fascist Regime, has failed to
95 understand that Fascism, besides being a system of
government, is also a system of thought.

11

What could be the best title of the passage?

A) The history of fascism

B) The philosophy of fascism

C) Fascism as a philosophy

D) Different perspectives of a concept

The best answer is (D).
The passage is about numerous aspects ("political", "spiritual", "ethical", "religious") of a notion ("fascism")

(A), (B), (C); Each of these deals with only one aspect of fascism: a case of TOO NARROW, even if this one aspect is a correct one.

12

According to the passage, what can be said about the "form" (Line 5) of fascism?

A) It possesses impractical content that brings fascism a recipe of truth in theory.

B) It is impossible to spiritually influence the world using human will-power without using this form.

C) It is a philosophy or intuition, a system of ideas which evolves itself into a system of logical contraction, or which concentrates itself in a vision or in a faith.

D) It can change depending upon when and where fascism is practiced.

The best answer is (D).
This is a pretty straightforward question. The form fascism takes can change ("co-related to the contingencies") depending upon when ("time") and where ("place") fascism is practiced.

(A); It is fascism, not its form, that has content ("it has at the same time an ideal content which

elevates it into a formula of truth"), thus whether the content is ideal or impractical is beside the point.
(B); It is impossible ("There is no way") to spiritually influence ("of exercising a spiritual influence") the world ("on the things of the world") using human will-power ("by means of a human will-power"); however, 'without using the form' cannot be understood as "without first having a clear conception of the particular and transient reality".
(C); 'It' in this choice refers to fascism, not its form.

13

Which choice gives the best evidence for the answer to the previous question?

A) "It has at the same time an ideal content which elevates it into a formula of truth in the higher region of the history of thought." (Lines 6-9)

B) "It has therefore a form co-related to the contingencies of time and place." (Lines 5-6)

C) "There is no way of exercising a spiritual influence on the things of the world by means of a human will-power commanding the wills of others." (Lines 9-12)

D) "It is action with an inherent doctrine which, arising out of a given system of historic forces, is inserted in it and works on it from within." (Lines 2-5)

The best answer is (B)
Refer to the explanation for the answer to the previous question.

14

Why did the author argue that fascism cannot be understood by looking at its approach to education?

A) because it is a blatant lie

B) because it is a living conception of the world and the world can change

C) because it is based on intuition

D) because it usually has dreadful consequences

The best answer is (B).
"Fascism would therefore not be understood in many of its manifestations (as, for example, in its organisations of the Party, its system of education, its discipline)". Thus whatever comes before this sentence will give the answer. It is a living conception of the world ("an organic conception of the world"), which can change. ("evolves itself into a system of logical contraction")

(A), (C), (D); Because of "therefore" as explained for (B), there is only one location where the answer can be found, and the points are "organic" and "evolves", but no information in (A),(C) or (D) has anything to do with "organic" or "evolves".

15

Which choice gives the best evidence for the answer to the previous question?

A) "but which is always, at least virtually, an organic conception of the world" (Lines 25-26)

B) "It is a philosophy or intuition, a system of ideas which evolves itself into a system of logical contraction, or which concentrates itself in a vision or in a faith." (Lines 23-25)

C) "There can be no conception of a State which is not fundamentally a conception of Life." (Lines 20-22)

D) "to have a knowledge of man we must know

Test 2

the reality of things and their laws" (Lines 19-20)

The best answer is (B).
Refer to the explanation for the answer to the previous question.

16

According to the passage, what is the connection between the various conceptions of fascism?

A) a simple listing of each conception in turn

B) **a series of conceptions leading to a final conception**

C) one conception to be elaborated on by another conception

D) a conception that serves as a foundation for all other conceptions

The best answer is (B).
Each paragraph deals with a single aspect of fascism. Thus, we need to carefully look at how each paragraph is logically connected with the others. Both of the first two sentences in the second and third paragraphs contain "therefore"; also, "this positive conception of life" in the first sentence of the fourth paragraph is already explained in the third paragraph; finally, the concept "spiritual" in the first sentence of the last paragraph is also already dealt with in detail in the second and fourth paragraphs.

(A); Since all the paragraphs are connected with each other, "a simple listing" is an absurd understanding.
(C); Even though all the paragraphs are related, each subsequent paragraph deals with a different aspect of fascism, so elaboration is not the way the passage is developed.

17

According to the passage, why is fascism a spiritual conception?

A) because each person in a fascist country is an embodiment of the nation itself

B) **because everybody in fascism is in absolutely spiritual surroundings in which his or her worth is suited for the surroundings**

C) because people in fascist societies believe that their value consists of their metaphysical essence

D) because people in fascism are not really alone in their ideology

The best answer is (B).
"It is therefore a spiritual conception, itself also a result of the general reaction of the Century against the languid and materialistic positivism of the Eighteenth Century". Thus, whatever comes before this sentence will provide the answer. Because everybody in fascism ("the individual") is in absolutely spiritual surroundings ("entirely spiritual existence")in which his or her worth("value") is suited for ("consists in") the surroundings.

(A); The focus of the last sentence in the fourth paragraph comes after "realizes" and the important concepts are "entirely spiritual existence" and "his value consists (in which)" but 'nation' cannot be translated as any of these.
(C); "Spiritual" is not exactly the same as "metaphysical"
(D); Refer to (A); "not alone in their ideology" doesn't mean they are in "entirely spiritual existence in which his value as a man consists."

Test 2

18

Which choice gives the best evidence for the answer to the previous question?

A) "He is this by a moral law which embraces and binds together individuals and generations in an established tradition and mission," (Lines 39-41)

B) "by self-abnegation and by the sacrifice of his particular interests, even by death, realises the entirely spiritual existence in which his value as a man consists." (Lines 46-50)

C) "a moral law which suppresses the instinct to lead a life confined to a brief cycle of pleasure in order, instead, to replace it within the orbit of duty in a superior conception of life, free from the limits of time and space" (Lines 41-46)

D) "itself also a result of the general reaction of the Century against the languid and materialistic positivism of the Eighteenth Century." (Lines 51-54)

The best answer is (B).
Refer to the explanation for the answer to the previous question.

19

As used in lines 47, "abnegation" most nearly means

A) denial
B) offering
C) retreat
D) diffidence

The best answer is (A).
We are looking for a concept that can be compared with "sacrifice".

'Offering' is almost the opposite of this, so (B) is out, and "retreating from one's interests" does not make sense, so (C) is out. Being unsure or not confident about one's interests is not comparable to sacrificing them.

20

According to the last paragraph of the passage, in Fascism, that Fascism is a religious conception can be translated that

A) Fascism is much more than just a system of control.
B) According to fascist ideology people must have their own religion.
C) Only religious people can belong to a fascist society.
D) In a fascist society nobody should be opportunistic about the religious policies of fascism.

The best answer is (A).
Refer to the answer to Question 11; The passage is about several aspects ("political", "spiritual", "ethical", "religious") of a notion ("fascism"). A system of control is "political", and fascism's other traits ("spiritual", "ethical", "religious") are more than just "political" ('a system of control').

(B); Fascism is "religious", but that doesn't mean that its constituents, its people, can or must have their own religion.
(C); Apply exactly the same logic as for (B); fascism is "religious", but that doesn't mean that only religious people can belong to a fascist society; non-religious people can live in a religious society… unless the author says otherwise.
(D); "Anyone who has stopped short at the mere consideration of opportunism in the religious policy of the Fascist Regime, has failed to understand that Fascism, besides being a system of government, is also a system of thought." So, in order to understand fascism correctly, people must be opportunistic about the religious policies of fascist regimes.

I call our world Flatland, not because we call it so, but to make its nature clearer to you, my happy readers, who are privileged to live in Space. Imagine a vast sheet of paper on which straight Lines, Triangles, Squares, Pentagons, Hexagons, and other figures, instead of remaining fixed in their places, move freely about, on or in the surface, but without the power of rising above or sinking below it, very much like shadows— only hard with luminous edges— and you will then have a pretty correct notion of my country and countrymen. Alas, a few years ago, I should have said "my universe:" but now my mind has been opened to higher views of things. In such a country, you will perceive at once that it is impossible that there should be anything of what you call a "solid" kind; but I dare say you will suppose that we could at least distinguish by sight the Triangles, Squares, and other figures, moving about as I have described them. On the contrary, we could see nothing of the kind, not at least so as to distinguish one figure from another. Nothing was visible, nor could be visible, to us, except Straight Lines; and the necessity of this I will speedily demonstrate. Place a penny on the middle of one of your tables in Space; and leaning over it, look down upon it. It will appear a circle. But now, drawing back to the edge of the table, gradually lower your eye (thus bringing yourself more and more into the condition of the inhabitants of Flatland), and you will find the penny becoming more and more oval to your view, and at last when you have placed your eye exactly on the edge of the table (so that you are, as it were, actually a Flatlander) the penny will then have ceased to appear oval at all, and will have become, so far as you can see, a straight line. The same thing would happen if you were to treat in the same way a Triangle, or a Square, or any other figure cut out from pasteboard. As soon as you look at it with your eye on the edge of the table, you will find that it ceases to appear to you as a figure, and that it becomes in appearance a straight line. Take for example an equilateral Triangle— who represents with us a Tradesman of the respectable class. Figure 1 represents the Tradesman as you would see him while you were bending over him from above; figures 2 and 3 represent the Tradesman, as you would see him if your eye were close to the level, or all but on the level of the table; and if your eye were quite on the level of the table (and that is how we see him in Flatland) you would see nothing but a straight line. When I was in Spaceland I heard that your sailors have very similar experiences while they traverse your seas and discern some distant island or coast lying on the horizon. The far-off land may have bays, forelands, angles in and out to any number and extent; yet at a distance you see none of these (unless indeed your sun shines bright upon them revealing the projections and retirements by means of light and shade), nothing but a grey unbroken line upon the water. Well, that is just what we see when one of our triangular or other acquaintances comes towards us in Flatland. As there is neither sun with us, nor any light of such a kind as to make shadows, we have none of the helps to the sight that you have in Spaceland. If our friend comes closer to us we see his line becomes larger; if he leaves us it becomes smaller; but still he looks like a straight line; be he a Triangle, Square, Pentagon, Hexagon, Circle, what you will— a straight Line he looks and nothing else. You may perhaps ask how under these disadvantageous circumstances we are able to distinguish our friends from one another: but the answer to this very natural question will be more fitly and easily given when I come to describe the inhabitants of Flatland. For the present let me defer this subject, and say a word or two about the climate and houses in our country.

Test 2

21

What could be the best title for the passage?

A) The merits of living on land that is flat
B) A comparison and contrast between Flatland and Spaceland
C) The difficulties associated with living in Flatland
D) The nature of Flatland

The best answer is (D).
The author states that this passage is about the nature of Flatland. ("I call our world Flatland, not because we call it so, but to make its nature clearer to you,")

(A), (B), (C); None of these means or can mean the "nature of the flatland" or anything that can be implied as such.

22

According to the author, why does a person look like a flat line?

A) because of perspective
B) because the observer is in space
C) because the observer is on a flat land
D) because of the way the observer looks at things

The best answer is (C).
"but still he looks like a straight line; be he a Triangle, Square, Pentagon, Hexagon, Circle, what you will— a straight Line he looks and nothing else.", "As there is neither sun with us, nor any light of such a kind as to make shadows, we have none of the helps to the sight that you have in Spaceland."

(A); That the observer is on a flat land is a fact, not a perspective.
(B); The observer is on flat land.

(D); Being on flat land is not 'a way' of looking at things.

23

According to the passage, which choice will determine whether or not an island and a ship look the same?

A) their shapes
B) their distance from the observer
C) the observer's reasoning
D) their surroundings

The best answer is (B).
"The far-off land may have bays, forelands, angles in and out to any number and extent; yet at a distance you see none of these"

(A), (C), (D); None of these can mean "distance."

24

Why does the author call his world flatland?

A) because this is actually the real shape of his world
B) because the readers live happily in Space
C) because the readers lack imagination even though they enjoy having certain rights
D) because the readers must be informed of something about the world

The best answer is (D).
By calling his or her land a flat land, the author is trying to tell something about the nature of Flatland ("I call our world Flatland, not because we call it so, but to make its nature clearer to you,"), which is that it is flat.

(A), (B), (C); None of these can mean that Flatland is flat, nor do these contain the concept of nature

Test 2

or trait, character, or characteristic or property.

25

What is the role of quotations around the word "solid" (Line 17) in the passage?

A) emphasis
B) indicating a dual meaning
C) irony
D) showing some level of misunderstanding

The best answer is (D).
"there should be anything of what you call a "solid" kind; but I dare say you will suppose that we could at least distinguish by sight the Triangles, Squares, and other figures, moving about as I have described them." The semicolon after "solid" kind expresses the author's worry that the audience might still think that some kinds of solid objects may exist, but in fact there are none. ("On the contrary, we could see nothing of the kind, not at least so as to distinguish one figure from another.")

(A); At the beginning of the passage, this is the function of the quotations, but as the passage progresses, the focus shifts from emphasis to a possible misunderstanding of the readers and the author's concern about this misunderstanding.
(B); Here, the possible dual meaning of the word is 1) a solid in the strict chemical sense and 2) a solid as a concrete object in the obvious every-day sense. However, in context, this solid has nothing to do with any chemical concept.
(C); A tricky choice, but since the readers' possible misunderstanding cannot be called irony, there is no irony here.

26

Which choice gives the best evidence for the answer to the previous question?

A) "but I dare say you will suppose that we could at least distinguish by sight the Triangles, Squares, and other figures, moving about as I have described them." (Lines 17-20)
B) "On the contrary, we could see nothing of the kind, not at least so as to distinguish one figure from another." (Lines 20-22)
C) "the necessity of this I will speedily demonstrate." (Lines 24-25)
D) "but now my mind has been opened to higher views of things." (Lines 13-14)

The best answer is (B).
Refer to the explanation for the answer to the previous question.

27

In context, which choice most nearly means the same as "solid" as used in line 17?

A) hardened
B) unmistakable
C) distinguishable
D) strong

The best answer is (C).
This is essentially the same question as Question 25. We need to focus on the semicolon after "solid" kind, and see that it is followed by the word "distinguish"; thus any choice that has the closest relevancy to "distinguish" is the answer. ("a "solid" kind; but I dare say you will suppose that we could at least distinguish by sight the Triangles, Squares, and other figures, moving about as I have described them")

Test 2

28

It can be inferred that in Flatland one way to tell apart objects of different shapes would be to

A) look at them from a distance
B) be helped by sunlight shining on them
C) find a solid object
D) get really close to the objects being observed

The best answer is (D).
"As soon as you look at it with your eye on the edge of the table, you will find that it ceases to appear to you as a figure, and that it becomes in appearance a straight line." Thus, there could be no other way.

(A); The opposite
(B); There is no sunlight in Flatland.
(C); There are no "solid" objects in Flatland.

29

According to the passage, why does the author mention Pentagon?

A) to talk about a specific characteristic of some shape
B) to expound on the difficulties involved in distinguishing specific shapes
C) to explain how the shape of an object is of no help when attempting to distinguish one from another
D) to describe the universal problem of too much geometric complication

The best answer is (C).
The author states that the exact form of an object is irrelevant when trying to distinguish among them. ("but still he looks like a straight line; be he a Triangle, Square, Pentagon, Hexagon, Circle, what you will— a straight Line he looks and nothing else.")

30

The answer to which question gives the best evidence for the answer to the previous question?

A) Question 22
B) Question 24
C) Question 27
D) Question 28

The best answer is (C).
Refer to the explanation for the answer to Question 27.

Test 2

In 'What was the Gunpowder Plot? The Traditional Story tested by Original Evidence,' Father Gerard has set forth all the difficulties he found while sifting the accessible evidence, and has deduced from his examination a result which, though somewhat vague in itself, leaves upon his readers a very distinct impression that the celebrated conspiracy was mainly, if not altogether, a fiction devised by the Earl of Salisbury for the purpose of maintaining or strengthening his position in the government of the country under James I. Such, at least, is what I gather of Father Gerard's aim from a perusal of his book. Lest, however, I should in any way do him an injustice, I proceed to quote the summary placed by him at the conclusion of his argument:—

"The evidence available to us appears to establish principally two points: that the true history of the Gunpowder Plot is now known to no man, and that the history commonly received is certainly untrue. "It is quite impossible to believe that the Government were not aware of the Plot long before they announced its discovery. "It is difficult to believe that the proceedings of the conspirators were actually such as they are related to have been. "It is unquestionable that the Government consistently falsified the story and the evidence as presented to the world, and that the points upon which they most insisted prove upon examination to be the most doubtful. "There are grave reasons for the conclusion that the whole transaction was dexterously contrived for the purpose which in fact it opportunely served, by those who alone reaped benefit from it, and who showed themselves so unscrupulous in the manner of reaping."

No candid person, indeed, can feel surprise that any English Roman Catholic, especially a Roman Catholic priest, should feel anxious to wipe away the reproach which the plot has brought upon those who share his faith. Not merely were his spiritual predecessors subjected to a persecution borne with the noblest and least self-assertive constancy, simply in consequence of what is now known to all historical students to have been the entirely false charge that the plot emanated from, or was approved by the English Roman Catholics as a body, but this false belief prevailed so widely that it must have hindered, to no slight extent, the spread of that organization which he regards as having been set forth by divine institution for the salvation of mankind. If Father Gerard has gone farther than this, and has attempted to show that even the handful of Catholics who took part in the plot were more sinned against than sinning, I, for one, am not inclined to condemn him very harshly, even if I am forced to repudiate alike his method and his conclusions. Erroneous as I hold them, Father Gerard's conclusions at least call for patient inquiry. Up to this time critics have urged that parts at least of the public declarations of the Government were inconsistent with the evidence, and have even pointed to deliberate falsification. Father Gerard is, as far as I know, the first to go a step farther, and to argue that much of the evidence itself has been tampered with, on the ground that it is inconsistent with physical facts, so that things cannot possibly have happened as they are said to have happened in confessions attributed to the conspirators themselves. I can only speak for myself when I say that after reading much hostile criticism of Father Gerard's book— and I would especially refer to a most able review of it, so far as negative criticism can go, in the Edinburgh Review of January last— I did not feel that all difficulties had been removed, or that without further investigation I could safely maintain my former attitude towards the traditional story. It is, indeed, plain, as the Edinburgh Review has shown, that Father Gerard is unversed in the methods of historical inquiry which have guided recent scholars. Yet, for all that, he gives us hard nuts to crack; and, till they are cracked, the story of Gunpowder Plot cannot be allowed to settle down in peace. It seems strange to find a writer so regardless of what is, in these days, considered the first canon of historical inquiry, that evidence worth having must be almost entirely the evidence of contemporaries who are in a position to know something about that which they assert.

Test 2

31

What is the role of the first paragraph in relation to the rest of the passage?

A) aside
B) background
C) introduction
D) generalization

The best answer is (C).
The first paragraph ends with a colon, which means whatever follows serves as an elaboration or addition.

(A), (B), (D); Not worth mentioning why these are wrong.

32

What is the author's intention for writing this passage?

A) to criticize some general problems common among reviewers of historical events
B) to depict how the government had falsified certain evidence
C) to attempt to give a fair and unbiased review of a historical commentary
D) to demonstrate what was wrong with the Gunpowder plot

The best answer is (C).
'What was the Gunpowder Plot? The Traditional Story tested by Original Evidence,' is the review on the Gunpowder Plot that the author will review in this passage. The author is trying to give this commentary a fair appraisal. ("Lest, however, I should in any way do him an injustice, I proceed to quote the summary placed by him at the conclusion of his argument.")

(A): too NEGATIVE to be the answer

(B); This passage is focused on Father Gerard's commentary: WRONG PERSPECTIVE.
(D); This passage is focused on Father Gerard's commentary: WRONG PERSPECTIVE.

33

According to the author, what might be Father Gerard's problem?

A) His bottom lines need patient investigation.
B) His method is not compatible with his conclusions.
C) He is simply not qualified to conduct a historical investigation.
D) He made the mistake of giving us a very difficult assignment to handle.

The best answer is (C).
The author strongly asserts that Father Gerard lacks the expertise necessary to be a historical investigator. ("that Father Gerard is unversed in the methods of historical inquiry which have guided recent scholars")

(A), (B), (D); None of these choices can mean or imply that "Father Gerard is unversed in the methods of historical inquiry."

34

Which of the following provides the best evidence for the answer to the previous question?

A) "Father Gerard is unversed in the methods of historical inquiry which have guided recent scholars." (Lines 80-82)
B) "It is unquestionable that the Government consistently falsified the story and the evidence as presented to the world, and that the points upon which they most insisted prove upon examination to be the most doubtful." (Lines 26-30)

New SAT Reading Prep

Test 2

C) "Yet, for all that, he gives us hard nuts to crack." (Lines 82-83)

D) "Erroneous as I hold them, Father Gerard's conclusions at least call for patient inquiry." (Lines 58-60)

The best answer is (A).
Refer to the explanation for the answer to the previous question.

35

According to the passage, who must be his spiritual predecessors?

A) spiritual leaders of old times

B) previous Roman Catholic priests

C) most religious people

D) those who might be persecuted for religious reasons

The best answer is (B).
We need to take a look at the sentences that precedes the one in which we find his spiritual predecessors "No candid person, indeed, can feel surprise that any English Roman Catholic, especially a Roman Catholic priest, should feel anxious to wipe away the reproach which the plot has brought upon those who share his faith." After talking about Roman Catholic priests, the author went on to talk about somebody spiritual ("his spiritual predecessors"), so his spiritual predecessors must be Roman Catholic priests.

(A), (C), (D); According to the flow of the context (B) is obviously the answer.

36

Which of the following is strongly suggested by the first sentence of the third paragraph of the passage?

A) The plot was a protestant blasphemy.

B) The plot was devised by Roman Catholics.

C) The consequences of the plot probably worked against the Roman Catholic creed.

D) The plot was designed to attack the main articles of faith held by Roman Catholics.

The best answer is (C).
The consequence of the plot probably worked against ("reproach") the Roman Catholic creed ("those who share his faith").

(A); "Reproach" cannot be understood as a Protestant blasphemy: WRONG INFERENCE.
(B); A Roman Catholic would not harm other Roman Catholics. At least there is no evidence for that in the passage.
(D); It is not clear whether or not the main articles of faith were the target of the attack: WRONG INFERENCE.

37

According to the passage, what is most likely to be the primary principle when someone is making a historical investigation?

A) Almost every piece of evidence must be contemporary.

B) Only contemporaries can produce any worthwhile evidence.

C) Only contemporaries who have expertise relevant to the evidence they are dealing with can offer valid opinions.

D) It is frequently ignored by people like Father Gerald.

The best answer is (C).

The Primary principle ("the first canon) of historical investigation ("of historical inquiry") is that only contemporaries with certain information on the evidence they are dealing with can probably provide that as useful. ("that evidence worth having must be almost entirely the evidence of contemporaries who are in a position to know something about that which they assert")

38

Which of the following provides the best evidence for the answer to the previous question?

A) "till they are cracked, the story of Gunpowder Plot cannot be allowed to settle down in peace." (Lines 83-85)

B) "the first canon of historical inquiry, that evidence worth having must be almost entirely the evidence of contemporaries who are in a position to know something about that which they assert." (Lines 87-90)

C) "It seems strange to find a writer so regardless of what is, in these days, considered the first canon of historical inquiry," (Lines 85-87)

D) "Father Gerard is unversed in the methods of historical inquiry which have guided recent scholars." (Lines 80-82)

The best answer is (B).
Refer to the explanation for the answer to the previous question.

39

In context, what is the author probably trying to say in the second sentence of the third paragraph of the passage?

A) The plot did not do anything wrong.

B) It was an injustice that those involved in the plot were unfairly persecuted rather than fairly prosecuted.

C) Roman Catholic priests should not be the only ones who are prosecuted.

D) Students of History usually have false understanding of the plot.

The best answer is (B).
According to the passage, incorrect information about the alleged plot resulted in false charges being made ("to have been the entirely false charge that the plot emanated from"); the people involved were wrongfully charged. ('might be unjust')

(A); The focus is not on the plot, but on the "false charge that the plot emanated from": WRONG PERSPECTIVE.
(C); The focus is not on Roman Catholic priests, but on the "false charge that the plot emanated from": WRONG PERSPECTIVE.
(D); The charge itself was false, not the students' understanding of it: WRONG PERSPECTIVE.

40

According to the passage, which of the following is the best appreciation of the author's attitude toward Father Gerald's conclusions?

A) hard to grasp

B) ill-conceived

C) with no practical evidence

D) patient

The best answer is (B).
According to the passage it is "that Father Gerard is unversed in the methods of historical inquiry which have guided recent scholars.", "a writer so regardless of what is, in these days, considered the first canon of historical inquiry,", The point is that it is ill-conceived. ("Father Gerard is unversed in…historical inquiry…", "a writer so regardless of…the first canon of historical inquiry,")

(A); The point is not whether or not it is hard to understand Father Gerard's review.

Test 2

(C); The point is not whether Gerard's review is practical or theoretical and with or without evidence.
(D): Too POSITIVE to be the answer

41

According to the passage, probably why does the author say "hard nut to crack"?

A) because Father Gerald has made the case very difficult to solve

B) because he raised important suspicions regarding certain fabrications

C) because the Catholics involved in the plot were the worst sinners of their time

D) because the case is unlikely to be solved in the foreseeable future

The best answer is (B).
Right after severely criticizing Father Gerard, the author said, "Yet, for all that, he gives us a hard nuts to crack." This comment seems to be rather positive about Father Gerard, and the only positive assessment the author gave of Father Gerard's point of view is that "much of the evidence itself has been tampered with," The point here is that there was some fabrication ("tampered"), and Father Gerard raised important suspicions about it ("on the ground that it is inconsistent with physical facts, so that things cannot possibly have happened as they are said to have happened in confessions attributed to the conspirators themselves")

(A), (C), (D): too NEGATIVE to be the answer

42

Which of the following provides the best evidence for the answer to the previous question?

A) "till they are cracked,...down in peace." (Lines 83-85)

B) "that Father Gerard is...recent scholars." (Lines 80-82)

C) "I did not feel that all difficulties had been removed, or...towards the traditional story." (Lines 75-78)

D) "the first to go a step farther,... conspirators themselves." (Lines 64-70)

The best answer is (D).
Refer to the explanation for the answer to the previous question.

Psychological warfare is waged before, during, and after war; it is not waged against the opposing psychological warfare operators; it is not controlled by the laws, usages, and customs of war; and it cannot be defined in terms of terrain, order of battle, or named engagements. It is a continuous process. Success or failure is often known only months or years after the execution of the operation. Yet success, though incalculable, can be overwhelming; and failure, though undetectable, can be mortal. Psychological warfare does not fit readily into familiar concepts of war. Military science owes much of its precision and definiteness to its dealing with a well-defined subject, the application of organized lawful violence. The officer or soldier can usually undertake his task of applying mass violence without having to determine upon the enemy. The opening of war, recognition of neutrals, the listing of enemies, proclamation of peace— such problems are considered political, and outside the responsibility of the soldier. Even in the application of force short of war, the soldier proceeds only when the character of the military operation is prescribed by higher (that is, political) authorities, and after the enemies are defined by lawful and authoritative command. In one field only, psychological warfare, is there endless uncertainty as to the very nature of the operation. Psychological warfare, by the nature of its instruments and its mission, begins long before the declaration of war. Psychological warfare continues after overt hostilities have stopped. The enemy often avoids identifying himself in psychological warfare; much of the time, he is disguised as the voice of home, of God, of the church, of the friendly press. Offensively, the psychological warfare operator must fight antagonists who never answer back— the enemy audience. He cannot fight the one enemy who is in plain sight, the hostile psychological warfare operator, because the hostile operator is greedily receptive to attack. Neither success nor defeat are measurable factors. Psychological strategy is planned along the edge of nightmare.

In a formal approach to this mysterious part of the clean-cut process of war, it might be desirable to start with Euclidian demonstrations, proceeding from definition to definition until the subject-matter had been delimited by logic. Alternatively it might be interesting to try a historical approach, describing the development of psychological warfare through the ages. The best approach is perhaps afforded by a simplification of both a logical and historical approach. For concrete examples it is most worthwhile to look at instances of psychological warfare taken out of history down to World War II. Then the definitions and working relationships can be traced and with these in mind— a somewhat more detailed and critical appraisal of World Wars I and II organizations and operations can be undertaken. If a historian or philosopher picks up this book, he will find much with which to quarrel, but for the survey of so hard-to-define a subject, this may be a forgivable fault. Psychological warfare and propaganda are each as old as mankind; but it has taken modern specialization to bring them into focus as separate subjects. The materials for their history lie scattered through thousands of books and it is therefore impossible to brief them. Any reader contemplating retirement from the army to a sedentary life is urged to take up this subject. A history of propaganda would provide not only a new light on many otherwise odd or trivial historical events; it would throw genuine illumination on the process of history itself. There are however numerous instances which can be cited to show applications of psychological warfare.

Test 2

43

What could be the best title of the passage?

A) The nature of a certain intriguing war enterprise
B) The reasons for the complications of psychological warfare
C) The relation between war and psychological warfare
D) The history of psychological warfare

The best answer is (A).
This passage is about the nature of psychological warfare. Psychological warfare can be understood as a certain intriguing war enterprise.

(B), (C), (D); All of these describe only one specific aspect of psychological warfare: a case of TOO NARROW

44

Which of the following is true of the connection between war and the soldier?

A) Soldiers usually resort to using force short of actually going to war.
B) Soldiers have absolutely nothing to with problems during war, which are not concerned with military force.
C) During a war soldiers are probably not likely to be involved in psychological warfare.
D) Conducting psychological warfare is not a clear-cut matter.

The best answer is (C).
Psychological warfare ("such problems") are not likely to involve soldiers ("are considered political, and outside the responsibility of the soldier").

(A); Soldier do use forces short of war ("Even in the application of force short of war, the soldier proceeds only when the character of the military operation is prescribed by higher (that is, political) authorities,"). However, there is no proof that this 'usually' happens.
(B); Be careful about the sentence structure. It doesn't say that soldiers have absolutely nothing to do with problems during war that are not concerned with military force. (B) says soldiers have absolutely nothing to with problems during war, and those problems are not concerned with military force. In other words, (B) says soldiers have absolutely nothing to do with any problems during war, and that is nonsense.
(D); No matter how true (D) might be, (D) has nothing to do with the soldier.

45

According to the passage, which of the following is true of the connection between war and psychological warfare?

A) The duration of psychological warfare depends on that of the corresponding war.
B) Psychological warfare necessarily lasts longer than the war itself.
C) Psychological warfare must stop if the enemy ceases its war effort.
D) In terms of the results produced psychological warfare is more effective than war itself.

The best answer is (B).
"Psychological warfare continues after overt hostilities have stopped."

(A); As shown in (B) all we know is that psychological warfare lasts longer than war itself, but we don't know how much longer, so we can't say the duration of psychological warfare depends on that of the corresponding war: for example, the psychological warfare can last 11 years for a ten-year war and 12 years for a nine-year war, and so on.
(C); This directly contradicts the evidence that proves that (B) is the answer.

(D); Although the passage says "Yet success, though incalculable, can be overwhelming", this doesn't mean that psychological warfare is more effective than the war itself, because there is no proof that it is more overwhelming.

46

Which choice gives the best evidence for the answer to the previous question?

A) "Offensively, the psychological warfare operator must fight antagonists who never answer back" (Lines 36-38)

B) "Psychological warfare; much of the time, he is disguised as the voice of home, of God, of the church, of the friendly press" (Lines 34-36)

C) "In one field only, psychological warfare, is there endless uncertainty as to the very nature of the operation." (Lines 27-29)

D) "Psychological warfare, by the nature of its instruments and its mission, begins long before the declaration of war. Psychological warfare continues after overt hostilities have stopped." (Lines 29-33)

The best answer is (D).
Refer to the explanation for the answer to the previous question.

47

Which of the following can be most likely be inferred about psychological warfare?

A) Before declaring war, a nation must prepare the details of how the war is going to be conducted.

B) Before declaring war nations must have prepared a detailed plan of how the war is going to be conducted.

C) Psychological warfare is much more complicated than war itself.

D) Psychological warfare requires more labor than war itself.

The best answer is (A).
The only clue to this question is "Psychological warfare, by the nature of its instruments and its mission, begins long before the declaration of war." The focus here is "the nature of its instruments" Since its mission is obvious, winning the war, the question here is 'what does the author mean by "the nature of its instruments"?' What are the instruments that psychological warfare employs to win the war? Take a look at the key word in (A), "details". What could be the details of any war: strategy, types of weapons, the number of soldiers, and so on. These are the ways to win a war; they are the instruments referred to above. This is one hell of a difficult case of PARAPHRASING, but it is not impossible.

(B): TOO NARROW
(C), (D); Neither of these can be understood as "its instruments."

48

Which choice gives the best evidence for the answer to the previous question?

A) "Military science owes much of its precision and definiteness to its dealing with a well-defined subject, the application of organized lawful violence." (Lines 12-15)

B) "He cannot fight the one enemy who is in plain sight, the hostile psychological warfare operator, because the hostile operator is greedily receptive to attack." (Lines 39-43)

C) "In one field only, psychological warfare, is there endless uncertainty as to the very nature of the operation." (Lines 27-29)

D) "Psychological warfare, by the nature of its instruments and its mission, begins long before the declaration of war." (Lines 29-31)

Test 2

The best answer is (D).
Refer to the explanation for the answer to the previous question.

49

According to the passage, which of the following is most similar to psychological warfare?

A) The strategy of a kid who takes full advantage of a math book in order to pass a test.

B) A governmental plan to spread the rumor that a newly proposed medical plan will definitely work this time.

C) A national undertaking to collect money for the construction of shelters in preparation for heavy bombing during a war.

D) A government's plan to infiltrate a heavily guarded missile factory of a friendly nation.

The best answer is (B).
In order to solve this kind of hypothetical question, we need to focus on the integral relation between the primary elements: in this case, war and psychological warfare. So we must find two concepts that correspond to war and to psychological warfare, respectively; what war is to the proposed medical plan, psychological warfare is to the governmental plan.

(A), (C), (D); None of these provides any sort of corresponding relationships.

50

Which choice gives the best evidence for the answer to the previous question?

A) "Neither success nor defeat are measurable factors." (Lines 42-43)

B) "A history of propaganda would provide not only a new light on many otherwise odd or trivial historical events." (Lines 73-75)

C) "Offensively, the psychological warfare operator must fight antagonists who never answer back" (Lines 36-38)

D) "There are however numerous instances which can be cited to show applications of psychological warfare." (Lines 76-78)

The best answer is (B).
Refer to the explanation for the answer to the previous question.

51

As used in line 24, "prescribed" most nearly means

A) cured
B) dictated
C) commended
D) depicted

The best answer is (B).
Think about the relationship between the authorities and the military operation. What do the authorities do to a military operation? They order it. Simple.

52

According to the passage, which of the following is a trait of psychological warfare?

A) Its greatest enemy is those who don't respond.

B) It advances as quickly as history progresses.

C) Its precision relies on the application of military strategy.

D) Its objectives might go beyond just winning a war.

The best answer is (D).

Test 2

There are many ways ("numerous instances which can be cited to show applications of psychological warfare") psychological warfare can be used, which means that winning war is not the only use it can be put to.

(A); The author calls them antagonists ("the psychological warfare operator must fight antagonists who never answer back— the enemy audience."), not the greatest enemy.

(B); The relevant piece of evidence that can be used in this case is "it would throw genuine illumination on the process of history itself." This might suggest that 'it' advances as history progresses, but not as quickly.

TEST 3

Answer Keys & Explanations

Test 3

There were three great European nations in ancient days, each of which furnished history with a hero: the Greeks, the Carthaginians, and the Romans.

Alexander was the hero of the Greeks. He was King of Macedon, a country lying north of Greece proper. He headed an army of his countrymen, and made an excursion for conquest and glory into Asia. He made himself master of all that quarter of the globe, and reigned over it in Babylon, till he brought himself to an early grave by the excesses into which his boundless prosperity allured him. His fame rests on his triumphant success in building up for himself so vast an empire, and the admiration which his career has always excited among mankind is heightened by the consideration of his youth, and of the noble and generous impulses which strongly marked his character.

The Carthaginian hero was Hannibal. We class the Carthaginians among the European nations of antiquity; for, in respect to their origin, their civilization, and all their commercial and political relations, they belonged to the European race, though it is true that their capital was on the African side of the Mediterranean Sea. Hannibal was the great Carthaginian hero. He earned his fame by the energy and implacableness of his hate. The work of his life was to keep a vast empire in a state of continual anxiety and terror for fifty years, so that his claim to greatness and glory rests on the determination, the perseverance, and the success with which he fulfilled his function of being, while he lived, the terror of the world.

The Roman hero was Caesar. He was born just one hundred years before the Christian era. His renown does not depend, like that of Alexander, on foreign conquests, nor, like that of Hannibal, on the terrible energy of his aggressions upon foreign foes, but upon his protracted and dreadful contests with, and ultimate triumphs over, his rivals and competitors at home. When he appeared upon the stage, the Roman Empire already included nearly all of the world that was worth possessing. There were no more conquests to be made. Caesar did, indeed, enlarge, in some degree, the boundaries of the empire; but the main question in his day was, who should possess the power which preceding conquerors had acquired.

The Roman Empire, as it existed in those days, must not be conceived of by the reader as united together under one compact and consolidated government. It was, on the other hand, a vast congeries of nations, widely dissimilar in every respect from each other, speaking various languages, and having various customs and laws. They were all, however, more or less dependent upon, and connected with, the great central power. Some of these countries were provinces, and were governed by officers appointed and sent out by the authorities at Rome. These governors had to collect the taxes of their provinces, and also to preside over and direct, in many important respects, the administration of justice. They had, accordingly, abundant opportunities to enrich themselves while thus in office, by collecting more money than they paid over to the government at home, and by taking bribes to favor the rich man's cause in court. Thus the more wealthy and prosperous provinces were objects of great competition among aspirants for office at Rome. Leading men would get these appointments, and, after remaining long enough in their provinces to acquire a fortune, would come back to Rome, and expend it in intrigues and maneuvers to obtain higher offices still.

Whenever there was any foreign war to be carried on with a distant nation or tribe, there was always a great eagerness among all the military officers of the state to be appointed to the command. They each felt sure that they should conquer in the contest, and they could enrich themselves still more rapidly by the spoils of victory in war, than by extortion and bribes in the government of a province in peace. Then, besides, a victorious general coming back to Rome always found that his military renown added vastly to his influence and power in the city. He was welcomed with celebrations and triumphs; the people flocked to see him and to shout his praise. He placed his trophies of victory in the temples, and entertained the populace with games and shows, and with combats of gladiators or of wild beasts, which he had brought home with him for this purpose in the train of his army. While he was thus enjoying his triumph, his political enemies would be thrown into the back ground and into the shade; unless, indeed, some one of them might himself

Test 3

be earning the same honors in some other field, to come back in due time, and claim his share of power and celebrity in his turn. In this case,
100 Rome would be sometimes distracted and rent by the conflicts and contentions of military rivals, who had acquired powers too vast for all the civil influences of the Republic to regulate or control.

1

What could be the best title of the passage?

A) The three greatest ancient nations

B) The three heroes in the greatest ancient nations

C) The history of Caesar

D) How Caesar rose to power

The best answer is (B).
The focus in on the heroes not on their nations because as it can easily be seen in the case of Caesar, the explanation gets very complicated ("They each felt sure that they should conquer in the contest, and they could enrich themselves still more rapidly by the spoils of victory in war, than by extortion and bribes in the government of a province in peace."); the nations only work as introductions to these three heroes.

(C), (D); Even though the passage devotes the greatest space to Caesar, even when it talks about him it deals with the differences between him and Alexander ("His renown does not depend, like that of Alexander, on foreign conquests"), and those of him and Hannibal ("nor, like that of Hannibal, on the terrible energy of his aggressions upon foreign foes,"). These cases are TOO NARROW; even though he writes about Caesar in more detail, the author compares all three heroes.

2

According to the passage, why did the author probably mention three heroes?

A) to talk about their significant differences

B) to stress the similarity that some nations have

C) to emphasize the differences between Caesar and the other two heroes

D) to lead into a more important topic

Test 3

The best answer is (B).
(A) and (B) can be very confusing, but in order for (A) to be the answer, there has to be proof for 'significant' differences. Although the author talked about the differences between the three heroes, the author never used any word or expression to be understood as 'significant'. Nor is any inference possible. On top of that, the passage began talking about the similarity of three nations. ("each of which furnished history with a hero")

3

Which of the following is the main difference between Alexander and Hannibal?

A) Only one of them conquered a vast land area.

B) Only one of them had to deal mostly with domestic problems rather than having to invade foreign nations.

C) Only one of them had a horrific image.

D) They had dissimilar reasons for their conquest.

The best answer is (C).
(B); This cannot be the answer precisely for the same reason why 1-(C), 1-(D) cannot be the answer.
(D); Since the passage ended giving some details about Caesar, and he is one of the heroes, there are no important other topics than the three heroes.)

4

Which of the following is the main difference between Alexander and Caesar?

A) Only one of them conquered a vast land area.

B) Only one of them had to deal with more of domestic problems than having to invade foreign nations.

C) Only one of them had a horrific image.

D) They had dissimilar reasons for their conquests.

The answer is (B).
Refer to the explanation for 1-(C), (D)

5

According to the passage, of all the differences mentioned, which difference is most outstanding and why?

A) Alexander's, because he conquered the largest land area.

B) Hannibal's, because he had the most horrible image of all.

C) Caesar's, because he was born just one hundred years before the Christian era.

D) Caesar's, because he was in a significantly different circumstance than the other two who were in a more typical situation.

The best answer is (D).
Even though the passage is about three heroes, not just one, Caesar, the author dedicates more words to explaining his situation because it had the most outstanding differences. ("His renown does not depend, like that of Alexander, on foreign conquests, nor, like that of Hannibal, on the terrible energy of his aggressions upon foreign foes, but upon his protracted and dreadful contests with, and ultimate triumphs over, his rivals and competitors at home")

6

Which of the following is true of the Roman Empire?

A) Some of the nations in it had political independence.

B) The central government possessed absolute power in every aspect of life.

C) Although its nations had many differences, they had one thing in common.

D) The nations were different from each other in every way except for the central government.

The best answer is (C).
Even though all the nations were different from each other ("widely dissimilar in every respect from each other, speaking various languages, and having various customs and laws."), they had one thing in common. ("They were all, however, more or less dependent upon, and connected with, the great central power.")

7

As used in line 53, "congeries" most nearly means

A) aggregate
B) host
C) collectivity
D) congregation

The best answer is (B).
We need to look at congeries and words around it ("a vast congeries of nations"), so it should go well with "vast" and "nations". We can easily tell "a vast congeries of" has to mean many, and (B) is the best choice to mean many.

(A); This has more to do with mass, than to do with number
(C); This can never mean any specific number; this is an abstract noun; 'collection' could have been a lot better as the answer.
(D); This can mean number, but of people not of nations.)

8

According to the passage, in Roman Empire probably who would get the most profit?

A) the officials in the central government at Rome
B) the king of each nation conquered by Rome
C) the governors sent to the provinces by Rome
D) the officials at Rome bribed by the governors appointed for the conquered nations

The best answer is (C).
The governors made a lot of money ("after remaining long enough in their provinces to acquire a fortune,"), and those who were bribed were not the officials in the central government, but the provincial governors. ("they could enrich themselves still more rapidly by the spoils of victory in war, than by extortion and bribes in the government of a province in peace.")

(A), (D); These are very plausible choices but the passage was very unclear about this ("They were all, however, more or less dependent upon, and connected with, the great central power.")
(B); This was never a focus of the passage. The passage was centered on the conqueror(s) not those who were conquered.

9

Which choice gives the best evidence for the answer to the previous question?

A) "after remaining long enough in their provinces to acquire a fortune," (Lines 71-72)
B) "These governors had to collect the taxes of their provinces, and also to preside over and direct, in many important respects, the administration of justice." (Lines 60-63)
C) "They were all, however, more or less dependent upon, and connected with, the great central power." (Lines 56-57)

D) "they paid over to the government at home, and by taking bribes to favor the rich man's cause in court." (Lines 66-67)

The best answer is (A).
Refer to the explanation for the answer to the previous question.

10

According to the passage, which of the following is true of victorious generals returning to Rome?

A) They were welcomed because everyone knew they would try to acquire political power.

B) Their influence as war generals was surpassed by their role in entertaining the populace.

C) Most of them showed their strength by fighting with gladiators or with wild beasts.

D) They considered war a way of gaining wealth.

The best answer is (D).
Refer to the explanation for 8-(C) ("they could enrich themselves still more rapidly by the spoils of victory in war, than by extortion and bribes in the government of a province in peace.")

The raw materials from which the food and tissue-building compounds of plants are synthetized include carbon dioxide, oxygen, water, nitrogen, phosphorus, sulfur, potassium, calcium, magnesium, and iron. The two gases first mentioned are derived directly from the air, through the respiratory organs of the plant. Water is taken into the plant chiefly from the soil, through its fibrous roots. All the other elements in the list are taken from the soil, nitrogen being derived from decaying organic matter (the original source of the nitrogen is, however, the atmosphere, from which the initial supply of nitrogen is obtained by direct assimilation by certain bacteria and perhaps other low forms of plant life), and the remaining ones from the mineral compounds of the soil.

Carbon dioxide and oxygen, being derived from the air, are always available to the leaves and stems of growing plants in unlimited supply; but the supply available to a seed when germinating in the soil, or to the roots of a growing farm crop, may sometimes become inadequate, especially in soils of a very compact texture, or "water-logged" soils. In such cases, the deficiency of these gaseous food elements may become a limiting factor in plant growth.

Water is often a limiting factor in plant growth. Experiments which have been repeated many times and under widely varying conditions show that when water is supplied to a plant in varying amounts, by increasing the percentage of water in the soil in which the plant is growing by regular increments up to the saturation point, the growth of the plant, or yield of the crop, increases up to a certain point and then falls off because the excess of water reduces the supply of air which is available to the plant roots. Hence, abundance of water is, in general, a most essential factor in plant growth.

Under normal conditions of air and moisture supply, however, the plant food elements which may be considered to be the limiting factors in the nutrition and growth of plants are the chemical elements mentioned in the list above.

The plant food materials which are taken from the soil by a growing plant must enter it by osmosis through the semi-permeable membranes

Test 3

which constitute the epidermis of the root-hairs,
and circulate through the plant either carried
in solution in the sap or by osmosis from cell to
cell. Hence, they must be in water-soluble form
before they can be utilized by plants. Obviously,
therefore, only those compounds of these elements
in the soil which are soluble in the soil water are
available as plant food. The greater proportion
of the soil elements are present there in the form
of compounds which are so slightly soluble in
water as to be unavailable to plants. The processes
by which these practically insoluble compounds
become gradually changed into soluble forms are
chiefly the "weathering" action of air and water
(particularly if the latter contains carbonic acid)
and the action of the organic acids resulting from
decaying animal or vegetable matter or secreted by
living plants.

11

What would be the best title of the passage?

A) Diverse chemical elements comprising plant food
B) Sources of plant food elements
C) Plant food elements
D) Indispensable chemical elements in plant growth

The best answer is (C).
The passage talks about different plant food materials ("carbon dioxide, oxygen, water, nitrogen, phosphorus, sulfur, potassium, calcium, magnesium, and iron"), chemical elements and compound: the way they are absorbed by plant: limiting factors as part of the nature of food materials: Osmosis as part of the way plant food materials are absorbed.

(A); a case of TOO NARROW
(B); a case of TOO NARROW
(D); The only possible relevance to this choice is "a most essential factor", which is abundance of water, which cannot be one of the 'chemical elements'.

12

Why were different chemical elements mentioned in the first paragraph?

A) to show the variety involved
B) to demonstrate the similarities between them
C) to delve into some biological differences
D) to establish some foundation for classification

The best answer is (D).
The author is talking about different ways ("derived directly from the air", "chiefly from the soil through its fibrous roots", "taken from the soil") in which different elements are absorbed by plants, and these different ways are the basis of

Test 3

classification of the elements as food. ("Obviously, therefore, only those compounds of these elements in the soil which are soluble in the soil water are available as plant food.")

(A); The focus is not the variety itself, but how all the elements are classified as different kinds of food.
(B); In order to be classified, the way the elements are absorbed is explained. This is a difference not a similarity.
(C); The different ways of absorption are not biological; they are physical in nature.)

13

What is the role of the second paragraph in connection to the first one?

A) cause and effect
B) specification
C) exemplification
D) comparison and contrast

The best answer is (B).
In the 2nd paragraph, the author is talking more ("always available") about the elements and compounds (oxygen and carbon dioxide) s/he already mentioned in the 1st paragraph.

(A); Something more specific cannot be the effect of something more general.
(C); Specification is not a form of exemplification; it works the other way around.
(D); Specification is not a form of comparison or contrast.

14

According to the passage, which of the following is true of oxygen and water?

A) They come from the same source.
B) They function in practically the same fashion.
C) They might have different availability.
D) Too much of either can work against the growth of a plant.

The best answer is (C).
According to 2nd paragraph, oxygen is "always available", but water might not be ("Hence, abundance of water is, in general, a most essential factor in plant growth.")

(A); Availability is not related with the source.
(B); Availability is not related with the function.
(D); Availability is not related with the limiting factor.

15

Which of the following is the most direct evidence for the answer to the previous question?

A) limiting factor
B) in varying amounts
C) always available
D) reduces the supply of air

The best answer is (C).
Refer to the explanation for the answer to the previous question.

Test 3

16

According to the passage, which of the following is the most unique feature of water in plant growth?

A) It is a constant limiting factor.

B) It inhibits the increment pattern of plant growth.

C) Its amount must vary to fit the needs of plant growth.

D) The efficiency of its role has to do with other essential element.

The best answer is (D).
The efficiency of water's role has to do with other elements ("when water is supplied to a plant in varying amounts, by increasing the percentage of water in the soil in which the plant is growing by regular increments up to the saturation point, the growth of the plant, or yield of the crop, increases up to a certain point", and then decreases because "the excess of water reduces the supply of air")

(A); There is no concept such as a constant limiting factor.
(B); Water doesn't always 'inhibit' the increment pattern of plant growth.
(C); The amount of water doesn't vary according to the needs of a plant ("by increasing the percentage of water in the soil in which the plant is growing by regular increments up to the saturation point, the growth of the plant, or yield of the crop, increases up to a certain point and then falls")

17

What would be the most probable reason the author said "however" (Line 12)?

A) because there are many limiting factors

B) because the definition of certain elements is dictated by some surrounding conditions

C) because the author didn't like the way the previous paragraph ends

D) because water is not the most important limiting factor

The best answer is (B).
"Under normal conditions of air and moisture supply, however, the plant food elements which may be considered to be the limiting factors in the nutrition and growth of plants are the chemical elements mentioned in the list above." In other words, If conditions change, limiting factors (a sort of classification) can change.

(A), (C), (D); None of these can mean or imply that "limiting factors" can change if "conditions of air and moisture supply" change.

18

Which of the following is the most direct evidence for the answer to the previous question?

A) limiting factor

B) in varying amounts

C) always available

D) under normal conditions

The best answer is (D).
Refer to the explanation for the answer to the previous question.

19

Why did the author mention "osmosis" (Line 51)?

A) to show one of many possible ways for nutrients to be absorbed into plants

B) to set up a criterion by which to improve efficiency

C) to talk about availability and limitation of a certain intake, which provides a criterion for classifying plant foods

D) to show how insoluble some elements in

water are, the solubility of which gives a significant ingredient of plant food classification

The best answer is (C).
Because plant food must be soluble in water ("they must be in water-soluble form before they can be utilized by plants") so only water-soluble plant food materials can be absorbed as plant food ("Obviously, therefore, only those compounds of these elements in the soil which are soluble in the soil water are available as plant food.") In other words, water-insoluble or slightly-soluble materials cannot be used as plant foods ("The greater proportion of the soil elements are present there in the form of compounds which are so slightly soluble in water as to be unavailable to plants."): water-soluble=availability, water-insoluble and slightly-insoluble=limitation.

(A); There are only two ways: water-soluble enough to be used as plant food or not water-soluble enough
(B); Whether or not something can be used as plant food is not a matter of efficiency or inefficiency
(D); The point is whether or not any material is water-soluble, not the solubility itself

20

What is the role of the last paragraph in the passage as a whole?

A) a solution to the problem presented by the passage

B) a very cautious conclusion

C) a decent elaboration of a concept proposed in the rest of the passage

D) adding a new perspective to the previous discussion

The best answer is (D).
The 1st paragraph is about different chemical elements and the ways they are taken in by plants. The 2nd paragraph is about some limiting factors and the conditions that create them. The 3rd paragraph is about water and how it can become a limiting factor. The 4th paragraph is about different conditions that create limiting factors. The 5th paragraph is about osmosis. So we need to know the connection between limiting factors and osmosis. As we carefully examine any possible connection between limiting factors and osmosis, it is obvious that there is no connection. previous discussion=limiting factor, a new perspective=osmosis

(A); Osmosis is not a solution to a limiting factor, which is not a problem.
(B); Osmosis is not a conclusion, careful or not
(C); Osmosis is not an elaboration of a limiting factor, decent or not.)

Test 3

The appearances in the heavens have from earliest historic ages filled men with wonder and awe; then they gradually became a source of questioning, and thinkers sought for explanations of the daily and nightly phenomena of sun, moon and stars. Scientific astronomy, however, was an impossibility until an exact system of chronology was devised. Meanwhile men puzzled over the shape of the earth, its position in the universe, what the stars were and why the positions of some shifted, and what those fiery comets were that now and again appeared and struck terror to their hearts. In answer to such questions, the Chaldean thinkers, slightly before the rise of the Greek schools of philosophy, developed the idea of the seven heavens in their crystalline spheres encircling the earth as their center. This conception seems to lie back of both the later Egyptian and Hebraic cosmologies, as well as of the Ptolemaic. Through the visits of Greek philosophers to Egyptian shores this conception helped to shape Greek thought and so indirectly affected western civilization. Thus our heritage in astronomical thought, as in many other lines, comes from the Greeks and the Romans reaching Europe (in part through Arabia and Spain), where it was shaped by the influence of the schools down to the close of the Middle Ages when men began anew to withstand authority in behalf of observation and were not afraid to follow whither their reason led them. But not all Greek philosophers, it seems, either knew or accepted the Babylonian cosmology. According to Plutarch, though Thales (640?-546? B.C.) and later the Stoics believed the earth to be spherical in form, Anaximander (610-546? B.C.) thought it to be like a "smooth stony pillar," Anaximenes (6th cent.) like a "table." Beginning with the followers of Thales or perhaps Parmenides (?-500 B.C.), as Diogenes Laërtius claims, a long line of Greek thinkers including Plato (428?-347? B.C.) and Aristotle (384-322 B.C.) placed the earth in the center of the universe. Whether Plato held that the earth "encircled" or "clung" around the axis is a disputed point; but Aristotle claimed it was the fixed and immovable center around which swung the spherical universe with its heaven of fixed stars and its seven concentric circles of the planets kept in their places by their transparent crystalline spheres. The stars were an even greater problem. Anaximenes thought they were "fastened like nails" in a crystalline firmament, and others thought them to be "fiery plates of gold resembling pictures." But if the heavens were solid, how could the brief presence of a comet be explained?

Among the philosophers were some noted as mathematicians whose leader was Pythagoras (c. 550 B.C.). He and at least one of the members of his school, Eudoxus (409?-356? B.C.), had visited Egypt, according to Diogenes Laërtius, and had in all probability been much interested in and influenced by the astronomical observations made by the Egyptian priests. On the same authority, Pythagoras was the first to declare the earth was round and to discuss the antipodes. He too emphasized the beauty and perfection of the circle and of the sphere in geometry, forms which became fixed for 2000 years as the fittest representations of the perfection of the heavenly bodies. There was some discussion in Diogenes' time as to the author of the theory of the earth's motion of axial rotation. Diogenes gives the honor to Philolaus (5th cent. B.C.) one of the Pythagoreans, though he adds that others attribute it to Icetas of Syracuse (6th or 5th cent. B.C.). Cicero, however, states the position of Hicetas of Syracuse as a belief in the absolute fixedness of all the heavenly bodies except the earth, which alone moves in the whole universe, and that its rapid revolutions upon its own axis cause the heavens apparently to move and the earth to stand still. Other thinkers of Syracuse may also have felt the Egyptian influence; for one of the greatest of them, Archimedes (c. 287-212 B.C.), stated the theory of the earth's revolution around the sun as enunciated by Aristarchus of Samos. (Perhaps this is the "hearth-fire of the universe" around which Philolaus imagined the earth to whirl.) In Arenarius, a curious study on the possibility of expressing infinite sums by numerical denominations as in counting the sands of the universe, Archimedes writes: "For you have known that the universe is called a sphere by several astrologers, its center the center of the earth, and its radius equal to a line drawn from the center of the sun to the center of the earth. This was written for the unlearned, as you have known from the astrologers…

Test 3

21

What would be the best title of the passage?

A) Astrological developments in ancient times

B) The development of astronomical thought

C) How Plato affected modern astronomy

D) The way Greek philosophers influenced modern science

The best answer is (B).
One of the best ways to answer this question is to refer to the explanations for all the other questions, but by especially referring to the following question and 10-A, we can easily see the answer; "thinkers sought for explanations of the daily and nightly phenomena of sun, moon and stars", 'Specification' (the rest of the passage))

22

What is the organization of the first sentence of the passage?

A) generalization and specification

B) comparison and contrast

C) cause and effect

D) transition in perspective

The best answer is (D).
The transition is rather obvious ("; then") from "wonder and awe" to "a source of questioning" and further to that "thinkers sought for explanations of the daily and nightly phenomena of sun, moon and stars"

23

According to the passage, what was Greek philosophers' attitude toward Babylonian cosmology?

A) A few of them were not interested.

B) Some of them didn't try hard enough to truly comprehend it.

C) Some of them appeared not to agree with it.

D) Its conceptualization was particularly difficult for them to grasp.

The best answer is (C).
Some Greek philosophers("not all Greek philosophers") appeared ("it seems") not to agree with it ("accepted the Babylonian cosmology.")

(A), (B), (D); These are all possible reasons for the answer (C), but only possible without any evidence: typical cases of WRONG INFERENCE.)

24

In context, which of the following is most probably the reason the Chaldean thinkers developed a multiple heaven theory?

A) because they did not know how to time certain astronomical events

B) because it was the best way for them to overcome their terror

C) because they had to answer some of their questions properly

D) because some horrible heavenly objects kept reappearing

The best answer is (A).
"Scientific astronomy, however, was an impossibility until an exact system of chronology was devised" and "Meanwhile" sentence continued to the introduction of "Chaldean thinkers". Thus,

those thinkers didn't have "an exact system of chronology"(a way to time).

25

Which choice gives the best evidence for the answer to the previous question?

A) "This conception seems to lie back of both the later Egyptian and Hebraic cosmologies, as well as of the Ptolemaic." (Lines 17-19)

B) "Scientific astronomy, however, was an impossibility until an exact system of chronology was devised." (Lines 6-8)

C) "Meanwhile men puzzled over the shape of the earth, its position in the universe, what the stars were and why the positions of some shifted, and what those fiery comets were that now and again appeared and struck terror to their hearts" (Lines 8-13)

D) "Through the visits of Greek philosophers to Egyptian shores this conception helped to shape Greek thought and so indirectly affected western civilization." (Lines 19-23)

The best answer is (B).
Refer to the explanation for the answer to the previous question.

26

Which of the following is true of Babylonian cosmology?

A) At the time of its inception it was less scientific than other approaches.

B) It had an influence far beyond the realm of scientific curiosity

C) It served as the foundation of Western civilization.

D) It was difficult for outsiders to understand, leading many to misunderstand it.

The best answer is (B).
This is essentially the same question as Question 4 ("Through the visits of Greek philosophers to Egyptian shores this conception helped to shape Greek thought and so indirectly affected western civilization.")

27

Which of the following gives the most direct evidence for the answer to the previous question?

A) not all Greek philosophers

B) so indirectly affected western civilization

C) men began anew to withstand authority

D) spherical in form

The best answer is (B).
This is essentially the same question as Question 4 ("Through the visits of Greek philosophers to Egyptian shores this conception helped to shape Greek thought and so indirectly affected western civilization.")

28

According to the passage, which of the following is probably the reason stars were bigger problems?

A) because they were obviously much greater in number than the earth

B) because their movements were more complicated than that of the earth

C) because of an unexplainable anomaly

D) because there was a big conflict between astronomy and mathematics

The best answer is (C).
Stars were a bigger ("even greater") problem because of an unexplainable anomaly ("But if the heavens were solid, how could the brief presence of a comet be explained?")

Test 3

(A), (B), (D); None of these can be inferred from the passage between "even greater" and "how could the brief")

29

Which of the following gives the most direct evidence for the answer to the previous question?

A) "Pythagoras was the first to declare the earth was round" (Lines 63-64)

B) "the fittest representations of the perfection of the heavenly bodies." (Lines 67-68)

C) "how could the brief presence of a comet be explained?" (Lines 53-54)

D) "Cicero, however, states the position of Hicetas of Syracuse as a belief in the absolute fixedness of all the heavenly bodies except the earth," (Lines 74-77)

The best answer is (C).
Refer to the explanation for the answer to the previous question.

30

Which of the following most directly shows the same attitude as displayed by enunciated?

A) Egyptian influence

B) curious

C) revolutions

D) the unlearned

The best answer is (D).
"enunciated by Aristarchus of Samos. (Perhaps this is the "hearth-fire of the universe" around which Philolaus imagined the earth to whirl.)" Since what is explained in the parenthesis is an example of wrong theory, we are looking for something wrong or ignorant.

31

Which of the following is not the strategy the author is using to convey his or her argument in the passage?

A) generalization and specification

B) comparison and contrast

C) cause and effect

D) exception and refutation

The best answer is (D).

(A): Generalization ("The appearances in the heavens have from earliest historic ages filled men with wonder and awe; then they gradually became a source of questioning, and thinkers sought for explanations of the daily and nightly phenomena of sun, moon and stars") and Specification (the rest of the passage)
(B): Comparison and Contrast ("Greek philosophers and Babylonian astronomy, Egyptian and Hebraic cosmologies, as well as of the Ptolemaic, Pythagorian philosophers and mathematicians")
(C): Cause and Effect ("In answer to such questions", "how could the brief presence of a comet be explained?")

Test 3

Electricity, next to Deity, is the most remarkable entity in the universe. Its marvelous and varied powers and utilities create a new epoch in scientific thought and discovery. Its study is replete with new and fascinating ideas and scientific theories. It contains the story of the universe more sublime than an epic, more wonderful than a romance. It organized the machinery of the worlds, and holds the secrets of nature and the mysteries of life in its invisible grasp. Electricity is the right hand of Deity, the tongue of the Spirit, the Word of Omnipotent power, the protean cosmic force and creative machinery of the universe. At the divine fiat it seized all atoms and space, it shook the ether into nebula, the nebula into worlds, the worlds into constellations, the constellations into a universe. It shaped planets and rounded suns and hurled them forth to circle in the chorus of the singing spheres. It gave form and functions to all matter from the rounded pebble to the stars; from the raindrop to the surging seas; from the chirping cricket to the sporting leviathan; from the helpless infant to the giant man. It is the messenger and executive of Creative Will to all created things. It is the ambassador of spirit to matter, the autocrat of communication between all the faculties of mind and all the functions of physical existence. It is the law of affinity in matter, of selection in atoms, and whispers to the body the intuitions of the Spirit and guides insensate worlds to do the will of Creative Omnipotence. Electricity is the wonderful medium and agent by which mind acts upon matter and works the miracle of life and growth. This mightiest servant of God and man, this genii greater than Aladdin's lamp, impresses all laws upon nature, and makes the universe obedient to the will of Deity, as man's body is obedient to the dictates of man's mind. This inscrutable word of power from the source of all power is beginning to supply the human race with an inexhaustible force that will revolutionize the earth and link all nations together as one family in a millennium of peace and good will. Human life seems to throb, pulsate, gleam and glow in this marvelous current of existence, which causes illumination, transportation, telegraphy, photography, surgery, horticulture, agriculture, metallurgy and manufacture to step forth as master magicians to work miracles for the comfort and happiness of mankind. Every new discovery, every step in the progress of electrical science conquers time, destroys distances, diffuses knowledge, dissipates ignorance, encourages friendship and draws men and nations closer and closer by physical ties and spiritual affinities. Where once noisy ponderous mechanism pounded the rocks to release the metals, electrical science with her unseen but resistless currents instantly separate the ore and the dross. Where the soot-begrimed engineer seizes the heavy iron throttle, she cleanly and softly touches a tiny button and the miracle is wrought— the heavy steed of steel receives its life not from smoking, hissing, fussing steam, but from an energy as silent as light and as potent as Omnipotence. This invisible electrical energy, without brush or color, paints the gorgeous beauties of the rainbow, and photographs in every ray of light and on every human eye the moving panorama of every passing scene. It telegraphs between mind and matter, between soul and body, between suns and planets, and gives life and energy to all the varied functions of this electric magnetic universe. This strange, miraculous power has taken its place as the supreme force of all forces, the ultimate elemental force from which all other physical forces are derived, and, without fuel or expense, flies with its burdens swifter than the flight of eagles. It is the last and greatest progeny of man genius and discovery, the seventh daughter of science, who dips her wand in the impossible and miraculous until miracles become prolific and common. Its power and expression are universal and its character and process superlatively grand. Its theatre of action is the universe and it comes to earth as the voice of Deity and the word of His Omnipotence. This science of the impossible, this daughter of miracles, is destined to outstrip all past achievements. The ponderous and noisy mechanisms will pass away, the barren rocks will change into most precious things, the sunlight will be converted into reservoirs of power, and every raindrop and waterfall, ocean tide and wind current, will reveal exhaustless sources of wealth and energy.

Test 3

32

What would be the best title of the passage?

A) The practical uses of electricity
B) What electricity can and cannot do
C) The miraculous and ambivalent power of electricity
D) **An incredible agent in the Universe**

The best answer is (D).
That electricity is incredible is reiterated throughout the passage ("most remarkable entity", "the right hand of Deity", "the Word of Omnipotent power", "the protean cosmic force and creative machinery of the universe", "It gave form and functions to all matter from the rounded pebble to the stars", "works the miracle of life and growth", "mightiest servant of God and man")

(A); This passage is very rhetorical about electricity. Refer to the explanation for (D)
(B), (C); There is nothing negative about electricity in this passage.

33

According to the passage, what can be said about electricity?

A) **There will be no scientific outcome greater than that of electricity.**
B) Its influence is as great as that of God.
C) It is the earliest and most significant scientific discovery.
D) It and God play complementary roles in human history.

The best answer is (A).
There will be no greater scientific outcome ("last and greatest progeny") than this.

(B); It is not as great as God. ("next to Deity")

(C); The directly opposite of "last"
(D); "Electricity is the right hand of Deity" and being an entity's hand implies subordination to that entity, and being subordinate is not compatible with 'complementary'.

34

Which of the following is the best interpretation of the author's attitude toward electricity?

A) **overwhelmed**
B) exhilarated
C) overzealous
D) detached

The best answer is (A).
Evidence for this can be found throughout the passage, but the most obvious example is "the most remarkable entity in the universe".

(B); The passage is extremely positive about electricity, but the author is trying to explain the reasons for this positive attitude, so anything as emotional as exhilarated cannot be the answer. ("marvelous and varied powers and utilities create a new epoch in scientific thought and discovery", "contains the story of the universe more sublime than an epic, more wonderful than a romance.", "organized the machinery of the worlds, and holds the secrets of nature and the mysteries of life in its invisible grasp", and so on)
(C); The answer must be positive, because the author's attitude anything but negative.
(D); The author is not emotional enough to be called exhilarated, but the tone of the passage is certainly not objective. In most situations making references to God suggests a somewhat subjective approach.

Test 3

35

Which of the following gives the least evidence for the answer to the previous question?

A) "This strange, miraculous power…the flight of eagles." (Lines 73-78)

B) "This mightiest servant…to the will of Deity," (Lines 34-37)

C) "Every new discovery,…physical ties and spiritual affinities." (Lines 50-55)

D) "Electricity, next to Deity, is the most remarkable entity in the universe." (Lines 1-2)

The best answer is (D).
Refer to the explanation for the answer to the previous question.

36

According to the context, what does the author most likely mean by mind acts upon matter?

A) Mind produces changes in the states of matter.

B) People employ mind to create useful things from matter.

C) Some people take advantage of matter with a mind to do things that would be totally incredible or impossible without God's help.

D) Mind can work wonders, sometimes even in the realm of the gods.

The best answer is (B).
Since there is no clue within the same sentence, we need to look for one elsewhere. The author continually refers to the power of electricity in abstract terms but eventually gets around to listing the various practical and useful things people can produce using electricity. ("most precious things", "reservoirs of power", "exhaustless sources of wealth and energy")

(A); The point is not simply changing states.
(C); There is no evidence that some people need God's help in doing (B).
(D); "Next to Deity", "This mightiest servant of God and man".

37

According to the passage, which of the following is NOT true of electricity?

A) It must be the most integral element that God works with.

B) It is the most important tool used by God to govern the Universe.

C) It serves God, but not man.

D) Without it, it might be hard for mind to act upon matter.

The best answer is (C).
Electricity serves not only God, but also man. ("This mightiest servant of God and man")

(A), (B); The meaning of integral is very similar to that of important. ("most remarkable entity", "the right hand of Deity", "the Word of Omnipotent power", "the protean cosmic force and creative machinery of the universe", "It gave form and functions to all matter from the rounded pebble to the stars", "works the miracle of life and growth", "mightiest servant of God and man")
(D); Because "electricity is the medium by which mind acts on matter", it can be said that without it, there is no medium, and without medium, it is very likely that mind cannot act.

Test 3

38

As used in line 39, "inscrutable" most likely means

A) mysterious
B) splendid
C) docile
D) devine

The best answer is (A).
The only significant context to be used is "this genii greater than Aladdin's lamp, impresses all laws upon nature, and makes the universe obedient to the will of Deity, as man's body is obedient to the dictates of man's mind.", "from the source of all power is beginning to supply the human race with an inexhaustible force that will revolutionize" and the points here are "genii greater", "all laws", the universe obedient", "the source of all power", "inexhaustible force", and "revolutionize" but (C) is the only word that is incompatible with these concepts, so we cannot infer the meaning of inscrutable only from the context.

39

Which of the following is mostly likely the role of "current" (Line 45)?

A) irony
B) sarcasm
C) metaphor
D) duality

The best answer is (D).
The word current obviously means 'flow' in this context, but since the author is talking about electricity as a whole, it generates a sensation of electric current, too.

40

If turned out to be true, which of the following would most directly undermine the author's argument?

A) Electricity is absolutely essential for the development of any inventions, in the future, near or distant.
B) Because of the many advances in electrical science and engineering, weapons have become more sophisticated and deadly.
C) Some people are hardcore atheists while others are uncommitted agnostics.
D) Some countries are not advanced enough to take full advantage of the advances in electrical science.

The best answer is (B).
The only word that expresses an obviously negative attitude toward electricity is 'deadly'.

41

Which of the following gives the best evidence for the answer to the previous question?

A) "This mightiest servant…the will of Deity," (Lines 34-37)
B) "an inexhaustible force…and good will." (Lines 41-43)
C) "Human life seems…, metallurgy and manufacture" (Lines 44-48)
D) "the heavy steed…potent as Omnipotence." (Lines 62-65)

The best answer is (B).
Refer to the explanation for the answer to the previous question.

As happens in all the sciences in which Geometry is applied to matter, the demonstrations concerning Optics are founded on truths drawn from experience. Such are that the rays of light are propagated in straight lines; that the angles of reflexion and of incidence are equal; and that in refraction the ray is bent according to the law of sines, now so well known, and which is no less certain than the preceding laws. The majority of those who have written touching the various parts of Optics have contented themselves with presuming these truths. But some, more inquiring, have desired to investigate the origin and the causes, considering these to be in themselves wonderful effects of Nature. In which they advanced some ingenious things, but not however such that the most intelligent folk do not wish for better and more satisfactory explanations. Wherefore I here desire to propound what I have meditated on the subject, so as to contribute as much as I can to the explanation of this department of Natural Science, which, not without reason, is reputed to be one of its most difficult parts. I recognize myself to be much indebted to those who were the first to begin to dissipate the strange obscurity in which these things were enveloped, and to give us hope that they might be explained by intelligible reasoning. But, on the other hand I am astonished also that even here these have often been willing to offer, as assured and demonstrative, reasonings which were far from conclusive. For I do not find that any one has yet given a probable explanation of the first and most notable phenomena of light, namely why it is not propagated except in straight lines, and how visible rays, coming from an infinitude of diverse places, cross one another without hindering one another in any way. I shall therefore essay in this book, to give, in accordance with the principles accepted in the Philosophy of the present day, some clearer and more probable reasons, firstly of these properties of light propagated rectilinearly; secondly of light which is reflected on meeting other bodies. Then I shall explain the phenomena of those rays which are said to suffer refraction on passing through transparent bodies of different sorts; and in this part I shall also explain the effects of the refraction of the air by the different densities of the Atmosphere. Thereafter I shall examine the causes of the strange refraction of a certain kind of Crystal which is brought from Iceland. And finally I shall treat of the various shapes of transparent and reflecting bodies by which rays are collected at a point or are turned aside in various ways. From this it will be seen with what facility, following our new Theory, we find not only the Ellipses, Hyperbolas, and other curves which Mr. Des Cartes has ingeniously invented for this purpose; but also those which the surface of a glass lens ought to possess when its other surface is given as spherical or plane, or of any other figure that may be. It is inconceivable to doubt that light consists in the motion of some sort of matter. For whether one considers its production, one sees that here upon the Earth it is chiefly engendered by fire and flame which contain without doubt bodies that are in rapid motion, since they dissolve and melt many other bodies, even the most solid; or whether one considers its effects, one sees that when light is collected, as by concave mirrors, it has the property of burning as a fire does, that is to say it disunites the particles of bodies. This is assuredly the mark of motion, at least in the true Philosophy, in which one conceives the causes of all natural effects in terms of mechanical motions. This, in my opinion, we must necessarily do, or else renounce all hopes of ever comprehending anything in Physics. And as, according to this Philosophy, one holds as certain that the sensation of sight is excited only by the impression of some movement of a kind of matter which acts on the nerves at the back of our eyes, there is here yet one reason more for believing that light consists in a movement of the matter which exists between us and the luminous body.

Test 3

42

What could be the best title of the passage?

A) The physical characteristics of rays

B) The reason for which rays move rectilinearly

C) The significance of the rectilinear motion of rays

D) Certain traits of light

E) The importance of matter in the movement of light

The best answer is (C).
The traits are "rectilinearly", "reflexion", refraction" all of which need "matter" to happen as explained throughout the passage.

(A), (B), (D); typical cases of TOO NARROW

43

According to the passage, in which aspect of light is the author most interested in?

A) that it needs matter to propagate

B) what happens when it propagates

C) that the rules of Geometry govern its movement

D) that studying it has led to improvements in the field of Optics

The best answer is (B).
The author clearly states his/her intention to talk about different phenomena which light causes or experiences as it propagates ("firstly of these properties of light propagated rectilinearly"; "reflected", "refraction", "the effects of the refraction of the air by the different densities of the Atmosphere", "the causes of the strange refraction". "the various shapes of transparent and reflecting bodies by which rays are collected at a point or are turned aside in various ways"

(A); The author is interested in what happens as light propagates, not what light needs to propagate; the author is interested in the motion of light. ("…the rays of light are propagated in straight lines;…the angles of reflexion and of incidence are equal;…in refraction the ray is bent according to the law of sines")
(C), (D): typical cases of TOO NARROW

44

What is the author's general attitude?

A) inquisitive

B) subjective

C) authoritative

D) qualified

The best answer is (B).
The argument is based essentially on cause and effect, and the author explains in a reasoned manner practically every phenomenon related to the propagation of light; however, we can count how many times the words "I" or "my" are used including, "This, in my opinion, we must necessarily do, or else renounce all hopes of ever comprehending anything in Physics."

45

According to the author, what is the connection between "light" and "matter"?

A) irrelevant

B) inclusive

C) unclear

D) inseparable

The best answer is (D).
The author is very confident about the connection between light and matter ("It is inconceivable to

doubt that light consists in the motion of some sort of matter.")

46

According to the passage, which of the following is a case in which exploring physics would become futile?

A) when physicists lose hope
B) **when it is not possible to explain any natural effect using physical movements**
C) when excited light possesses traits similar to fire
D) when collecting light using a concave mirror no longer exhibits the property of burning fire

The best answer is (B).
The author strongly believes that every natural effect can be explained by physical motion ("This is assuredly the mark of motion, at least in the true Philosophy, in which one conceives the causes of all natural effects in terms of mechanical motions"). If this were not the case, understanding anything would be hopeless. ("This, in my opinion, we must necessarily do, or else renounce all hopes of ever comprehending anything in Physics.")

(A); The point is not that physicists might lose hope, but that "comprehending anything in Physics" would becomes hopeless; a case of WRONG PERSPECTIVE.
(C); This is stated in the passage. ("when light is collected, as by concave mirrors, it has the property of burning as a fire does, that is to say it disunites the particles of bodies.")
(D); There is no reason to conclude that the study of Physics in general would become futile ("hopeless") because of this one problem: no evidence, a case of WRONG INFERENCE

47

Which of the following gives the best evidence for the answer to the previous question?

A) "one considers its effects…the particles of bodies." (Lines 68-72)
B) "the sensation of sight…at the back of our eyes," (Lines 79-82)
C) "in which one conceives…mechanical motions." (Lines 73-75)
D) **"This, in my opinion,…in Physics." (Lines 75-77)**

The best answer is (D).
Refer to the explanation for the answer to the previous question.

48

According to the passage, which choice can be logically added to the end of the passage?

A) a wider varieties of light motions
B) a wider varieties of light
C) **a way to corroborate the author's argument**
D) a way to refute a possible counterargument against the author's

The best answer is (C).
The author needs to explain what that one reason more is, ("one reason more for believing that light consists in a movement of the matter which exists between us and the luminous body") and this reason is 'a way to corroborate the author's argument.

(A), (B), (D); These don't fit "one reason more for believing that light consists in a movement of the matter which exists between us and the luminous body.

Test 3

49

Which choice would the author be most likely to agree with?

A) Light must be some kind of matter.

B) Without matter, light cannot exist.

C) A light source must exist as a form of matter.

D) Matter is the cause of light.

The best answer is (B).
Refer to the previous question.

50

According to the passage, why did the author probably mention the connection between Optics and experience along with the connection between Geometry and matter?

A) in order to introduce a more detailed topic

B) in order to introduce the connection between Optics and matter

C) in order to talk about how Optics was invented

D) in order to establish some background for a further explanation of why light must move through matter

The best answer is (B).
From the beginning, of the passage the author uses Optics as an example of how matter is closely connected with light. ("As happens in all the sciences in which Geometry is applied to matter, the demonstrations concerning Optics are founded on truths drawn from experience.")

(A), (C), (D); None of these implies any connection between matter and light "founded on truths drawn from experience." and this experience is connected with "such." ("that the rays of light are propagated in straight lines; that the angles of reflexion and of incidence are equal; and that in refraction the ray is bent according to the law of sines")

51

Which choice gives the best evidence for the answer to the previous question?

A) "the ray is bent according to the law of sines," (Lines 7-8)

B) "it is not propagated except in straight lines," (Lines 34-35)

C) "light which is reflected on meeting other bodies." (Lines 43-44)

D) "majority of those who have written touching the various parts of Optics have contented themselves with presuming these truths." (Lines 9-12)

The best answer is (A).
Refer to the previous question.

TEST 4

Answer Keys & Explanations

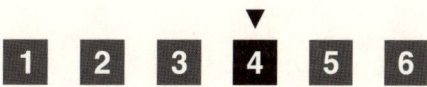

Archimedes writes: "For you have known that the universe is called a sphere by several astrologers, its center the center of the earth, and its radius equal to a line drawn from the center of the sun to the center of the earth. This was written for the unlearned, as you have known from the astrologers…. [Aristarchus of Samos] concludes that the world is many times greater than the estimate we have just given. He supposes that the fixed stars and the sun remain motionless, but that the earth following a circular course, revolves around the sun as a center, and that the sphere of the fixed stars having the same sun as a center, is so vast that the circle which he supposes the earth to follow in revolving holds the same ratio to the distance of the fixed stars as the center of a sphere holds to its circumference." These ancient philosophers realized in some degree the immensity of the universe in which the earth was but a point. They held that the earth was an unsupported sphere the size of which Eratosthenes (c. 276-194 B.C.) had calculated approximately. They knew the sun was far larger than the earth, and Cicero with other thinkers recognized the insignificance of earthly affairs in the face of such cosmic immensity. They knew too about the seven planets, had studied their orbits, and worked out astronomical ways of measuring the passage of time with a fair amount of accuracy. Hipparchus and other thinkers had discovered the fact of the precession of the equinoxes, though there was no adequate theory to account for it until Copernicus formulated his "motion of declination." The Pythagoreans accepted the idea of the earth's turning upon its axis, and some even held the idea of its revolution around the motionless sun. Others suggested that comets had orbits which they uniformly followed and therefore their reappearance could be anticipated. Why then was the heliocentric theory not definitely accepted? In the first place, such a theory was contrary to the supposed facts of daily existence. A man did not have to be trained in the schools to observe that the earth seemed stable under his feet and that each morning the sun swept from the east to set at night in the west. Sometimes it rose more to the north or to the south than at other times. How could that be explained if the sun were stationary? Study of the stars was valuable for navigators and for surveyors, perhaps, but such disturbing theories should not be propounded by philosophers. Cleanthes, according to Plutarch, "advised that the Greeks ought to have prosecuted Aristarchus the Samian for blasphemy against religion, as shaking the very foundations of the world, because this man endeavoring to save appearances, supposed that the heavens remained immovable and that the earth moved through an oblique circle, at the same time turning about its own axis." Few would care to face their fellows as blasphemers and impious thinkers on behalf of an unsupported theory. Eighteen hundred years later Galileo would not do so, even though in his day the theory was by no means unsupported by observation. Furthermore, one of the weaknesses of the Greek civilization militated strongly against the acceptance of this hypothesis so contrary to the evidence of the senses. Experimentation and the development of applied science was practically an impossibility where the existence of slaves made manual labor degrading and shameful. Men might reason indefinitely; but few, if any, were willing to try to improve the instruments of observation or to test their observations by experiments. At the same time another astronomical theory was developing which was an adequate explanation for the phenomena observed up to that time. This theory of epicycles and eccentrics worked out by Apollonius of Perga (c. 225 B.C.) and by Hipparchus (c. 160 B.C.) and crystallized for posterity in Ptolemy's great treatise on astronomy, the Almagest, (c. 140 A.D.) became the fundamental principle of the science until within the last three hundred years. The theory of the eccentric was based on the idea that heavenly bodies following circular orbits revolved around a center that did not coincide with that of the observer on the earth. That would explain why the sun appeared sometimes nearer the earth and sometimes farther away. The epicycle represented the heavenly body as moving along the circumference of one circle (called the epicycle) the center of which moves on another circle (the deferent). With better observations additional epicycles and eccentric were used to represent the newly observed phenomena till in the later Middle Ages the universe became a "—Sphere with Centric and Eccentric scribbled o'er, Cycle and Epicycle, Orb in Orb"—

Test 4

1

According to the passage, which of the following exemplifies earthly affairs?

A) the size of the earth
B) the distance between the earth and the Sun
C) the orbit of the earth
D) the revolution of the earth around the sun

The best answer is (D).
Any affair is an action, not an object. And the author is talking about "orbit". The only action from these four choices is (D).

2

In context, which of the following most clearly shows the author's intention for mentioning daily existence?

A) to show that it is impossible to verify whether it is valid or not
B) to imply that sometimes, it cannot be used as a basis for theorization.
C) to indicate that experiencing it can be a very subjective
D) to explain that, in most cases, without it, theorization is impossible, especially in the realm of science

The best answer is (B).
"Daily existence" or daily experience might not be a valid basis for a corresponding theorization ("such a theory was contrary to the supposed facts of daily existence"). In other words, what you see is not what you get.

3

According to the passage, which of the following is NOT a direct obstacle to fully accepting the heliocentric theory?

A) the theory of epicycles
B) the observations of a navigator on a vessel at sea
C) everyday experience
D) religion

The best answer is (A).
The theory of epicycles cannot be a direct obstacle because it was only "another astronomical theory" that was "developing which was an adequate explanation for the phenomena observed up to that time."

(B), (C); Refer to the explanation for the answer to the previous question.
(D); Religion was probably the greatest obstacle ("advised that the Greeks ought to have prosecuted Aristarchus the Samian for blasphemy against religion, as shaking the very foundations of the world, because this man endeavoring to save appearances, supposed that the heavens remained immovable and that the earth moved through an oblique circle,")

4

Which of the following provides the best evidence for the answer to the previous question?

A) "such a theory was contrary to the supposed facts of daily existence." (Lines 41-42)
B) "At the same time another astronomical theory was developing" (Lines 72-74)
C) "seemed stable under his feet" (Line 44)
D) "Sometimes it rose more to the north or to the south than at other times." (Lines 46-47)

Test 4

The best answer is (B).
Refer to the explanation for the answer to the previous question.

5

In context, why was using applied science almost out of the question?

A) Performing the procedures necessary in the applied science was regarded as shameful.

B) Philosophers did not have the instruments necessary to conduct accurate scientific experiments.

C) Slaves could not work in the field of science.

D) Getting involved in applied science was considered blasphemous.

The best answer is (A).
This is almost exactly stated in the passage ("the development of applied science was practically an impossibility where the existence of slaves made manual labor degrading and shameful.")

(B); A lack of suitable instruments was not the point.
(C); There was nothing that prevented slaves from working in applied science.
(D); Not everything "degrading and shameful" is blasphemous.

6

Which of the following provides the most direct evidence for the answer to the previous question?

A) "Few would care to face their fellows as blasphemers" (Lines 58-59)

B) "an adequate explanation for the phenomena observed up to that time." (Lines 74-75)

C) "on behalf of an unsupported theory." (Lines 59-60)

D) "where the existence of slaves made manual labor degrading and shameful." (Lines 68-69)

The best answer is (B).
Refer to the explanation for the answer to the previous question.

7

Why does the author probably mention within the last three hundred years?

A) A major breakthrough must have occurred around that time.

B) There must have been some reason why the Almagest could no longer serve as a fundamental basis for a meaningful theory.

C) Something happened to the idea of eccentric theory so that it was no longer dependable.

D) Heliocentric theorists couldn't defend themselves against blasphemous criticism.

The best answer is (B).
According to the passage, what is known is only that the theory of epicycles was accepted "until within the last three hundred years" and nothing more; anything other than that is all WRONG INFERENCE ((A), (C), (D)).

8

Which of the following would be the best way to comprehend the connection between the heliocentric and the eccentric theory?

A) They were compatible with each other to a certain degree.

B) They could have worked in harmony with each other in that one could have taken care of the other's weaknesses.

C) Although both were related to the concept of a center, they were referring to different

Test 4

centers.

D) They were both correct, but they were applied in the wrong manner.

The best answer is (C).
The center in heliocentric theory is the sun, whereas the center in eccentric theory is "based on the idea that heavenly bodies following circular orbits revolved around a center that did not coincide with that of the observer on the earth."

9

As used in line 78, "crystallized" most nearly means

A) solidified

B) concentrated

C) clarified

D) clear to understand

The best answer is (D).
We need to look at the flow of the context; A theory ("This theory of epicycles and eccentrics") was crystallized for the next generation (people) ("posterity").

(A), (B); The context is not related to any chemical reaction.
(C); There is no indication in the passage that the theory was confusing, at least in the centuries after it was formulated.

10

According to the passage, what would be the correct attitude of a modern astronomer toward the Almagest?

A) absolutely inspiring

B) mostly suspicious

C) somewhat correct

D) extremely doubtful

The best answer is (C).
For centuries after it was formulated it worked adequately well ("became the fundamental principle of the science until within the last three hundred years"), and it did explain some of the heavenly phenomena in question. ("That would explain why the sun appeared sometimes nearer the earth and sometimes farther away")

(A), (B), (D); "became the fundamental principle of the science until within the last three hundred years."

He has dissolved Representative Houses repeatedly, for opposing with manly firmness his invasions on the rights of the people.

He has refused for a long time, after such
5 dissolutions, to cause others to be elected; whereby the Legislative powers, incapable of Annihilation, have returned to the People at large for their exercise; the State remaining in the mean time exposed to all the dangers of invasion from
10 without, and convulsions within.

He has endeavoured to prevent the population of these States; for that purpose obstructing the Laws for Naturalization of Foreigners; refusing to pass others to encourage their migrations hither,
15 and raising the conditions of new Appropriations of Lands.

He has obstructed the Administration of Justice, by refusing his Assent to Laws for establishing Judiciary powers.

20 He has made Judges dependent on his Will alone, for the tenure of their offices, and the amount and payment of their salaries.

He has erected a multitude of New Offices, and sent hither swarms of Officers to harrass our
25 people, and eat out their substance.

He has kept among us, in times of peace, Standing Armies without the Consent of our legislatures.

He has affected to render the Military
30 independent of and superior to the Civil power.

He has combined with others to subject us to a jurisdiction foreign to our constitution, and unacknowledged by our laws; giving his Assent to their Acts of pretended Legislation:

35 For Quartering large bodies of armed troops among us:

For protecting them, by a mock Trial, from punishment for any Murders which they should commit on the Inhabitants of these States:

40 For cutting off our Trade with all parts of the world:

For imposing Taxes on us without our Consent:

For depriving us in many cases, of the benefits
45 of Trial by Jury:

For transporting us beyond Seas to be tried for pretended offences

For abolishing the free System of English Laws in a neighbouring Province, establishing
50 therein an Arbitrary government, and enlarging its Boundaries so as to render it at once an example and fit instrument for introducing the same absolute rule into these Colonies:

Test 4

11

As used in line 1, "dissolved" most nearly means

A) divided
B) solved
C) annihilated
D) destroyed

The best answer is (D).
We need to know what The English King ("He") would have done to the Colonial "Representative Houses repeatedly."

(A); contextually awkward
(B); contextually impossible
(C); too strong a magnitude

12

What can be said about Representative Houses?

A) They resisted the power of the King but only in moderation.
B) They could not resist as strongly as they had wanted to.
C) They defied the King's interference with determination.
D) They tried to make a compromise.

The best answer is (C).
Representative Houses defied ("opposing") King's interference ("his invasions on the rights of the people.") with determination ("with manly firmness").

(A), (B), (D); "opposing…with manly firmness"

13

Why is State mentioned in the passage?

A) to show how the King perceives his power over it.
B) to imply the importance of the absence of Representative Houses
C) to speculate on the impact of the King's enterprise against the population of the States
D) to predict the future of the States without Representative Houses

The best answer is (B).
The passage says the English King ("he") "has refused for a long time, after such dissolutions, to cause others to be elected" so "the state" means the state without "Representative Houses."

(A), (C); Neither of these implies that the State has no Representative Houses
(D); The State refers to the current State without Representative Houses, not to a future expectation.

14

Which of the following provides the best evidence for the answer to the previous question?

A) "Annihilation" (Line 6)
B) "convulsions" (Line 10)
C) "manly firmness" (Line 2)
D) "at large" (Line 7)

The best answer is (B).
(B) is the only choice that shows what happens without Representative Houses.

Test 4

15

Which of the following is NOT what the King did to hamper a certain social phenomenon?

A) hindered immigration
B) created some new restrictions
C) inhibited some legal institutions
D) created a general sense of injustice

The best answer is (D).
The rest of the choices are all clearly mentioned in the passage.
(D); TOO BROAD to be from the passage

(A): "refusing to pass others to encourage their migrations hither"
(B): "raising the conditions of new Appropriations of Lands."
(C): "to prevent the population of these States", "obstructing the Laws for Naturalization of Foreigners"

16

Which of the following is the best interpretation of what the King did to obstruct the justice system of the States?

A) What he did was intentional from the beginning.
B) His actions were not limited to a specific aspect of the system.
C) Controlling the general population was his top priority.
D) Manipulating judges' incomes was the most effective measure he took to accomplish his goal.

The best answer is (B).
The author is talking about many ways that the English king is obstructing colonial justice system. ("He has dissolved Representative Houses repeatedly,", "He has endeavoured to prevent the population of these States", "He has obstructed the Administration of Justice, by refusing his Assent to Laws for establishing Judiciary powers", "He has kept among us, in times of peace, Standing Armies without the Consent of our legislatures.", "He has combined with others to subject us to a jurisdiction foreign to our constitution, and unacknowledged by our laws", "For depriving us in many cases, of the benefits of Trial by Jury:")

(A); Whether or not the King's actions were intentional cannot be inferred from this passage alone: WRONG INFERENCE
(C), (D): TOO NARROW

17

Which of the following is what the author means by substance?

A) privacy
B) freedom
C) economy
D) history

The best answer is (B).
According to the passage, the English King was "eating out" what American people had. ("substance") Whatever American people had at the time must be stated or implied in the passage; possibilities are freedom, peace, Representative Houses, a justice system and so on. (B) is the only possibility based on this reasoning.

18

According to the passage, what can be said about the military created by the King?

A) It derived its power from the ordinary citizens.
B) Its power surpasses that of citizens by a huge

margin.

C) The citizenry was probably not involved in establishing it.

D) It was an obstacle to the conduct of normal civil life.

The best answer is (C).
The English king created a military that had no relationship with the citizens. ("He has affected to render the Military independent of and superior to the Civil power.")

(A), (D); Because (C) is the answer, these choices cannot be the answer.
(B); Its power obviously surpassed that of the citizens ("superior"); how large the margin of superiority was cannot be inferred from this passage alone: WRONG INFERENCE

19

The author describes King's attitude regarding the military as.

A) hostile

B) aggressive

C) arrogant

D) agitated

The best answer is (C).
The king arrogantly ("affected") made the Military "independent of and superior to the Civil power."

The only choice to reflect the King's "affected" behavior is (C).

20

Which of the following is the best evidence for the answer to the previous question?

A) "affected" (Line 20)

B) "render" (Line 20)

C) "independent" (Line 21)

D) "superior" (Line 21)

The best answer is (A).
Refer to the explanation for the answer to the previous question.

Test 4

Finally, to those nations who would make themselves our adversary, we offer not a pledge but a request: that both sides begin anew the quest for peace, before the dark powers of destruction
5 unleashed by science engulf all humanity in planned or accidental self-destruction.

We dare not tempt them with weakness. For only when our arms are sufficient beyond doubt can we be certain beyond doubt that they will never be
10 employed.

But neither can two great and powerful groups of nations take comfort from our present course—both sides overburdened by the cost of modern weapons, both rightly alarmed by the steady spread
15 of the deadly atom, yet both racing to alter that uncertain balance of terror that stays the hand of mankind's final war.

So let us begin anew—remembering on both sides that civility is not a sign of weakness, and
20 sincerity is always subject to proof. Let us never negotiate out of fear. But let us never fear to negotiate.

Let both sides explore what problems unite us instead of belaboring those problems which divide
25 us.

Let both sides, for the first time, formulate serious and precise proposals for the inspection and control of arms—and bring the absolute power to destroy other nations under the absolute control of
30 all nations.

Let both sides seek to invoke the wonders of science instead of its terrors. Together let us explore the stars, conquer the deserts, eradicate disease, tap the ocean depths, and encourage the arts and
35 commerce.

Let both sides unite to heed in all corners of the earth the command of Isaiah—to "undo the heavy burdens . . . [and] let the oppressed go free."

And if a beachhead of cooperation may push
40 back the jungle of suspicion, let both sides join in creating a new endeavor, not a new balance of power, but a new world of law, where the strong are just and the weak secure and the peace preserved.

45 All this will not be finished in the first one hundred days. Nor will it be finished in the first one thousand days, nor in the life of this administration, nor even perhaps in our lifetime on this planet. But let us begin.

50 In your hands, my fellow citizens, more than mine, will rest the final success or failure of our course. Since this country was founded each generation of Americans has been summoned to give testimony to its national loyalty. The graves of
55 young Americans who answered the call to service surround the globe.

Now the trumpet summons us again—not as a call to bear arms, though arms we need—not as a call to battle, though embattled we are—but a
60 call to bear the burden of a long twilight struggle, year in and year out, "rejoicing in hope, patient in tribulation"—a struggle against the common enemies of man: tyranny, poverty, disease, and war itself.

65 Can we forge against these enemies a grand and global alliance, North and South, East and West, that can assure a more fruitful life for all mankind? Will you join in that historic effort?

In the long history of the world, only a few
70 generations have been granted the role of defending freedom in its hour of maximum danger. I do not shrink from this responsibility—I welcome it. I do not believe that any of us would exchange places with any other people or any other generation. The
75 energy, the faith, the devotion which we bring to this endeavor will light our country and all who serve it—and the glow from that fire can truly light the world.

And so, my fellow Americans: ask not what
80 your country can do for you—ask what you can do for your country.

My fellow citizens of the world: ask not what America will do for you, but what together we can do for the freedom of man.

85 Finally, whether you are citizens of America or citizens of the world, ask of us here the same high standards of strength and sacrifice which we ask of you. With a good conscience our only sure reward, with history the final judge of our deeds, let us go
90 forth to lead the land we love, asking His blessing and His help, but knowing that here on earth God's work must truly be our own.

Test 4

21

What is the author's attitude toward negotiations related to the control of deadly weapons?

A) Beyond doubt he is totally against them.

B) Everything depends on certain conditions being met in advance.

C) He welcomes them wholeheartedly, but with certain conditions.

D) He is not fearful of them for his own unique reasons.

The best answer is (C).
The author welcomes such negotiations throughout the passage ("a request: that both sides begin anew the quest for peace", "never negotiate out of fear. But let us never fear to negotiate", "let both sides join in creating a new endeavor, not a new balance of power, but a new world of law", "Can we forge against these enemies a grand and global alliance, North and South, East and West, that can assure a more fruitful life for all mankind? Will you join in that historic effort?"), but he sets certain general conditions. ("never … out of fear")

(A); Since the author states his enthusiastic support for such negotiations at several points in the passage, this choice is absurd.
(B); As explained for (C), even though the author is a little cautious about negotiating, he does not indicate that his willingness to negotiate depends on some preset conditions.
(D); It is true that the author is not fearful about negotiating ("Let us never negotiate out of fear. But let us never fear to negotiate"), but this is not due to any unique or personal reasons.

22

According to the passage, what is the role of science in the author's argument?

A) It is an obstacle that stands in the way of negotiating controls on weapons.

B) It provides a unique opportunity to start peace talks and negotiations on arms control.

C) It is something that must be balanced for the sake of world peace.

D) It is a field in which many positive advances can be made.

The best answer is (D).
The author knows that science played a leading role creating deadly weapons ("before the dark powers of destruction unleashed by science engulf all humanity in planned or accidental self-destruction."), so the author is obviously believes that science has some negative aspects, but that does not mean it is an obstacle (A) or something that needs to be balanced (C), and many positive advances are possible in science. ("Let both sides seek to invoke the wonders of science instead of its terrors. Together let us explore the stars, conquer the deserts, eradicate disease, tap the ocean depths, and encourage the arts and commerce.")

(B); POSITIVE
(C); The concept of balance in the field of science is very vague and cannot be inferred from the passage.

23

Why does the author want to deal with deadly weapons from a position of confidence?

A) because the author is afraid of them

B) because war would be inevitable without it

C) because dealing with them without it would be too expensive

D) because dealing with them without it might

be uncomfortable

The answer is (B).
The author believes it is necessary to deal with deadly weapons from a position of strength ("We dare not tempt them with weakness") because ("For") war would be inevitable ("can we be certain … that they will never be employed.") without it (=confidence). ("only when our arms are sufficient beyond doubt")

(A); The author doesn't want to deal with them from a position of "weakness".
(C); The author doesn't want to use the weapons ("can we be certain … that they will never be employed."). Money is irrelevant.
(D); "That they will never be employed." has nothing to do with comfort.

24

Which of the following is the most direct evidence for the answer to the previous question?

A) "But neither can two great and powerful groups of nations take comfort from our present course" (Lines 11-12)

B) "Let both sides unite to heed in all corners of the earth the command of Isaiah—to "undo the heavy burdens . . . [and] let the oppressed go free." (Lines 36-38)

C) "the strong are just and the weak secure and the peace preserved." (Lines 42-44)

D) "For only when our arms are sufficient beyond doubt can we be certain beyond doubt that they will never be employed." (Lines 7-10)

The best answer is (D).
Refer to the explanation for the answer to the previous question.

25

In the context of the passage what is the most probable role of beachhead?

A) extreme criticism
B) genuine hope
C) irony
D) playfulness

The best answer is (C).
Since the author needs the cooperation of the two sides, America and the Soviet Union, the beachhead is something very good and important, but in context it can create a jungle of suspicion.

(A), (B), (D); None of these can show the duality explained in (C).

26

According to the passage, what is the most significant difference between "a new balance of power" and "a new world of law"? (Lines 41-42)

A) Combining the two is a solution to many of the world's problems.

B) Only one of the two can guarantee what the author is aiming for.

C) The former might be a by-product of the old world.

D) One of them might not be easy to achieve because of the jungle of suspicion.

The best answer is (B).
The author wants "not a new balance of power, but a new world of law" because only the latter can provide an opportunity for the author to achieve his goals. ("where the strong are just and the weak secure and the peace preserved.")

(A); The author clearly states "not a new balance of power, but a new world of law."

Test 4

(C); The author made a distinction between "a new balance of power" and "a new world of law" not between "a new balance of power" and any old balance of power.

(D); According to the passage, the jungle of suspicion has nothing to do with whether or not either of the two is hard to achieve.

27

In context, what does the first one hundred days signify?

A) a period of time during the author's administration

B) the first half of the duration of any significant change

C) a period shorter than one thousand days

D) a relatively short period of time

The best answer is (D).
The author's attitude is to take time ("patient in tribulation"); he does not want the audience, Americans, to be in a hurry or impatient.

(A); As explained for (D), the point is to be patient; it is not about the author's time in power: WRONG PERSPECTIVE.
(B); As explained for (D), the point is to be patient; it is not about any change: WRONG PERSPECTIVE.
(C); As explained for (D), the point is to be patient; it is not about comparing specific lengths of time: WRONG PERSPECTIVE.

28

Why did the author say "more than mine" (Lines 50-51)?

A) because what the author wants to accomplish is not a job for one person

B) because the author knows he is not strong enough to do the job required

C) because the author needs the collaboration of his fellow citizens

D) because the achievement of the author's goal do not depend on just old Americans

The best answer is (A).
The author needs more than one person ("each generation of Americans has been summoned to give testimony to its national loyalty.") to achieve his stated goals.

(B); It is not clear why the author mentions "each generation", whether he needs 'the strength of the generation' or not.
(C); This is a tricky choice because normally if we need a generation to do anything, it will be because we need some form of collaboration among the generations of people, but the author gave no clue about this collaboration. This is a typical case of taking advantage of wrong COMMON SENSE.
(D); Whether the "generation" is old or new is not the point: WRONG PERSPECTIVE.

29

Which of the following is the best evidence for the answer to the previous question?

A) "The graves of young Americans who answered the call to service surround the globe." (Lines 54-56)

B) "a beachhead of cooperation may push back the jungle of suspicion," (Lines 39-40)

C) "Since this country was founded each generation of Americans has been summoned to give testimony to its national loyalty." (Lines 52-54)

D) "nor in the life of this administration, nor even perhaps in our lifetime on this planet. But let us begin." (Lines 47-49)

The best answer is (C).
Refer to the explanation for the answer to the previous question.

30

Which of the following is the main goal of the passage?

A) to achieve world peace in order to maintain civilization as it is

B) to encourage a certain group of people to become part of an attempt to maintain something of consequence

C) to defend freedom around the world at all cost

D) to secure world peace by using only peaceful means

The best answer is (B).
The goal of the passage is to maintain freedom and peace ("My fellow citizens of the world: ask not what America will do for you, but what together we can do for the freedom of man.", "in creating a new endeavor, not a new balance of power, but a new world of law, where the strong are just and the weak secure and the peace preserved.") by encouraging two sides, America and the Soviet Union, ("both sides") to cooperate.

(A); According to the passage, world peace is the main goal as explained in (B), but not because we need to maintain civilization as it is.
(C); Freedom is to be defended, but not at all cost.
(D); World Peace is to be secured, but not only using peaceful means.

31

Which of the following is the best evidence for the answer to the previous question?

A) "only a few generations have been granted the role of defending freedom in its hour of maximum danger." (Lines 69-71)

B) "My fellow citizens of the world: ask not what America will do for you, but what together we can do for the freedom of man." (Lines 82-84)

C) "knowing that here on earth God's work must truly be our own." (Lines 91-92)

D) "Let us never negotiate out of fear. But let us never fear to negotiate." (Lines 20-22)

The best answer is (B).
Refer to the explanation for the answer to the previous question.

As everybody knows nowadays, the knowledge we possess of life before the beginnings of human memory and tradition is derived from the markings and fossils of living things in the stratified rocks. We find preserved in shale and slate, limestone, and sandstone, bones, shells, fibres, stems, fruits, footmarks, scratchings and the like, side by side with the ripple marks of the earliest tides and the pittings of the earliest rain-falls. It is by the sedulous examination of this Record of the Rocks that the past history of the earth's life has been pieced together. That much nearly everybody knows to-day. The sedimentary rocks do not lie neatly stratum above stratum; they have been crumpled, bent, thrust about, distorted and mixed together like the leaves of a library that has been repeatedly looted and burnt, and it is only as a result of many devoted lifetimes of work that the record has been put into order and read. The whole compass of time represented by the record of the rocks is now estimated as 1,600,000,000 years. The earliest rocks in the record are called by geologists the Azoic rocks, because they show no traces of life. Great areas of these Azoic rocks lie uncovered in North America, and they are of such a thickness that geologists consider that they represent a period of at least half of the 1,600,000,000 which they assign to the whole geological record. Let me repeat this profoundly significant fact. Half the great interval of time since land and sea were first distinguishable on earth has left us no traces of life. There are ripplings and rain marks still to be found in these rocks, but no marks nor vestiges of any living thing. Then, as we come up the record, signs of past life appear and increase. The age of the world's history in which we find these past traces is called by geologists the Lower Palæozoic age. The first indications that life was astir are vestiges of comparatively simple and lowly things: the shells of small shellfish, the stems and flowerlike heads of zoophytes, seaweeds and the tracks and remains of sea worms and crustacea. Very early appear certain creatures rather like plant-lice, crawling creatures which could roll themselves up into balls as the plant-lice do, the trilobites. Later by a few million years or so come certain sea scorpions, more mobile and powerful creatures than the world had ever seen before. None of these creatures were of very great size. Among the largest were certain of the sea scorpions, which measured nine feet in length. There are no signs whatever of land life of any sort, plant or animal; there are no fishes nor any vertebrated creatures in this part of the record. Essentially all the plants and creatures which have left us their traces from this period of the earth's history are shallow-water and intertidal beings. If we wished to parallel the flora and fauna of the Lower Palæozoic rocks on the earth today, we should do it best, except in the matter of size, by taking a drop of water from a rock pool or scummy ditch and examining it under a microscope. The little crustacea, the small shellfish, the zoophytes and algæ we should find there would display a quite striking resemblance to these clumsier, larger prototypes that once were the crown of life upon our planet. It is well, however, to bear in mind that the Lower Palæozoic rocks probably do not give us anything at all representative of the first beginnings of life on our planet. Unless a creature has bones or other hard parts, unless it wears a shell or is big enough and heavy enough to make characteristic footprints and trails in mud, it is unlikely to leave any fossilized traces of its existence behind. Today there are hundreds of thousands of species of small soft-bodied creatures in our world which it is inconceivable can ever leave any mark for future geologists to discover. In the world's past, millions of millions of species of such creatures may have lived and multiplied and flourished and passed away without a trace remaining. The waters of the warm and shallow lakes and seas of the so-called Azoic period may have teemed with an infinite variety of lowly, jelly-like, shell-less and boneless creatures, and a multitude of green scummy plants may have spread over the sunlit intertidal rocks and beaches. The Record of the Rocks is no more a complete record of life in the past than the books of a bank are a record of the existence of everybody in the neighbourhood. It is only when a species begins to secrete a shell or a spicule or a carapace or a lime-supported stem, and so put by something for the future, that it goes upon the Record. But in rocks of an age prior to those which bear any fossil traces, graphite, a form of uncombined carbon, is sometimes found, and some authorities consider that it may have been separated out from combination through the vital activities of unknown living things.

Test 4

32

What could be the best title of the passage?

A) The varieties of life on earth

B) Fossils as the primary source for tracing the history of life on earth

C) Life on earth

D) Evolution of life on earth

The best answer is (C).
The author is talking about how we know about past life ("the knowledge we possess of life before the beginnings of human memory and tradition is derived from the markings and fossils of living things in the stratified rocks"), the origin of the markings of life ("The first indications that life was astir are vestiges of comparatively simple and lowly things: the shells of small shellfish, the stems and flowerlike heads of zoophytes, seaweeds and the tracks and remains of sea worms and crustacea."), and some speculation about certain aspects of early life.

(A): a typical case of TOO NARROW
(B); Fossils are constantly used as a source of information, but there is no evidence that they are the primary source.
(D): a typical case of TOO NARROW

33

As used in line 10, "sedulous" most nearly means

A) cautious

B) meticulous

C) diligent

D) analytical

The best answer is (C).
"and it is only as a result of many devoted lifetimes of work that the record has been put into order and read." So we are looking for something that is compatible with "many devoted lifetimes of work", but we simply don't have that in our choices. In other words, no contextual approach is possible in this case.

34

According to the passage, which of the following is true about the traces left by past life forms?

A) They are haphazard all through the history of the earth.

B) They continue to be discovered and at an increasing rate.

C) They seem to be concentrated in a certain time period.

D) They are very accurate indications of how long ago life came into being on Earth.

The best answer is (C).
There was no sign of life for a while ("Half the great interval of time since land and sea were first distinguishable on earth has left us no traces of life…no marks nor vestiges of any living thing"), but at a certain point, evidence of life appeared and it became limited to a period. ("Then, as we come up the record, signs of past life appear and increase. The age of the world's history in which we find these past traces is called by geologists the Lower Palæozoic age.")

35

Which choice gives the best evidence for the answer to the previous question?

A) "As everybody knows nowadays, the knowledge we possess of life before the beginnings of human memory and tradition is derived from the markings and fossils of living things in the stratified rocks," (Lines 1-4)

B) "Very early appear certain creatures rather

like plant-lice, crawling creatures which could roll themselves up into balls as the plant-lice do, the trilobites." (Lines 42-45)

C) "Then, as we come up the record, signs of past life appear and increase." (Lines 34-35)

D) "The age of the world's history in which we find these past traces is called by geologists the Lower Palæozoic age." (Lines 35-37)

The best answer is (D).
Refer to the explanation for the answer to the previous question.

36

As used in line 33, "vestiges" most nearly means

A) image
B) amount
C) number
D) trace

The best answer is (D).
All we have to do is read a couple of sentences before the word in question. "Half the great interval of time since land and sea were first distinguishable on earth has left us no traces of life. There are ripplings and rain marks still to be found in these rocks, but no marks nor vestiges of any living thing" If we carefully compare the two sentences, we can tell that no traces of life mean the same as "nor vestiges of any living thing".

37

According to the passage, what can be learned from shells of small shellfish?

A) that life on Earth has existed for a very long time.
B) that fossils are the first sign of life on Earth

C) that fossils are very useful
D) that there are a wide varieties of fossils

The best answer is (B).
"The first indications that life was astir are vestiges of comparatively simple and lowly things: the shells of small shellfish" Thus, shells of small shellfish worked as the first sign ("indication") of life activities. ("life was astir")

(A); No matter how long life may have existed on Earth, "first indication" gives no indication of how long life has existed.
(C); No matter how useful the fossils of small shellfish might be, "first indication" cannot tell us anything about the usefulness of these fossils.
(D); The fossils of small shellfish were not compared with those of any other species.

38

Which choice gives the best evidence for the answer to the previous question?

A) "The first indications that life was astir are vestiges of comparatively simple and lowly things:" (Lines 37-39)

B) "We find preserved in shale and slate, limestone, and sandstone, bones, shells, fibres, stems, fruits, footmarks, scratchings and the like," (Lines 5-7)

C) "it wears a shell or is big enough and heavy enough to make characteristic footprints and trails in mud," (Lines 70-72)

D) "The little crustacea, the small shellfish, the zoophytes and algæ we should find there would display a quite striking resemblance to these clumsier," (Lines 61-64)

The best answer is (A).
Refer to the explanation for the answer to the previous question.

Test 4

39

Which of the following might be the best interpretation of the author's attitude?

A) authoritative
B) mainly speculative
C) detached
D) emotional

The best answer is (A).
The evidence for this is scattered throughout the passage. "Essentially all the plants and creatures which have left us their traces from this period of the earth's history are shallow-water and intertidal beings." The author makes this argument as if it needs no additional proof and as if the reader already understands the points being made; the author is maintaining a "Don't question me" attitude.
"As everybody knows nowadays, the knowledge we possess of life before the beginnings of human memory and tradition is derived from the markings and fossils of living things in the stratified rocks"
"That much nearly everybody knows to-day."
By saying "everybody", the author ensures that it is not possible to debate the argument.)

40

Which choice gives the best evidence for the answer to the previous question?

A) "We find preserved in shale and slate, limestone, and sandstone, bones, shells, fibres, stems, fruits," (Lines 5-7)
B) "There are ripplings and rain marks still to be found in these rocks, but no marks nor vestiges of any living thing." (Lines 32-34)
C) "The first indications that life was astir are vestiges of comparatively simple and lowly things:" (Lines 37-39)
D) "Essentially all the plants and creatures which have left us their traces from this period of the earth's history are shallow-water and intertidal beings." (Lines 54-56)

The best answer is (D).
Refer to the explanation for the answer to the previous question.

41

What is the general organization of the passage?

A) presenting a misconception followed by a number of examples to be refuted later in the passage
B) proving a general statement by supporting it with a fair amount of elaboration and providing an interesting conclusion
C) proposing a theory supported by a substantial amount of detail which eventually leads to a new topic
D) supplying unclear information to be clarified by facts as the passage progresses

The best answer is (B).
At the very beginning of the passage, the author makes a general statement ("As everybody knows nowadays, the knowledge we possess of life before the beginnings of human memory and tradition is derived from the markings and fossils of living things in the stratified rocks,"), and then talks in detail about the various kinds of fossils. ("We find preserved in shale and slate, limestone, and sandstone, bones, shells, fibres, stems, fruits, footmarks, scratchings and the like, side by side with the ripple marks of the earliest tides and the pittings of the earliest rain-falls") The author then makes a few other arguments, but throughout the passage sticks mostly to elaborating on the main point. ("they have been crumpled, bent, thrust about, distorted and mixed together like the leaves of a library", "The whole compass of time represented by the record of the rocks is now estimated as 1,600,000,000 years", "the shells of small shellfish, the stems and flowerlike heads of

zoophytes, seaweeds and the tracks and remains of sea worms and crustacea", "The little crustacea, the small shellfish, the zoophytes and algæ we should find there would display a quite striking resemblance to these clumsier, larger prototypes that once were the crown of life upon our planet", "The waters of the warm and shallow lakes and seas of the so-called Azoic period may have teemed with an infinite variety of lowly, jelly-like, shell-less and boneless creatures, and a multitude of green scummy plants may have spread over the sunlit intertidal rocks and beaches.")

The history of European civilization is the history of a certain political institution which united and expressed Europe, and was governed from Rome. This institution was informed at its
5 very origin by the growing influence of a certain definite and organized religion: this religion it ultimately accepted and, finally, was merged in. The institution— having accepted the religion, having made of that religion its official expression,
10 and having breathed that religion in through every part until it became the spirit of the whole— was slowly modified, spiritually illumined and physically degraded by age. But it did not die. It was revived by the religion which had become its
15 new soul. It re-arose and still lives. This institution was first known among men as Republica; we call it today "The Roman Empire." The Religion which informed and saved it was then called, still is called, and will always be called "The Catholic
20 Church." Europe is the Church, and the Church is Europe. It is immaterial to the historical value of this historical truth whether it be presented to a man who utterly rejects Catholic dogma or to a man who believes everything the Church
25 may teach. A man remote in distance, in time, or in mental state from the thing we are about to examine would perceive the reality of this truth just as clearly as would a man who was steeped in its spirit from within and who formed an
30 intimate part of Christian Europe. The Oriental pagan, the contemporary atheist, some supposed student in some remote future, reading history in some place from which the Catholic Faith shall have utterly departed, and to which the habits
35 and traditions of our civilization will therefore be wholly alien, would each, in proportion to his science, grasp as clearly as it is grasped today by the Catholic student who is of European birth, the truth that Europe and the Catholic Church
40 were and are one thing. The only people who do not grasp it (or do not admit it) are those writers of history whose special, local, and temporary business it is to oppose the Catholic Church, or who have a traditional bias against it. These men
45 are numerous, they have formed, in the Protestant and other anti-Catholic universities, a whole school of hypothetical and unreal history in which, though the original workers are few, their copyists

Test 4

are innumerable: and that school of unreal history
is still dogmatically taught in the anti-Catholic
centres of Europe and of the world. Now our
quarrel with this school should be, not that it is
anti-Catholic—that concerns another sphere of
thought— but that it is unhistorical. To neglect the
truth that the Roman Empire with its institutions
and its spirit was the sole origin of European
civilization; to forget or to diminish the truth
that the Empire accepted in its maturity a certain
religion; to conceal the fact that this religion was
not a vague mood, but a determinate and highly
organized corporation; to present in the first
centuries some non-existent "Christianity" in place
of the existent Church; to suggest that the Faith
was a vague agreement among individual holders
of opinions instead of what it historically was, the
doctrine of a fixed authoritative institution; to fail
to identify that institution with the institution still
here today and still called the Catholic Church;
to exaggerate the insignificant barbaric influences
which came from outside the Empire and did
nothing to modify its spirit; to pretend that the
Empire or its religion have at any time ceased to
be— that is, to pretend that there has ever been
a solution of continuity between the past and the
present of Europe— all these pretensions are parts
of one historical falsehood. In all by which we
Europeans differ from the rest of mankind there is
nothing which was not originally peculiar to the
Roman Empire, or is not demonstrably derived
from something peculiar to it.

42

What would be the best title of the passage?

A) Religion in Europe

B) The significance of the Roman Empire in the history of Europe

C) Several factors necessary for processing the history of Europe and Roman Empire

D) History, religion and the Roman Empire in Europe

The best answer is (B).
The passage is about the Roman Empire so (A) is out. Since from the first sentence another focus of the passage is history ("The history of European civilization is the history of a certain political institution which united and expressed Europe, and was governed from Rome", "It is immaterial to the historical value of this historical truth whether it be presented to a man who utterly rejects Catholic dogma or to a man who believes everything the Church may teach"), so (D) is a case of TOO BROAD.
As shown in "Europe is the Church, and the Church is Europe. It is immaterial to the historical value of this historical truth whether it be presented to a man who utterly rejects Catholic dogma or to a man who believes everything the Church may teach."
this passage is about "the historical value of this historical truth". Also, this historical truth is directly related to Catholic Church and this church is closely related to the Roman Empire. ("The Religion which informed and saved it (="Roman Empire") was then called, still is called, and will always be called "The Catholic Church.")

Test 4

43

According to the passage, what is the connection between the Church and the Roman Empire in Europe?

A) They were intertwined with each other so strongly that they dictated every major aspect of European history.

B) One of them was inconceivable without the other.

C) The Church survived in Europe with the help of Roman Empire.

D) The Roman Empire had a strong faith in the Catholic Church.

The best answer is (B).
That "It was revived by the religion which had become its new soul." shows how closely the Roman Empire and the Catholic Church were related.

(A); The perspective of the Roman Empire is missing.
(C); 'Survived' alone does not suggest a strong relationship in keeping with "revived" and "new soul".
(D); This needs further elaboration, and that elaboration is (B).

44

Which of the following provides the best evidence for the answer to the previous question?

A) "Europe is the Church, and the Church is Europe." (Lines 20-21)

B) "It was revived by the religion which had become its new soul." (Lines 13-15) its new soul." (Lines 13-15)

C) "The Religion which informed and saved it was then called, still is called, and will always be called "The Catholic Church." (Lines 17-19)

D) "But it did not die." (Line 13)

The best answer is (B).
Refer to the explanation for the answer to the previous question.

45

As used in line 21, "immaterial" most nearly means

A) spiritual

B) metaphysical

C) unsubstantial

D) priceless

The best answer is (C).
The author claims that two totally different kinds of men could not help but see "this truth" ("a man who utterly rejects Catholic dogma") ("A man remote in distance, in time, or in mental state from the thing we are about to examine") "would perceive the reality of this truth just as clearly as would" "a man who was steeped in its spirit from within and who formed an intimate part of Christian Europe" ("a man who believes everything the Church may teach."); there is no difference at all. Both would "clearly" see that "Europe is the Church, and the Church is Europe".

(A); an obvious eye-catcher: dictionary meaning
(B), (D); Neither of these can mean 'meaningless' or 'nothing'.

46

In talking about the historical value of the true connection between Europe and Church, why were two very different men mentioned?

A) to illustrate how people's opinions might differ depending on their historical era

B) to create an extreme contrast

C) to emphasize the universal importance of the

Test 4

D) to show the difference between the genuine historical value and people's perception of it

The best answer is (C).
This question is an extension of the two previous questions. The author uses these two men to demonstrate that "this truth" is not dependent on one's background or point of view. ("A man remote in distance, in time, or in mental state from the thing we are about to examine would perceive the reality of this truth just as clearly as would a man who was steeped in its spirit from within and who formed an intimate part of Christian Europe."); in other words, the author is saying that every (rational) person will accept the truth.

47

As used in line 54, "unhistorical" most nearly means

A) not historically organized
B) not famous
C) false
D) not imaginative

The best answer is (C).
We need to find the clues which indicate what the author means by unhistorical: "a traditional bias", "a whole school of hypothetical and unreal history". The closest choice will be wrong or false.

(A), (B), (D); None of these can be understood as wrong or false.

48

How does the author view those who deny that the Roman Empire with its institutions and its spirit was the sole origin of European civilization?

A) immature
B) liars
C) vague
D) not authoritative

The best answer is (B).
This question is also an extension from the previous question; those with unhistorical views are those who do not accept "this truth" and anybody who contradicts the truth and gives 'false' information is a liar. ("those writers of history whose special, local, and temporary business it is to oppose the Catholic Church, or who have a traditional bias against it. These men are numerous, they have formed, in the Protestant and other anti-Catholic universities, a whole school of hypothetical and unreal history", "to neglect the truth that the Roman Empire with its institutions and its spirit was the sole origin of European civilization")

49

Which of the following provides the best evidence for the answer to the previous question?

A) "neglect the truth" "diminish the truth" "conceal the fact" (Lines 54-59)
B) "the Empire accepted in its maturity a certain religion;" (Lines 58-59)
C) "pretend that there has ever been a solution of continuity between the past and the present of Europe" (Lines 73-75)
D) "a determinate and highly organized corporation" (Lines 60-61)

The best answer is (A).
Refer to the explanation for the answer to the

Test 4

previous question.

50

In context, which of the following could work against the author by using the same strategy employed by the author?

A) "a traditional bias against it" (Line 44)

B) "in proportion to his science" (Lines 36-37)

C) "that school of unreal history is still dogmatically taught" (Lines 49-50)

D) "the Catholic Faith shall have utterly departed" (Lines 33-34)

The best answer is (A).
The author claims that those who have opinions that are not in keeping with those set out in the passage are biased, but those who oppose the author can claim that it is the author who is biased; this is possible because the author failed to provide any evidence for the bias supposedly present in others.

51

Which of the following could be the best interpretation of the author's attitude?

A) perceptive

B) qualified

C) authoritative

D) scientific

The best answer is (C).
The author criticizes those who do not accept "this truth" without providing any reason why this criticism is justified. Thus, the author is very subjective, and not analytical at all.

TEST 5

Answer Keys & Explanations

Analyses of the tissues of plants show that they contain all of the elements that are to be found in the soil on which they grew. Any of these elements which are present in the soil in soluble form are
5 carried into the plants with the soil water in which they are dissolved, whether they are needed by the plant for its nutrition or not. But in the case of those elements which are not taken out of the sap to be used by the plant cells in their activities,
10 the total amount taken from the soil is much less than is that of the elements which are used in the synthetic processes of the plant. Hence, much larger proportions of some elements than of others are taken from the soil by plants. The
15 proportions of the different elements which are used by plants as raw materials for the manufacture of the products needed for their growth varies with the different species; but a certain amount of each of the so-called "essential elements" (see below) is
20 necessary to every plant, because each such element has a definite role which it performs in the plant's growth. A plant cannot grow to maturity unless a sufficient supply of each essential element comes to it from the soil.
25 From the standpoint of their relative value as raw materials for plant food, the elements which are present in the soil may be divided into three classes; namely, the non-essential, the essential and abundant, and the critical elements.
30 The first class includes silicon, aluminium, sodium, manganese, and certain other rarer elements which sometimes are found in soils of some special type, or unusual origin. These elements seem to have no role to play in the
35 nutrition of plants; although silicon is always present in plant ash and sodium salts are found in small quantities in all parts of practically all plants. Nearly all species of plants can be grown to full maturity in the entire absence of these elements
40 from their culture medium. Occasional exceptions to this statement in the case of special types of plants are known, and are of interest in special studies of plant adaptations, but need not be considered here.
45 The second group includes iron, calcium, magnesium, and, generally, sulfur. All of these elements are essential for plant growth, but are usually present in the soil in ample quantities to insure a sufficient supply in available form for all
50 plant needs. Recent investigations have shown, however, that there are many soils in which sulfur is present in such limited quantities that many agricultural crops, when grown on these soils, respond favorably to the application of sulfur-
55 containing fertilizers. In such cases, sulfur is a "critical" element.
The "critical" elements are those which are essential to the growth of all plants and which are present in most soils in relatively small proportions
60 and any one may, therefore, be the limiting factor in plant growth so far as plant food is concerned. These are nitrogen, phosphorus, potassium, and (possibly) sulfur.

Test 5

1

What could be the best title for the passage?

A) The value of the soil elements as plant food

B) The role of the soil elements in plant synthesis.

C) Why some elements are essential to plant survival

D) The water solubility of elements essential for plant nutrition

The best answer is (A).
What we need to look for here is "value" or "role" or significance.

(B); Plant synthesis is a WRONG PERSPECTIVE. It almost sounds as if a plant is synthesized from scratch: plant food, or plant nutrients are the correct perspective.
(C); TOO NARROW
(D); WRONG PERSPECTIVE)

2

Which of the following is true of the elements in soil?

A) The classification of them depends on their relative availability in soil.

B) The criterion for the classification of them is crystal clear.

C) A certain classification sometimes depends on the availability of relevant element to that classification.

D) Their availability in soil is directly related to their value.

The best answer is (C).
Some essential elements are "abundant." ("are usually present in the soil in ample quantities to insure a sufficient supply in available form for all plant needs")

"The "critical" elements not readily available ("essential to the growth of all plants and which are present in most soils in relatively small proportions")

(A); Not all non-essential elements present in the soil are available to plants to the same degree ("although silicon is always present in plant ash and sodium salts are found in small quantities in all parts of practically all plants.")
(B); whether or not an element is critical depends on certain factors. ("In such cases, sulfur is a "critical" element.")

3

According to the passage, what is the connection between essential elements and limiting factors?

A) Some essential elements may well be limiting factors.

B) Whether some elements are essential or not has no relevance to whether they are limiting factors.

C) Some of the limiting factors can be essential elements.

D) When certain essential elements lose one of their characteristics, they can become limiting factors.

The best answer is (A).
The essential elements that are not abundant are limiting factors. ("the essential and abundant, and the critical elements."

(B); the concept of "limiting" is directly related to the availability of the element.
(C): The other way around; some of the essential elements are limiting factors: "critical elements"
(D); Impossible to infer from the passage alone.

Test 5

4

Which of the following is the most direct evidence for the answer to the previous question?

A) "relative value" (Line 25) and "essential to the growth" (Line 58)

B) "in relatively small proportions and any one may, therefore, be the limiting factor in plant growth" (Lines 59-61)

C) "the essential and abundant, and the critical elements." (Lines 28-29)

D) "unusual origin" (Line 33) and "a definite role" (Line 21)

The best answer is (C).
Refer to the explanation for the answer to the previous question.

5

Which of the following questions is not clearly answered by the passage?

A) What is the connection between essential elements and limiting factors?

B) Why are essential elements readily available in soil?

C) What is the connection between essential and critical elements?

D) What is the function of non-essential elements?

The best answer is (D).
The author is not confident about the role of non-essential elements. ("These elements seem to have no role to play in the nutrition of plants")

(A); Of essential elements, those that exist in "relatively small proportions" are limiting factors, and these are also "critical" elements.
(B); The reason is clearly stated. ("in ample quantities to insure a sufficient supply in available form for all plant needs.")
(C); Refer to the explanation for (A).

6

Which of the following pieces of evidence might prove that non-essential elements might have something to do with plant growth?

A) "Occasional exceptions" (Line 40)

B) "entire absence" (Line 39)

C) "unusual origin" (Line 33)

D) "grow to maturity" (Line 22)

The best answer is (A).
"Nearly all species of plants can be grown to full maturity in the entire absence of these elements from their culture medium. Occasional exceptions to this statement in the case of special types of plants are known,"

7

Which of the following might work as the best logical analysis for the answer to the previous question?

A) Quantity makes quality more significant.

B) Nature doesn't put things where they are not needed.

C) No value, no use.

D) There are only three different kinds of elements.

The best answer is (B).
Even though it looks as if the non-essential elements do not seem to have any role in plant growth, they exist and are found in plants. Thus, it cannot be confidently said that they absolutely have no role at all, Besides, there are some occasional exceptions; therefore, we can safely say there are no elements without a reason or a role.

New SAT Reading Prep

Test 5

8

Which of the following might be the best assessment about non-essential elements?

A) They may well be relatively more available than essential elements.

B) They might be indirectly related with plant growth.

C) Their availability might have a lot to do with their significance.

D) Their apparent role in some cases might be due to specific adaptations in the certain plants.

The best answer is (D).
Their apparent role ("Occasional exceptions to this statement in the case of special types of plants are known") in some cases might come from some changes ("…plant adaptations") in the related plants.

9

Which of the following is the most direct evidence for the answer to the previous question?

A) "plant adaptations" (Line 43)

B) "special types" (Line 41)

C) "other rarer elements" (Line 31)

D) "special studies" (Lines 42-43)

The best answer is (A).
Refer to the explanation for the answer to the previous question.

10

Why most probably might the author not be interested in the significance of certain elements?

A) because no plant needs them to fully develop

B) because they do not exist in any significant amount in soil

C) because the special plants that need them are not rare enough

D) because their role in most plants' growth is not biologically evident, yet

The best answer is (D).
In this passage the most important thing to the author must be the relative value of elements in the soil. ("From the standpoint of their relative value as raw materials for plant food,")

(A), (B), (C); None of these mean or can be translated as "value" or "role."

Test 5

For taking away our Charters, abolishing our most valuable Laws, and altering fundamentally the Forms of our Governments:

For suspending our own Legislatures, and declaring themselves invested with power to legislate for us in all cases whatsoever.

He has abdicated Government here, by declaring us out of his Protection and waging War against us.

He has plundered our seas, ravaged our Coasts, burnt our towns, and destroyed the lives of our people.

He is at this time transporting large Armies of foreign Mercenaries to complete the works of death, desolation and tyranny, already begun with circumstances of Cruelty & perfidy scarcely paralleled in the most barbarous ages, and totally unworthy the Head of a civilized nation.

He has constrained our fellow Citizens taken Captive on the high Seas to bear Arms against their Country, to become the executioners of their friends and Brethren, or to fall themselves by their Hands.

He has excited domestic insurrections amongst us, and has endeavoured to bring on the inhabitants of our frontiers, the merciless Indian Savages, whose known rule of warfare, is an undistinguished destruction of all ages, sexes and conditions.

In every stage of these Oppressions We have Petitioned for Redress in the most humble terms: Our repeated Petitions have been answered only by repeated injury. A Prince whose character is thus marked by every act which may define a Tyrant, is unfit to be the ruler of a free people.

Nor have We been wanting in attentions to our Brittish brethren. We have warned them from time to time of attempts by their legislature to extend an unwarrantable jurisdiction over us. We have reminded them of the circumstances of our emigration and settlement here. We have appealed to their native justice and magnanimity, and we have conjured them by the ties of our common kindred to disavow these usurpations, which, would inevitably interrupt our connections and correspondence. They too have been deaf to the voice of justice and of consanguinity. We must, therefore, acquiesce in the necessity, which denounces our Separation, and hold them, as we hold the rest of mankind, Enemies in War, in Peace Friends.

We, therefore, the Representatives of the united States of America, in General Congress, Assembled, appealing to the Supreme Judge of the world for the rectitude of our intentions, do, in the Name, and by Authority of the good People of these Colonies, solemnly publish and declare, That these United Colonies are, and of Right ought to be Free and Independent States; that they are Absolved from all Allegiance to the British Crown, and that all political connection between them and the State of Great Britain, is and ought to be totally dissolved; and that as Free and Independent States, they have full Power to levy War, conclude Peace, contract Alliances, establish Commerce, and to do all other Acts and Things which Independent States may of right do. And for the support of this Declaration, with a firm reliance on the protection of divine Providence, we mutually pledge to each other our Lives, our Fortunes and our sacred Honor.

Test 5

11

Which of the following is probably NOT part of the actions of "he" as described in the passage?

A) territorial invasion
B) legal obstruction
C) organizational interference
D) military monopoly

The best answer is (D).
Even though the English King committed a variety of evil deeds including military actions ("He is at this time transporting large Armies of foreign Mercenaries to complete the works of death, desolation and tyranny", "He has constrained our fellow Citizens taken Captive on the high Seas to bear Arms against their Country, to become the executioners of their friends and Brethren,"), none of these indicates that he had a monopoly on military power. Probably, he didn't need a monopoly because he was the King by the grace of God.

12

According to the passage, what is most likely the nature of "his" military actions?

A) inhumane
B) treacherous
C) unparalleled
D) captivating

The best answer is (B).

(A); "cruelty": Being cruel doesn't necessarily mean inhumane
(B); "perfidy"
(C); "scarcely paralleled"
(D); POSITIVE

13

Why did the author refer to a "barbarous age"?

A) because s/he was afraid of what was happening in the present age
B) in order to make a comparison between this age and another barbarous age
C) in order to emphasize how bad the situation was in a certain era
D) because the nature of the English regime had traditionally been compared to that of savages

The best answer is (C).
Obviously the author wants to compare the contemporary situation with "the most barbarous ages" in terms of "cruelty and perfidy" so the author was emphasizing what was happening ("cruelty and perfidy") at that time.

(A); The point is not fear, but "cruelty and perfidy."
(B); The various kinds of barbarous ages were not the focus: COMPARISON AND CONTRAST.
(D); What was barbarous ("cruelty and perfidy") was not just the English government, but also the King himself: WRONG PERSPECTIVE.

14

In context, which of the following is the best interpretation of the attitude of the American resistance to the English?

A) It was mainly military in nature.
B) It was evenly balanced between diplomatic and aggressive in nature.
C) It displayed constant enterprise of a somewhat peaceful nature.
D) Unsuccessful at times but with some exceptions.

The best answer is (C).

Test 5

Americans constantly ("In every stage...repeated Petitions...") "tried ("have Petitioned for Redress ") peacefully. ("in the most humble terms")

(A), (B): "in the most humble terms"
(D): "answered only by repeated injury"

15

Which of the following is the best evidence for the answer to the previous question?

A) "these unsurpations" (Line 44)
B) "In every stage...Petitioned...most humble terms:" (Lines 30-31)
C) "attentions to our Brittish brethren" (Lines 36-37)
D) "warned them...of attempts" (Lines 37-38)

The best answer is (B).
Refer to the explanation for the answer to the previous question.

16

According to the passage, what can be said about the British response to American resistance?

A) retaliatory in nature
B) compromising if necessary
C) brutal at all cost
D) more severe than the resistance against it

The best answer is (D).
The resistance of the Americans was peaceful ("in the most humble terms"), but English response was cruel. ("answered only by repeated injury")

(A); "Repeated injury" doesn't necessarily mean that it was retaliatory in nature.
(B); This is far too POSITIVE to be the correct answer.

(C); "Repeated injury" can mean that it was brutal, but it doesn't necessarily imply brutality 'at all cost'

17

Which of the following is the best evidence for the answer to the previous question?

A) "constrained" "taken captive" (Lines 19-20)
B) "paralleled" "totally unworthy" (Lines 17-18)
C) "humble" "repeated injury" (Line 31, 33)
D) "insurrections" "merciless" (Line 24, 26)

The best answer is (C).
Refer to the explanation for the answer to the previous question.

18

In context, what is the author's attitude toward British public?

A) hostile
B) enthusiastic
C) apathetic
D) affectionate

The best answer is (D).
The author calls British people "brethren."

(A), (B), (C); None of these can be translated as "brethren" or brotherly, like brother.

19

Which of the following is the best evidence for the answer to the previous question?

A) "unwarrantable jurisdiction" (Line 39)
B) "Petitioned for Redress" (Line 31)

C) "marked...a Tyrant" (Line 34)
D) "our Brittish brethren" (Line 37)

The best answer is (D).
Refer to the explanation for the answer to the previous question.

20

What is the connection of the last paragraph to the passage as a whole?

A) reiteration
B) specification
C) a novel conclusion
D) generalization

The best answer is (A).
Almost everything mentioned in the last paragraph is a repetition of something mentioned earlier in the passage.
"Petitioned for Redress in the most humble terms:" ("the rectitude of our intentions")
"We must, therefore, acquiesce in the necessity, which denounces our Separation, and hold them, as we hold the rest of mankind, Enemies in War, in Peace Friends." ("that they are Absolved from all Allegiance to the British Crown" and "that all political connection between them and the State of Great Britain, is and ought to be totally dissolved")
"He has excited domestic insurrections amongst us, and has endeavoured to bring on the inhabitants of our frontiers, the merciless Indian Savages, whose known rule of warfare, is an undistinguished destruction of all ages, sexes and conditions." ("they have full Power to levy War, conclude Peace, contract Alliances, establish Commerce, and to do all other Acts and Things")

The editor of these essays was busy in the autumn of last year collating the opinions attached by different people to the word 'progress'. One Sunday afternoon he happened to be walking
5   with two friends in Oxford, one a professor of philosophy, the other a lady. The professor of philosophy declared that to him human progress must always mean primarily the increase of knowledge; the editor urged the increase of power
10 as its most characteristic feature, but the lady added at once that to her progress had always meant, and could only mean, increase in our appreciation of the humanity of others. The first two thoughts, harmonized and directed by the
15 third, may be taken to cover the whole field, and this volume to be merely a commentary upon them. What we have to consider is, when and how this idea of progress, as a general thing affecting mankind as a whole, first appeared in the world,
20 how far it has been realized in history, and how far it gives us any guidance and hope for the future. In the midst of a catastrophe which appears at first sight to be a deadly blow to the ideal, such an inquiry has a special interest and may have some
25 permanent value.
    Words are the thought of ages crystallized, or rather embodied with a constantly growing soul. The word 'Progress', like the word 'Humanity', is one of the most significant. It is a Latin word, not
30 used in its current abstract sense until after the Roman incorporation of the Mediterranean world. It contains Greek thought summed up and applied by Roman minds. Many of the earlier Greek thinkers, Xenophanes and Empedocles as well as
35 Plato and Aristotle, had thought and spoken of a steady process in things, including man himself, from lower to higher forms; but the first writer who expounds the notion with sufficient breadth of view and sufficiently accurate and concrete
40 observation to provide a preliminary sketch, was the great Roman poet who attributed all the best that was in him to the Greeks and yet has given us a highly original picture of the upward tendency of the world and of human society upon it. He,
45 too, so far as one can discover, was the first to use the word 'progress' in the sense of our inquiry. The passage in Lucretius at the end of his fifth book on the Nature of Things is so true and brilliant

and anticipates so many points in later thought that it is worth quoting at some length, and the poet's close relation with Cicero, the typical Greco-Roman thinker, gives his ideas the more weight as an historical document.

He begins by describing a struggle for existence in which the less well-adapted creatures died off, those who wanted either the power to protect themselves or the means of adapting themselves to the purposes of man. In this stage, however, man was a hardier creature than he afterwards became. He lived like the beasts of the field and was ignorant of tillage or fire or clothes or houses. He had no laws or government or marriage, and though he did not fear the dark, he feared the real danger of fiercer beasts. Men often died a miserable death, but not in multitudes on a single day as they do now by battle or shipwreck.

The next stage sees huts and skins and fire which softened their bodies, and marriage and the ties of family which softened their tempers. And tribes began to make treaties of alliance with other tribes.

Speech arose from the need which all creatures feel to exercise their natural powers, just as the calf will butt before his horns protrude. Men began to apply different sounds to denote different things, just as brute beasts will do to express different passions, as any one must have noticed in the cases of dogs and horses and birds. No one man set out to invent speech.

Fire was first learnt from lightning and the friction of trees, and cooking from the softening and ripening of things by the sun.

Then men of genius invented improved methods of life, the building of cities and private property in lands and cattle. But gold gave power to the wealthy and destroyed the sense of contentment in simple happiness. It must always be so whenever men allow themselves to become the slaves of things which should be their dependants and instruments.

They began to believe in and worship gods, because they saw in dreams shapes of preterhuman strength and beauty and deemed them immortal; and as they noted the changes of the seasons and all the wonders of the heavens, they placed their gods there and feared them when they spoke in the thunder. Metals were discovered through the burning of the woods, which caused the ores to run. Copper and brass came first and were rated above gold and silver. And then the metals took the place of hands, nails, teeth, and clubs, which had been men's earliest arms and tools. Weaving followed the discovery of the use of iron.

Sowing, planting, and grafting were learnt from nature herself, and gradually the cultivation of the soil was carried farther and farther up the hills.

Men learnt to sing from the birds, and to blow on pipes from the whistling of the zephyr through the reeds: and those simple tunes gave as much rustic jollity as our more elaborate tunes do now.

Then, in a summary passage at the end, Lucretius enumerates all the chief discoveries which men have made in the age-long process— ships, agriculture, walled cities, laws, roads, clothes, songs, pictures, statues, and all the pleasures of life— and adds, 'these things practice and the experience of the unresting mind have taught mankind gradually as they have progressed from point to point'.

Test 5

21

Why did the author probably have three opinions put together in the first paragraph?

A) to include as many diverse perspectives as possible

B) to investigate any possible difference(s) between vocations or ways of life

C) because one of them served as a base on which to build toward to the next step of the discussion

D) because they are by nature among the best material that can be used for an introduction

The best answer is (C).
The ideas of the two friends were processed in a certain way ("The first two thoughts, harmonized and directed") by the lady's idea ("by the third") which led to the next step in the discussion. ("may be taken to cover the whole field,")

(A); There is no evidence that the three opinions were significantly different from each other; the author did not say so or even imply it.
(B); Whatever differences may have existed in the opinions of these three people, there is no evidence that these differences were a result of their different vocations or ways of life: WRONG INFERENCE.
(D); The opinions of the three people might be well thought out, but we have no proof that they are among the best; the author did not say so or even imply it.

22

In context, which of the following is the best interpretation of "whole field"?

A) philosophy

B) everyday life

C) defining a concept

D) a certain compromise

The best answer is (C).
Since the author is interested in "collating the opinions attached by different people to the word 'progress'", we need something related to collating opinions about the word, "progress." ('concept')

(A), (B); These are the two sources of the opinions that need to be collated.
(D); There was no compromise because there was no conflict between their opinions or vocations or ways of life.

23

According to the passage, what is the most probable role of the three opinions mentioned in paragraph 1?

A) It provides an introduction to the main discussion of the concept, progress.

B) It provides the most significant argument to be commented upon.

C) It provides a foundation of scholarly enterprise to be expanded on later.

D) It provides a way of harmonizing and indicating a direction.

The best answer is (A).
As the author explores the meaning and uses of the word, "progress", he goes into it in increasing depth as the passage progresses ("begins by describing a struggle for existence in which the less well-adapted creatures died off, those who wanted either the power to protect themselves or the means of adapting themselves to the purposes of man", "The next stage sees huts and skins and fire which softened their bodies, and marriage and the ties of family which softened their tempers.", "Then men of genius invented improved methods of life, the building of cities and private property in lands and cattle"), so it can be safely said that the three opinions worked as an introduction.

(B); There is no proof that it is the most significant argument.

Test 5

(C); The lady's opinion is not the result of a scholarly enterprise; There is no proof.
(D); Only the third opinion provided a way to harmonize and indicated a direction to follow.

24

According to the passage, what can be said about humanity?

A) It must have the same history as the word soul.

B) The clarity of its meaning has been improving for a long time.

C) Words such as this normally change their meanings constantly.

D) Its change in meaning might be related to it being used in the field of politics.

The best answer is (B).
From mentioning "Latin word", every explanation is about "progress", not about "humanity". Also there are only two pieces of information about "humanity"("Words are the thought of ages crystallized, or rather embodied with a constantly growing soul", "one of the most significant"); the clarity of what it means has been improving ("crystallized") for a long time ("of ages"); We can say this because "humanity" is a word, too.

(A); it has the same "significance"
(C); "words are….embodied with a constantly growing soul", but this doesn't mean that they normally 'change their meanings': WRONG INFERENCE.
(D); This choice is related to "progress" not to "humanity" ("It (=progress) is a Latin word, not used in its current abstract sense until after the Roman incorporation(political) of the Mediterranean world") so there is no political relevance related to "humanity"; it is "progress" to which there is political relevance.

25

According to the passage, which of the following is most likely to be the first step in this application of these Roman minds in Question 23?

A) a correct and broad examination with hierarchical approaches

B) making a better use of rhythmic languages rather than prose even though they were to express the practical side of progress

C) taking full advantage of the concept of progress in a very contemporary perspective

D) tapping into the concept of the survival of the fittest

The best answer is (D).
The explanation that comes after Q 23 is an elaboration on Q 23. In other words, it explains how Greek thoughts had been summed up and applied by Roman minds. In the process of explaining that, "He ("typical Greco-Roman thinker") begins by describing a struggle for existence in which the less well-adapted creatures died off, …."

(A), (B), (C); None of these has anything to do with "a struggle for existence."

26

Which of following offers the best evidence for the answer to the previous question?

A) "Then men of genius invented improved methods of life, the building of cities and private property in lands and cattle." (Lines 83-85)

B) "He begins by describing a struggle for existence in which the less well-adapted creatures died off," (Lines 54-55)

C) "Fire was first learnt from lightning and the friction of trees," (Lines 80-81)

D) "which had been men's earliest arms and

Test 5

tools. Weaving followed the discovery of the use of iron." (Lines 101-103)

The best answer is (B).
Refer to the explanation for the answer to the previous question.

27

Which of the following is most likely the author's objective by saying "hardier" (Line 59), "but not in multitudes on a single day as they do now by battle or shipwreck" (Lines 65-66)?

A) to inform the reader of a sense of change in a certain direction

B) to directly reflect the extent at which humanity used to be uncivilized

C) to demonstrate one aspect of the more dangerous modern way of life

D) to stress how futile progress can be

E) to reveal the future direction of human progress

The best answer is (A).
According to Q 24 modern man is "less hardy now than he once was, and dies in multitudes on a single day as by battle or shipwreck", and this may well be a direction of change.

(B); The author does not state or imply the degree at which modern man is more civilized than he used to be.
(C); What is stated after "but" signifies that modern life is more dangerous, but since modern man is less hardy; modern man is less likely to survive in a harsh environment; There are two aspects.
(D); Q 24 tells how the past changes into the present, but it tells nothing about how the present will develop into the future: a typical case of WRONG INFERENCE.

28

Why did the author mention speech?

A) to link inevitable events in history such as treaties and wars

B) to demystify why humans are different from other species

C) to attribute certain phenomena

D) to expound a particular pathway

The best answer is (D).
The author states speech was not an invention of only one man. ("No one man set out to invent speech.") Inventing speech by collaboration is a particular pathway.

(A); Arising "from the need which all creatures feel to exercise their natural powers" doesn't mean that it is inevitable.
(B); paragraph 5 is about similarity between humans and animals, not the difference. ("just as")
(C); to attribute certain phenomena to what?
IN other words, this means finding the cause of inventing speech, which is "the need which all creatures feel to exercise their natural powers."

29

Why does the author most probably mention fire and cooking?

A) to show how humans have exploited nature in order to progress

B) to give an example of a direct case of cause and effect

C) to lead to a more significant stage of change in human history

D) as the possible beginning of environmental destruction

E) as a very plausible origin of war

Test 5

The best answer is (C).
After mentioning "fire" and "cooking" the author says "Then men of genius invented improved methods of life,"; In other words, we can safely say that the author believes that "fire" and "cooking" led to an improved way of life; in further words, the author used "fire" and "cooking" to go on to talk about a more developed state of progress.

(A), (B), (D); None of these choices means what (C) means: typical cases of EYE CATCHERS appealing to our common sense.

30

Which of the following words most directly signifies the implied effect gold has on human beings?

A) "the wealthy" (Line 86)

B) "slaves" (Line 89)

C) "contentment" (Line 87)

D) "instruments" (Line 90)

The best answer is (B).
By saying "It must always be so whenever men allow themselves to become the slaves of things which should be their dependants and instruments, the author showed that humans are enslaved by their own "dependants and instruments".

(A); Becoming wealthy is not the effect the author is focuses on here.
(B); Because of gold, "the sense of contentment" was "destroyed."
(D); "Instruments" themselves are not the effect of gold, but they are the causes of the effect. Gold is an example of the instruments.

31

According to the passage, why did people start to be religious?

A) because they were afraid of unexplainable dreams

B) because they were frightened by the changing seasons

C) because some figures in their dreams possessed what they did not have

D) because gods were very noisy when they spoke

The best answer is (C).
Humans became religious ("They began to believe in and worship gods") because some figures in their dreams ("they saw in dreams shapes of ") possessed what they didn't have. ("preterhuman strength and beauty and deemed them immortal")

(A); Just because something is "preterhuman", we don't have to be afraid of it: no evidence.
(B); "And as they noted the changes of the seasons and all the wonders of the heavens, they placed their gods there and feared them when they spoke in the thunder"; so it was the gods that humans were frightened by ("feared"), not the changing seasons.
(D); It is true that the gods were noisy when they spoke ("they spoke in the thunder"), but humans didn't become religious because of that: no evidence.

32

According to the passage, which of the following might be the best interpretation of songs and statues?

A) They are the best representatives of the pleasures of life.

B) They might have provided something that humans needed as they moved through history.

New SAT Reading Prep 264

Test 5

C) People at the time moved around more frequently than they do at the present time.

D) They are probably the products of human esthetics.

The best answer is (B).
"These things practice and the experience of the unresting mind have taught mankind gradually as they have progressed from point to point" tells us that humans might have needed some rest or comfort or "pleasure" in the form of "songs" and "statues" as well as other material things. ("ships, agriculture, walled cities, laws, roads, clothes, …, and all the pleasures of life")

(A); No proof for them being 'the best'
(C); As used in this context "from point to point" does not mean movement in geographic sense.
(D); The author indicates no direct connection between esthetics and "pleasure".

Nothing is more certain than that each generation longs for a reassurance as to the value and charm of life, and is secretly afraid lest it lose its sense of the youth of the earth. This is doubtless one reason why it so passionately cherishes its poets and artists who have been able to explore for themselves and to reveal to others the perpetual springs of life's self-renewal. And yet the average man cannot obtain this desired reassurance through literature, nor yet through glimpses of earth and sky. It can come to him only through the chance embodiment of joy and youth which life itself may throw in his way. It is doubtless true that for the mass of men the message is never so unchallenged and so invincible as when embodied in youth itself. One generation after another has depended upon its young to equip it with gaiety and enthusiasm, to persuade it that living is a pleasure, until men everywhere have anxiously provided channels through which this wine of life might flow, and be preserved for their delight. The classical city promoted play with careful solicitude, building the theater and stadium as it built the market place and the temple. The Greeks held their games so integral a part of religion and patriotism that they came to expect from their poets the highest utterances at the very moments when the sense of pleasure released the national life. In the medieval city the knights held their tourneys, the guilds their pageants, the people their dances, and the church made festival for its most cherished saints with gay street processions, and presented a drama in which no less a theme than the history of creation became a matter of thrilling interest. Only in the modern city have men concluded that it is no longer necessary for the municipality to provide for the insatiable desire for play. In so far as they have acted upon this conclusion, they have entered upon a most difficult and dangerous experiment; and this at the very moment when the city has become distinctly industrial, and daily labor is continually more monotonous and subdivided. We forget how new the modern city is, and how short the span of time in which we have assumed that we can eliminate public provision for recreation. A further difficulty lies in the fact that this industrialism has gathered together multitudes of eager young creatures from all quarters of the earth as a labor supply for the countless factories and workshops, upon which the present industrial city is based. Never before in civilization have such numbers of young girls been suddenly released from the protection of the home and permitted to walk unattended upon city streets and to work under alien roofs; for the first time they are being prized more for their labor power than for their innocence, their tender beauty, their ephemeral gaiety. Society cares more for the products they manufacture than for their immemorial ability to reaffirm the charm of existence. Never before have such numbers of young boys earned money independently of the family life, and felt themselves free to spend it as they choose in the midst of vice deliberately disguised as pleasure.

This stupid experiment of organizing work and failing to organize play has, of course, brought about a fine revenge. The love of pleasure will not be denied, and when it has turned into all sorts of malignant and vicious appetites, then we, the middle aged, grow quite distracted and resort to all sorts of restrictive measures. We even try to dam up the sweet fountain itself because we are affrighted by these neglected streams; but almost worse than the restrictive measures is our apparent belief that the city itself has no obligation in the matter, an assumption upon which the modern city turns over to commercialism practically all the provisions for public recreation. Quite as one set of men has organized the young people into industrial enterprises in order to profit from their toil, so another set of men and also of women, I am sorry to say, have entered the neglected field of recreation and have organized enterprises which make profit out of this invincible love of pleasure. In every city arise so-called "places"—" gin-palaces," they are called in fiction; in Chicago we euphemistically say merely "places,"— in which alcohol is dispensed, not to allay thirst, but, ostensibly to stimulate gaiety, it is sold really in order to empty pockets. Huge dance halls are opened to which hundreds of young people are attracted, many of whom stand wistfully outside a roped circle, for it requires five cents to procure within it for five minutes the sense of allurement and intoxication which is sold in lieu of innocent pleasure. These coarse and illicit merrymakings remind one of the unrestrained jollities of Restoration London, and they are indeed their direct descendants, properly commercialized, still confusing joy with lust, and gaiety with debauchery.

Test 5

33

What could be the best title of the passage?

A) The history of youth and the city
B) The changing effect of youth upon the city
C) The similarities between youth and the city
D) **Youth in the city**

The best answer is (D).
This passage is about youth and the influence of the city on youth.

(A); History is irrelevant.
(B); It is the city that influences youth, not the other way around ("In every city arise so-called "places"—" gin-palaces," they are called in fiction; in Chicago we euphemistically say merely "places,"— in which alcohol is dispensed, not to allay thirst")
(C); Refer to the explanation for (B)

34

Why did the author talk about poets and artists?

A) to show the importance of esthetic qualities
B) **to emphasize the significance of youth**
C) to lead into a different topic which later becomes more important
D) to establish a connection between different concepts, which the average person would be unable to recognize

The best answer is (B).
Poets and artists can take good advantage of their youth and show that young people. ("have been able to explore for themselves and to reveal to others the perpetual springs of life's self-renewal")

(A); The concept of youth is missing.
(C); Youth is the only important topic.
(D); Youth is the only concept under discussion.

35

Which choice does "it" (Line 5) refer to?

A) **each generation**
B) sense
C) youth
D) earth

The best answer is (A).
The sentence before the sentence containing "it" and the sentence containing "it" are parallel to each other, and both sentences have the same subject.

36

According to the passage, what can be said about earth and sky?

A) It would be impossible to feel young just by looking at them.
B) Anybody can sense the feeling of youth by getting a glimpse of them.
C) **Seeing them might remind the observer of what his/her youth was like but probably only by accident.**
D) They give most people a general sense of the natural beauty of youth.

The best answer is (C).
"And yet the average man cannot obtain this desired reassurance through literature, nor yet through glimpses of earth and sky. It can come to him only through the chance embodiment of joy and youth which life itself may throw in his way."

(A); "Chance embodiment" does not mean 'impossible'.
(B); "Chance embodiment" does not mean 'anybody'.
(D); "Chance embodiment" does not mean 'a general sense of the natural beauty of youth'.

Test 5

37

According to the passage, which choice gives the best evidence for the role of theaters and stadiums when they were first built in cities?

A) "turned into all sorts of malignant and vicious appetites," (Lines 68-69)

B) "provided channels through which this wine of life might flow," (Lines 20-21)

C) "make profit out of this invincible love of pleasure." (Lines 83-84)

D) "ostensibly to stimulate gaiety," (Lines 88-89)

The best answer is (B).
"The classical city promoted play with careful solicitude, building the theater and stadium as it built the market place and the temple."; theaters and stadiums are examples of the things men have created to "provide channels through which this wine of life might flow, and be preserved for their delight".

(A); NEGATIVE
(C); Money (profit) is not the point.
(D); NEGATIVE)

38

According to the author, what can be said about pleasure?

A) All the pleasure is malicious.

B) Most pleasure is a means to help old people remember what their youth was like.

C) Intoxication is the worst kind of pleasure.

D) There are basically two different kinds.

The best answer is (D).
There are two distinctly different kinds of pleasure: the negative kind ("the sense of allurement and intoxication") and the positive kind. ("in lieu of innocent pleasure")

(A); Not all pleasure is malicious; for example, "gaiety" is not.
(B); How much pleasure is a means to help old people remember what their youth was like is unknown even if pleasure is such a means.
(C); The different kinds of pleasure were never compared in terms of good or evil.

39

Which choice gives the best evidence for the answer to the previous question?

A) "The Greeks held their games so a part of religion and patriotism that they came to expect from their poets the highest utterances at the very moments" (Lines 24-27)

B) "when it has turned into all sorts of malignant and vicious appetites, then we, the middle aged, grow quite distracted and resort to all sorts of restrictive measures." (Lines 68-71)

C) "it requires five cents to procure within it for five minutes the sense of allurement and intoxication which is sold in lieu of innocent pleasure." (Lines 93-95)

D) "the sense of pleasure released the national life." (Lines 27-28)

The best answer is (C).
Refer to the explanation for the answer to the previous question.

40

According to the passage, what can be said about gaiety?

A) The young have more of it than the old.

B) It is absolutely irrelevant to young people.

C) It is more similar to joy than to lust.

Test 5

D) It cannot be obtained from such places as stadiums.

The best answer is (C).
This question is an extension of Question 38; gaiety is a positive kind of pleasure. So (D) is out, so is (B).
From "still confusing joy with lust, and gaiety with debauchery" we can say joy goes with gaiety, and lust goes with debauchery.

(A); The young and the old cannot be compared in terms of the amount of gaiety each group feels because, if old people regain their feeling of youth, they can still experience gaiety ("Nothing is more certain than that each generation longs for a reassurance as to the value and charm of life, and is secretly afraid lest it lose its sense of the youth of the earth.", "they are being prized more for their labor power than for their innocence, their tender beauty, their ephemeral gaiety.") and by the same token, young people might lose their sense of gaiety through debauchery.

41

According to the passage, what is the connection between the city and the youth?

A) They used to be strongly related in every sense.
B) The city is a fountain of youth, and the fountain becomes more powerful as history progresses.
C) The city is responsible for maintaining the youth.
D) The city possesses many minor tracks to promote the beauty of the youth.

The best answer is (C).
"One generation after another has depended upon its young to equip it with gaiety and enthusiasm, to persuade it that living is a pleasure, until men everywhere have anxiously provided channels through which this wine of life might flow, and be preserved for their delight. The classical city promoted play with careful solicitude, building the theater and stadium as it built the market place and the temple." This part of the passage tells us that the city ("theater", "stadium", "market place", and "the temple") provided a way to maintain the youth. ("channels through which this wine of life might flow")

(A); No evidence that is related to 'every sense'
(B); No evidence that it is getting more powerful; actually its power to function as a fountain of youth is waning. ("A further difficulty lies in the fact that this industrialism has gathered together multitudes of eager young creatures from all quarters of the earth as a labor supply for the countless factories and workshops, upon which the present industrial city is based")
(D); Whether any means to promote the beauty of youth is major or minor is not the focus of the passage.

42

As used in line 22, "solicitude" most nearly means

A) concern
B) anxiety
C) hope
D) solitude

(A) is the best answer.
The only usable clue is "anxiously" but 'anxiety' is an eye-catcher because it is too negative to fit into the context. We need to find a word that has a meaning similar to 'anxiety' but less negative.

In a sense, the experience of the past may, unfortunately, provide a clue to the future. The last two great wars have shown an increasing emphasis on ideology or political faith as driving forces
[5] behind warfare, rather than the considerations of coldly calculated diplomacy. Wars become more serious, and less gentlemanly; the enemy must be taken into account not merely as a man, but as a fanatic. To the normal group-loyalty of any good
[10] soldier to his army, right or wrong, there is added the loyalty to the Ism or the Leader. Warfare thus goes back to the Wars of Faith. It is possible that techniques from the Christian-Mohammedan or from the Protestant-Catholic wars of the past
[15] could be reexamined with a view to establishing those parts of their tested experience which may seem to be psychologically and militarily sound in our own time. How fast can converts be made from the other side? In what circumstances
[20] should an enemy word of honor be treated as valid? How can heretics (today, read "subversive elements") be uprooted? Does the enemy faith have weak points which permit enemy beliefs to be turned against personnel at the appropriate
[25] times? What unobjectionable forms should leaflets and broadcasts follow in mentioning subjects which are reverenced by the enemy but not by ourselves? The expansion of the Islamic Faith-and-Empire provides a great deal of procedural
[30] information which cannot be neglected in our time. It has been said that men's faith should not be destroyed by violence, and that force alone is insufficient to change the minds of men. If this were true, it would mean that Germany can never
[35] be de-Nazified, and that there is no hope that the democratic peoples captured by totalitarian powers can adjust themselves to their new overlords or, if adjusted, can be converted back to free principles. In reality warfare by Mohammed's captains and
[40] successors demonstrated two principles of long-range psychological warfare which are still valid today:

A people can be converted from one faith to the other if given the choice between conversion
[45] and extermination, stubborn individuals being rooted out. To effect the initial conversion, participation in the public ceremonies and formal language of the new faith must be required. Sustained counterintelligence must remain on the
[50] alert against backsliders, but formal acceptance will become genuine acceptance if all public media of expression are denied the vanquished faith.

If immediate wholesale conversion would require military operations that were too extensive
[55] or severe, the same result can be effected by toleration of the objectionable faith, combined with the issuance of genuine privileges to the new, preferred faith. The conquered people are left in the private, humble enjoyment of their old
[60] beliefs and folkways; but all participation in public life, whether political, cultural or economic, is conditioned on acceptance of the new faith. In this manner, all up-rising members of the society will move in a few generations over to the new
[65] faith in the process of becoming rich, powerful, or learned; what is left of the old faith will be a gutter superstition, possessing neither power nor majesty.

These two rules worked once in the rise of Islam. They were applied again by Nazi overlords
[70] during World War II, the former in Poland, the Ukraine and Byelorussia, the latter in Holland, Belgium, Norway and other Western countries. The rules will probably be seen in action again. The former process is difficult and bloody, but quick;
[75] the latter is as sure as a steam-roller. If Christians, or democrats, or progressives— whatever free men may be called— are put in a position of underprivilege and shame for their beliefs, and if the door is left open to voluntary conversion, so
[80] that anyone who wants to can come over to the winning side, the winning side will sooner or later convert almost everyone who is capable of making trouble. (In the language of Vilfredo Pareto, this would probably be termed "capture of the rising
[85] elite"; in the language of present-day Marxists, this would be described as "utilization of potential leadership cadres from historically superseded classes"; in the language of practical politics, it means "cut in the smart boys from the opposition,
[90] so that they can't set up a racket of their own.")

Test 5

43

What could be the best title of the passage?

A) Why certain types of psychological warfare fail

B) Different types of psychological warfare

C) A focus on psychological warfare

D) The operation of a certain endeavor related to war

The best answer is (D).
The passage is about psychological warfare ("In reality warfare by Mohammed's captains and successors demonstrated two principles of long-range psychological warfare which are still valid today") and how it works. ("To effect the initial conversion, participation in the public ceremonies and formal language of the new faith must be required")

(A), (B) (C); None of these can be understood as how psychological warfare works.

44

According to the passage, which of the following could be the driving force in the conduct of a war?

A) a winning diplomatic strategy

B) something practical

C) a combination of something ideological and something practical

D) an ideological approach

The best answer is (D).
The driving force in the conduct of a war is clearly stated in the passage. ("The last two great wars have shown an increasing emphasis on the ideology or political faith as driving forces behind warfare, rather than the considerations of coldly calculated diplomacy.")

(A); An "ideology or political faith" do not have to be part of a winning diplomatic strategy; it is not impossible to win without them; however, there is no evidence for this in the passage.
(B); An "ideology" cannot be something practical.
(C); An "ideology" does not have to be a combination of something ideological and something practical.

45

Which choice gives the best evidence for the answer to the previous question?

Which choice gives the best evidence for the answer to the previous question?

A) Lines 53-56 ("If immediate…faith,")

B) Lines 85-89 ("in the language…classes.")

C) Lines 3-5 ("emphasis…behind warfare.")

D) Lines 37-38 ("if…free principles.")

The best answer is (C).
Refer to the explanation for the answer to the previous question.

46

According to the passage, what would it be that needs to be done if simple persuasion proved ineffective?

A) stand the enemy's faith

B) grant significant and practical privileges to followers of the victor's new, preferred faith

C) end the war on terms that put restrictions on the enemy

D) make a greater effort to persuade the enemy

The best answer is (A).
If overall persuasion ("immediate wholesale conversion") proved ineffective ("would require

Test 5

military operations that were too extensive or severe") the enemy's faith might have to be stood. ("the same result can be effected by toleration of the objectionable faith")

(B), (C), (D); None of these contain the concept of "toleration".

47

Which choice gives the best evidence for the answer to the previous question?

A) Lines 58-61 ("The conquered…in public life")
B) Lines 53-56 ("If immediate…faith,")
C) Lines 56-58 ("combined…preferred faith.")
D) Lines 73-75 ("The former…steam-roller.")

The best answer is (C).
Refer to the explanation for the answer to the previous question.

48

As used in line 53, "wholesale" most nearly means

A) economic
B) expansive
C) sustained
D) effective

The best answer is (B).
We need to look for a clue to see the contextual flow, and we can see "extensive", the only choice that goes well with extensive is (B), and the dictionary meaning of wholesale is compatible with (B); we are lucky.

49

According to the passage, which of the following is true of a new faith after a war?

A) Every conquered person must either follow it or suffer cherishing the old faith.
B) Even when clinging to their prewar faith, the conquered people cannot be totally free from the influence of the new faith.
C) There are two rules in effect that help control a prewar faith.
D) What happened in Norway was a good example of what happens when a new faith is reluctantly embraced.

The best answer is (B).
Even when clinging to the prewar faith ("… left in the private, humble enjoyment of their old beliefs and folkways), the conquered people cannot be totally free from the new faith. ("but all participation in public life, whether political, cultural or economic, is conditioned on acceptance of the new faith")

50

Which choice gives the best evidence for the answer to the previous question?

A) "The rules will probably be seen in action again." (Line 73)
B) "The conquered people are left in the private, humble enjoyment of their old beliefs and folkways;" (Lines 58-60)
C) "The former process is difficult and bloody, but quick; the latter is as sure as a steam-roller." (Lines 73-75)
D) "But all participation in public life, whether political, cultural or economic, is conditioned on acceptance of the new faith." (Lines 60-62)

Test 5

The best answer is (D).
Refer to the explanation for the answer to the previous question.

51

As used in in line 82, "is capable of making trouble" most nearly means

A) can cause a revolution after the war is over

B) can change their minds

C) can never be converted

D) cannot endure further suffering as a conquered people

The best answer is (B).
"The winning side will sooner or later convert almost everyone who is capable of making trouble". "Everyone" means the ones that need to be converted: either those with old faith or those who have returned to the old faith; the only possible choice that means or implies this is (B).

(A); 'Revolution' is too strong to be the answer.
(C); 'Never' is too strong to be the answer.
(D); 'Further suffering' is too strong to be the answer.

52

According to the passage, which of the following is most probably what the author means by "a racket of their own" (Line 90)?

A) a new faith that is compatible with the victor's

B) a new political activity which the victor will probably not accept

C) a faith that is unacceptable because it is too radical

D) social behavior that is unacceptable because it directly contradicts the victor's vision for a new society

The best answer is (B).
"Cut in the smart boys from the opposition, so that they can't set up a racket of their own." Thus, a racket is probably something similar to "opposition", something 'the victor will probably not accept".

(A); POSITIVE
(C); 'Unacceptable' is acceptable, but not 'too radical' because the nature of this racket is unknown.
(D); "Racket" can well be 'an acceptable social activity', but it doesn't have to 'directly contradict the victor's vision for a new society.'

TEST 6

Answer Keys & Explanations

"Sense with keenest edge unused Yet unsteel'd by scathing fire: Lovely feet as yet unbruised On the ways of dark desire!" These words written by a poet to his young son express the longing which has at times seized all of us, to guard youth from the mass of difficulties which may be traced to the obscure manifestation of that fundamental susceptibility of which we are all slow to speak and concerning which we evade public responsibility, although it brings its scores of victims into the police courts every morning. At the very outset we must bear in mind that the senses of youth are singularly acute, and ready to respond to every vivid appeal. We know that nature herself has sharpened the senses for her own purposes, and is deliberately establishing a connection between them and the newly awakened susceptibility of sex; for it is only through the outward senses that the selection of an individual mate is made and the instinct utilized for nature's purposes. It would seem, however, that nature was determined that the force and constancy of the instinct must make up for its lack of precision, and that she was totally unconcerned that this instinct ruthlessly seized the youth at the moment when he was least prepared to cope with it; not only because his powers of self-control and discrimination are unequal to the task, but because his senses are helplessly wide open to the world. These early manifestations of the sex susceptibility are for the most part vague and formless, and are absolutely without definition to the youth himself. Sometimes months and years elapse before the individual mate is selected and determined upon, and during the time when the differentiation is not complete— and it often is not— there is of necessity a great deal of groping and waste. This period of groping is complicated by the fact that the youth's power for appreciating is far ahead of his ability for expression. "The inner traffic fairly obstructs the outer current," and it is nothing short of cruelty to over-stimulate his senses as does the modern city. This period is difficult everywhere, but it seems at times as if a great city almost deliberately increased its perils. The newly awakened senses are appealed to by all that is gaudy and sensual, by the flippant street music, the highly colored theater posters, the trashy love stories, the feathered hats, the cheap heroics of the revolvers displayed in the pawn-shop windows. This fundamental susceptibility is thus evoked without a corresponding stir of the higher imagination, and the result is as dangerous as possible. We are told upon good authority that "If the imagination is retarded, while the senses remain awake, we have a state of esthetic insensibility,"— in other words, the senses become sodden and cannot be lifted from the ground. It is this state of "esthetic insensibility" into which we allow the youth to fall which is so distressing and so unjustifiable. Sex impulse then becomes merely a dumb and powerful instinct without in the least awakening the imagination or the heart, nor does it overflow into neighboring fields of consciousness. Every city contains hundreds of degenerates who have been over-mastered and borne down by it; they fill the casual lodging houses and the infirmaries. In many instances it has pushed men of ability and promise to the bottom of the social scale. Warner, in his American Charities, designates it as one of the steady forces making for failure and poverty, and contends that "the inherent uncleanness of their minds prevents many men from rising above the rank of day laborers and finally incapacitates them even for that position." He also suggests that the modern man has a stronger imagination than the man of a few hundred years ago and that sensuality destroys him the more rapidly. It is difficult to state how much evil and distress might be averted if the imagination were utilized in its higher capacities through the historic paths.

Test 6

1

What could be the best title of the passage?

A) The inevitable entanglement of youth and the city

B) How city influences youth

C) The numerous obstacles in the city

D) Why it is so difficult to find a future spouse in the city

The best answer is (B).
Answers to all the other questions point to the answer of this question.

2

Which choice would most likely be the author's attitude toward natural disasters such as an earthquake, if s/he maintained the same attitude s/he has about youth?

A) S/he would immediately restore all losses caused by them.

B) S/he would individually hold responsible every individual affected by them.

C) S/he would argue for collective responsibility to deal with the necessary reconstruction.

D) Only natural disasters that occur in the city are of any consequence.

The best answer is (C).
This question is strongly related with Question 8. Since the author believes that a lack of imagination is widespread phenomenon, s/he would act as if no single individual should be held responsible.

3

According to the passage, when the time comes to choose a mate, what is the solution to the problems caused by a lack of maturity?

A) sensuality

B) imagination

C) youth itself

D) a careful selection process

The best answer is (B).
The problem of choosing mate ("This period of groping is complicated by the fact that the youth's power for appreciating is far ahead of his ability for expression.") is a problem of susceptibility without imagination ("This fundamental susceptibility is thus evoked without a corresponding stir of the higher imagination, and the result is as dangerous as possible.") and thus this can be solved with imagination. ("We are told upon good authority that "If the imagination is retarded, while the senses remain awake, we have a state of esthetic insensibility"")

(A),(C),(D); None of these can be translated as imagination.

4

Which choice gives the best evidence for the answer to the previous question?

A) "If the imagination is…a state of esthetic insensibility," (Lines 53-55)

B) "It is this state of "esthetic insensibility" …so unjustifiable." (Lines 57-59)

C) "Every city contains hundreds of…the infirmaries" (Lines 63-66)

D) "Sometimes months and years elapse…a great deal of groping and waste." (Lines 32-37)

Test 6

The best answer is (A).
Refer to the explanation for the answer to the previous question.

5

The author sees the "fundamental susceptibility" mentioned in line 7-8 as

A) fundamentally malignant because it lacks imagination

B) **something that could work better under certain conditions**

C) absolutely indispensable

D) unconditionally risky no matter where it comes from

The best answer is (B).
This fundamental susceptibility would work better if the higher imagination were employed. ("This fundamental susceptibility is thus evoked without a corresponding stir of the higher imagination, and the result is as dangerous as possible")

(A); No matter how negative it is, the level of malignancy cannot be inferred from the passage. ("as dangerous as possible.")
(C); POSTITIVE
(D); No evidence for it being unconditionally risky. ("as dangerous as possible.")

6

According to the passage, why would finding a spouse be more problematic than not finding one?

A) because males have difficulty expressing their needs

B) because qualifications do not always match expectations

C) because the inner conflict between the two opposite genders obstructs the surroundings

D) partly because some of their surroundings tends to produce more problems than they did before

The best answer is (D).
The surroundings (="the city") would make more problems ("This period is difficult everywhere, but it seems at times as if a great city almost deliberately increased its perils.")

(A); The difference between males and females is not the point: COMPARISON AND CONTRAST.
(B); Qualifications suffer because of sexual impulses ("In many instances it has pushed men of ability and promise to the bottom of the social scale."), and they have nothing to do with expectations.
(C); "This period of groping is complicated by the fact that the youth's power for appreciating is far ahead of his ability for expression. "The inner traffic fairly obstructs the outer current". Thus, the inner traffic here is "the youth's power for appreciating" not 'the inner conflict between the two opposite genders', and "the outer current" here is "his ability for expression", not 'the outer surroundings'.

7

Which choice gives the best evidence for the answer to the previous question?

A) "The inner traffic fairly obstructs the outer current," (Lines 39-40)

B) "it is nothing short of cruelty to over-stimulate his senses as does the modern city." (Lines 40-42)

C) "This fundamental susceptibility is thus evoked without a corresponding stir of the higher imagination," (Lines 49-51)

D) "This period is difficult everywhere, but it seems at times as if a great city almost deliberately increased its perils." (Lines 42-44)

Test 6

The best answer is (A).
Refer to the explanation for the answer to the previous question.

8

Why did the author mention "casual lodging"?

A) to stress how inexpensive accommodations are in the city

B) to show how common a certain phenomenon is

C) to illustrate why a certain type of accommodation is more popular than other types

D) to suggest that youngsters regard lodgings as something very easy to get

The best answer is (B).
The author makes sure we understand that this particular phenomenon is very commonplace. ("Every city", "hundreds of degenerates", "In many instances", "the steady forces")

(A),(C), (D); None of these can be understood as common, widespread, or dominant.

9

As used in line 56, "sodden" most nearly means

A) invigorated

B) darkened

C) moisturized

D) dull

The best answer is (D).
The dictionary meaning of sodden is soggy or wet, but since we are looking for the contextual meaning, we need to look at the clues ("esthetic insensibility", "cannot be lifted from the ground", "dumb", "without in the least awakening the imagination"), and the choice that has a meaning that matches all these clues is the answer.

10

According to the passage, what is true of esthetic insensibility?

A) The fundamental susceptibility will always lead to it.

B) It can be mostly found on the ground.

C) One needs some sort of mental power to snap out of it.

D) It comes from a lack of artistic training.

The best answer is (C).
This question is an extension of Question 3. Since esthetic insensibility is caused by a lack of imagination, we need imagination to escape from our esthetic insensibility. ("If the imagination is retarded, while the senses remain awake, we have a state of esthetic insensibility")

(A); There is no evidence that justifies using 'always'
(B); There is no evidence that justifies using 'mostly'
(D); Artistic training is never the point.

Test 6

This is a day of national consecration, and I am certain that on this day my fellow Americans expect that on my induction into the Presidency I will address them with a candor and a decision
[5] which the present situation of our people impels. This is preeminently the time to speak the truth, the whole truth, frankly and boldly. Nor need we shrink from honestly facing conditions in our country today. This great Nation will endure
[10] as it has endured, will revive and will prosper. So, first of all, let me assert my firm belief that the only thing we have to fear is fear itself—nameless, unreasoning, unjustified terror which paralyzes needed efforts to convert retreat into
[15] advance. In every dark hour of our national life a leadership of frankness and of vigor has met with that understanding and support of the people themselves which is essential to victory. And I am convinced that you will again give that support
[20] to leadership in these critical days. In such a spirit on my part and on yours we face our common difficulties. They concern, thank God, only material things. Values have shrunk to fantastic levels; taxes have risen; our ability to pay has
[25] fallen; government of all kinds is faced by serious curtailment of income; the means of exchange are frozen in the currents of trade; the withered leaves of industrial enterprise lie on every side; farmers find no markets for their produce; and
[30] the savings of many years in thousands of families are gone. More important, a host of unemployed citizens face the grim problem of existence, and an equally great number toil with little return. Only a foolish optimist can deny the dark realities of
[35] the moment. And yet our distress comes from no failure of substance. We are stricken by no plague of locusts. Compared with the perils which our forefathers conquered because they believed and were not afraid, we have still much to be thankful
[40] for. Nature still offers her bounty and human efforts have multiplied it. Plenty is at our doorstep, but a generous use of it languishes in the very sight of the supply.

Primarily this is because the rulers of the
[45] exchange of mankind's goods have failed, through their own stubbornness and their own incompetence, have admitted their failure and have abdicated. Practices of the unscrupulous money changers stand indicted in the court of
[50] public opinion, rejected by the hearts and minds of men. True they have tried, but their efforts have been cast in the pattern of an outworn tradition. Faced by failure of credit they have proposed only the lending of more money. Stripped of the lure of
[55] profit by which to induce our people to follow their false leadership, they have resorted to exhortations, pleading tearfully for restored confidence. They only know the rules of a generation of self-seekers. They have no vision, and when there is no vision
[60] the people perish. Yes, the money changers have fled from their high seats in the temple of our civilization. We may now restore that temple to the ancient truths. The measure of that restoration lies in the extent to which we apply social values
[65] more noble than mere monetary profit. Happiness lies not in the mere possession of money; it lies in the joy of achievement, in the thrill of creative effort. The joy, the moral stimulation of work no longer must be forgotten in the mad chase of
[70] evanescent profits. These dark days, my friends, will be worth all they cost us if they teach us that our true destiny is not to be ministered unto but to minister to ourselves—to our fellow men. Recognition of that falsity of material wealth as
[75] the standard of success goes hand in hand with the abandonment of the false belief that public office and high political position are to be valued only by the standards of pride of place and personal profit; and there must be an end to a conduct
[80] in banking and in business which too often has given to a sacred trust the likeness of callous and selfish wrongdoing. Small wonder that confidence languishes, for it thrives only on honesty, on honor, on the sacredness of obligations, on faithful
[85] protection, and on unselfish performance; without them it cannot live.

Test 6

11

What is the main topic of the passage?

A) America would be in danger without immediate and productive measures.

B) America can make a comeback as a world superpower.

C) There is a way for the nation to get back on course.

D) Money changers have created most of the major problems in the world.

The best answer is (C).
The author is basically very positive ("Nor need we shrink from honestly facing conditions in our country today. This great Nation will endure as it has endured, will revive and will prosper. So, first of all, let me assert my firm belief that the only thing we have to fear is fear itself"), but s/he claims that there are things that need to be done, changes that need to be made. ("Values have shrunk to fantastic levels; taxes have risen; our ability to pay has fallen; government of all kinds is faced by serious curtailment of income; the means of exchange are frozen in the currents of trade")

12

According to the passage, who are most likely the rulers of the exchange of mankind's goods?

A) incompetent economists

B) immoral business people

C) corrupt politicians

D) whoever is responsible for the current ordeal

The best answer is (D).
Since "the rulers of the exchange of mankind's goods" "have failed, through their own stubbornness and their own incompetence," (A), (B), and (C) are not impossible, but TOO NARROW.

13

In context, what is the most probable reason for which what nature's offer weakens before it is actually used?

A) the way nature runs its course

B) historical inevitability

C) human interference

D) conflicts among international rivals

The best answer is (C).
"Plenty is at our doorstep, but a generous use of it languishes in the very sight of the supply. Primarily this is because the rulers of the exchange of mankind's goods have failed, through their own stubbornness and their own incompetence, have admitted their failure and have abdicated."; Thus the reason is that "the rulers of the exchange of mankind's goods have failed," In other words, human failure is the cause, and the only choice that can be understood as human failure is (C).

(A), (B), (D); WRONG PERSPECTIVES

14

According to the passage, what could happen to people without vision?

A) They could physically die.

B) Their nation could disappear.

C) They could vanish into historical oblivion.

D) Money changers could abandon them.

The best answer is (C).
"They have no vision, and when there is no vision the people perish." The only choice that contains any concept compatible with "perish" is (C).

(A); "perish" in this context does not mean physical death: WRONG PERSPECTIVE
(B); It is the people who will "perish", not their

Test 6

"nation": WRONG PERSPECTIVE
(D): WRONG PERSPECTIVE

15

As used in line 48, "abdicated" most nearly means

A) forgot
B) gave up
C) lessened
D) came back

The best answer is (B).
In context, we need to find what goes well with goods. The only reasonable choice is to give up "goods"

16

As used in line 48, "unscrupulous" most nearly means

A) insufficient
B) incapable
C) bungling
D) unprincipled

The best answer is (D).
Those who can be "indicted" will be (D). No other choices are compatible with "indicted"

17

In the beginning of the passage, which of the following is most likely the reason that the author mentions the importance of candor?

A) because in general, it is the most important trait politicians must possess along with the sense of morality
B) because without it, it is practically impossible to comprehend what is happening in world economy
C) because the current economic situations in the U.S. is too dire to do anything about
D) because the status quo in a nation needs it to be looked at as it is

The best answer is (D).
"My fellow Americans expect that on my induction into the Presidency I will address them with a candor and a decision which the present situation of our people impels." The status quo ("the present situation") needs ("impels") to be looked at as it is.

(A), (B); The concept of "the present situation" is missing.
(C): too negative to be the answer

18

Which of the following is the major contrast the author employs throughout the passage?

A) the economy and politics
B) the U.S. and the world
C) money and spirit
D) idea and philosophy

The best answer is (C).
The author criticizes a certain type of people ("the rulers of the exchange of mankind's goods", "the unscrupulous money changers") and encourages a type of attitude ("So, first of all, let me assert my firm belief that the only thing we have to fear is fear itself—"), so the contrast is drawn between material wealth and an attitude that can overcome fear.

(A); The economy can be translated as money, but politics cannot be understood as an attitude with which to overcome fear.
(B): WRONG PERSPECTIVE

Test 6

(D); The concept of "money" is missing.

19

Which of the following is the author's general attitude?

A) very pessimistic

B) carefully optimistic

C) reluctantly compromising

D) hopeful but with some fear

The best answer is (B).
The author is very positive ("Nor need we shrink from honestly facing conditions in our country today. This great Nation will endure as it has endured, will revive and will prosper. So, first of all, let me assert my firm belief that the only thing we have to fear is fear itself") but not without caution ("Values have shrunk to fantastic levels; taxes have risen; our ability to pay has fallen; government of all kinds is faced by serious curtailment of income; the means of exchange are frozen in the currents of trade; the withered leaves of industrial enterprise lie on every side; farmers find no markets for their produce; and the savings of many years in thousands of families are gone. More important, a host of unemployed"), the author's reservations do not overwhelm his/her positive attitude. ("The only thing we have to fear is fear itself")

20

What is most likely the reason the author mentions locusts?

A) to directly criticize evil money changers

B) to lead the audience to a more important concept

C) to portray the magnitude of the natural disasters

D) to compare a biological crisis with an economic crises

The best answer is (B).
"And yet our distress comes from no failure of substance. We are stricken by no plague of locusts." Thus, even though there is "distress", this "distress" has nothing to do with locusts. So what is it? The author is making the reader think. The question the author is asking is essentially this; what are we stricken by? The answer is the important concept the author is leading the reader toward.

It is improbable that more nonsense has been written about aesthetics than about anything else: the literature of the subject is not large enough for that. It is certain, however, that about no subject with which I am acquainted has so little been said that is at all to the purpose. The explanation is discoverable. He who would elaborate a plausible theory of aesthetics must possess two qualities—artistic sensibility and a turn for clear thinking. Without sensibility a man can have no aesthetic experience, and, obviously, theories not based on broad and deep aesthetic experience are worthless. Only those for whom art is a constant source of passionate emotion can possess the data from which profitable theories may be deduced; but to deduce profitable theories even from accurate data involves a certain amount of brain-work, and, unfortunately, robust intellects and delicate sensibilities are not inseparable. As often as not, the hardest thinkers have had no aesthetic experience whatever. I have a friend blessed with an intellect as keen as a drill, who, though he takes an interest in aesthetics, has never during a life of almost forty years been guilty of an aesthetic emotion. So, having no faculty for distinguishing a work of art from a handsaw, he is apt to rear up a pyramid of irrefragable argument on the hypothesis that a handsaw is a work of art. This defect robs his perspicuous and subtle reasoning of much of its value; for it has ever been a maxim that faultless logic can win but little credit for conclusions that are based on premises notoriously false. Every cloud, however, has its silver lining, and this insensibility, though unlucky in that it makes my friend incapable of choosing a sound basis for his argument, mercifully blinds him to the absurdity of his conclusions while leaving him in full enjoyment of his masterly dialectic. People who set out from the hypothesis that Sir Edwin Landseer was the finest painter that ever lived will feel no uneasiness about an aesthetic which proves that Giotto was the worst. So, my friend, when he arrives very logically at the conclusion that a work of art should be small or round or smooth, or that to appreciate fully a picture you should pace smartly before it or set it spinning like a top, cannot guess why I ask him whether he has lately been to Cambridge, a place he sometimes visits. On the other hand, people who respond immediately and surely to works of art, though, in my judgment, more enviable than men of massive intellect but slight sensibility, are often quite as incapable of talking sense about aesthetics. Their heads are not always very clear. They possess the data on which any system must be based; but, generally, they want the power that draws correct inferences from true data. Having received aesthetic emotions from works of art, they are in a position to seek out the quality common to all that have moved them, but, in fact, they do nothing of the sort. I do not blame them. Why should they bother to examine their feelings when for them to feel is enough? Why should they stop to think when they are not very good at thinking? Why should they hunt for a common quality in all objects that move them in a particular way when they can linger over the many delicious and peculiar charms of each as it comes? So, if they write criticism and call it aesthetics, if they imagine that they are talking about Art when they are talking about particular works of art or even about the technique of painting, if, loving particular works they find tedious the consideration of art in general, perhaps they have chosen the better part.

Test 6

21

What would be the best title of the passage?

A) Art and sensibility
B) An esthetic hypothesis
C) Art and criticism
D) How art criticism is produced

The best answer is (B).
This passage is about esthetics, so we need to find a choice that makes reference to esthetics; the possible choices are (B), (C), (D).

(C); TOO BROAD; esthetics is only one kind of criticism.
(D); Art criticism can be understood as esthetics, but the passage is not about how it is made, but what it is: WRONG PERSPETIVE
Also, the author states they are two different things. ("they write criticism and call it aesthetics")
(A); Sensibility is much TOO BROAD to be understood as esthetics.

22

Which of the following is not a prerequisite for creating a reasonable esthetic theory?

A) esthetic understandability
B) a certain level of intelligence
C) the capacity to view art as a resource of some kind
D) clearly artistic thinking

The best answer is (D).
In order to provide ("deduce") reasonable esthetic theories ("profitable theories"), we need two qualities ("must possess two qualities— artistic sensibility and a turn for clear thinking.")

(D); "Clear thinking" is not 'clearly artistic thinking'.

(C); "constant source of passionate emotion"
(A), (B); These are the two qualities explained for (D).

23

According to the passage, which of the following is a problem with the prerequisite mentioned in the previous question?

A) the incompatibility of relevant preconditions
B) the extreme difficulty involved in establishing a particular quality
C) the naiveté of the public
D) the low probability of artistic experiences

The best answer is (A).
The author clearly states that it is sad ("unfortunately") that the two necessary qualities are incompatible ("are not inseparable".)

(B); The point is the separability of the two qualities.
(C): WRONG PERSPECTIVE
(D): WRONG PERSPECTIVE

24

What is true of the author's very smart friend mentioned in the passage?

A) He has never been convicted of any emotional crime.
B) He is far too intelligent to see anything beautiful.
C) His brain might somehow be preventing him from experiencing esthetic emotion.
D) He is not cut out for appreciating art.

The best answer is (C).
All we know is that the two qualities are separable, and the friend is lacking in one quality, esthetic

Test 6

sensibility.

(A); "Guilty" has nothing to do with any crime, emotional or otherwise.
(B); What moves us need not be beautiful: sad things can also move people.
(D); His problem is not necessarily genetic or inherited; it could have been acquired.

25

Which of the following is the mistake the author's friend makes as shown by the answer to the previous question?

A) He considers practical things as esthetic.

B) He confuses construction tools with those used for creating art.

C) He does not have the ability to speculate on the difference between tools and works of art.

D) He is unable to apply his or her intelligence to artistic contemplation.

The best answer is (A).
The author's friend only has keen intelligence ("So, having no faculty for distinguishing a work of art from a handsaw"), he considers ("is apt to rear up a pyramid of irrefragable argument on the hypothesis") something practical ("handsaw") as esthetic ("a work of art").

(B); A work of art is not a tool for creating art.
(C); "Having no faculty for distinguishing a work of art from a handsaw" is different from not having the ability to speculate on the difference between hand tools and works of art.
(D); There is no proof or any way to speculate that his problem stems from his inability to use his intelligence; it could just as easily be because of his intelligence.

26

Which of the following gives the best evidence for the answer to the previous question?

A) "my friend, when he arrives very logically at the conclusion that a work of art should be small or round or smooth," (Lines 42-44)

B) "he is apt to rear up a pyramid of irrefragable argument on the hypothesis that a handsaw is a work of art." (Lines 26-28)

C) "Sir Edwin Landseer was the finest painter that ever lived" (Lines 39-40)

D) "to appreciate fully a picture you should pace smartly before it or set it spinning like a top," (Lines 44-46)

The best answer is (B).
Refer to the explanation for the answer to the previous question.

27

Which of the following is the main dilemma clearly expressed in the passage?

A) Two essential qualities are unfortunately incompatible.

B) Many people are not intelligent or sensible enough to be properly artistic.

C) It is extremely difficult to distinguish between something artistic and a criticism.

D) Some people do not really care about what is truly esthetic.

The best answer is (A).
Throughout the passage the author dedicates a lot of space to talking about the two separable qualities even using his friend as an example.

Test 6

28

Which of the following gives the best evidence for the answer to the previous question?

A) "they find tedious the consideration of art in general, perhaps they have chosen the better part." (Lines 72-73)

B) "more enviable than men of massive intellect but slight sensibility, are often quite as incapable of talking sense about aesthetics." (Lines 50-53)

C) "mercifully blinds him to the absurdity of his conclusions while leaving him in full enjoyment of his masterly dialectic." (Lines 36-38)

D) "unfortunately, robust intellects and delicate sensibilities are not inseparable." (Lines 18-19)

The best answer is (D).
Refer to the explanation for the answer to the previous question.

29

What is the most probable role of the questions in the later part of the passage?

A) to clarify why the main dilemma is in fact a dilemma

B) to lead to another perspective of the same argument

C) to rhetorically allude to a novel problem

D) to allow the author to retreat from his/her original position in order to make an apparent compromise

The best answer is (D).
Up to the point where all these questions appear, the author was entirely focused on the two separable qualities, and thought it was "unfortunate" that these qualities were "not inseparable"; In other words, the author thought that a person needed both qualities in order to come up with a "profitable" esthetic theory. However, by posing these rhetorical questions, the author is stepping back a bit ("I do not blame them"). Earlier in the passage the author was more than a little negative about the ability of those who lack one of the two qualities ("having no faculty for distinguishing a work of art from a handsaw").

(A); By asking those questions, the author is trying to explain why some people cannot achieve a proper esthetic understanding.
(B); This is a tricky choice, because it seems very possible that this could be the answer, but this one is not as good as (D); the author's main goal is not the compromise (no evidence), so we cannot say 'lead to'.
(C); The author is not alluding to a problem. ("Why should they stop to think when they are not very good at thinking?", "Why should they hunt for a common quality in all objects that move them in a particular way when they can linger over the many delicious and peculiar charms of each as it comes?", "perhaps they have chosen the better part")

30

What does the author probably mean by "the better part" at the end of the passage?

A) what those with extreme intelligence can do

B) what those with artistic sensibility can do

C) what those with low intelligence can do

D) what those lacking in something can do

The best answer is (D).
In a few of these questions, the author was quite clear who s/he was talking about ("Why should they stop to think when they are not very good at thinking?"), but in most of the questions the author was not so clear: those without artistic sensibility (or with low artistic sensibility) or those with low intelligence? Therefore, it is safe to say that the author is talking about either of the two.

(A); The adjective should be 'low' rather than 'extreme' intelligence. ("Why should they stop to think when they are not very good at thinking?")
(B); The phrase should be 'a low level of artistic sensibility' or 'low intelligence'.
(C); This is only one of the two possibilities. Refer to the explanation for (A), (B), and (D).

Test 6

In the last fifty years there has been much very fine and interesting speculation on the part of scientific men upon the age and origin of our earth. Here we cannot pretend to give even a summary of such speculations because they involve the most subtle mathematical and physical considerations. The truth is that the physical and astronomical sciences are still too undeveloped as yet to make anything of the sort more than an illustrative guesswork. The general tendency has been to make the estimated age of our globe longer and longer. It now seems probable that the earth has had an independent existence as a spinning planet flying round and round the sun for a longer period than 2,000,000,000 years. It may have been much longer than that. This is a length of time that absolutely overpowers the imagination. Before that vast period of separate existence, the sun and earth and the other planets that circulate round the sun may have been a great swirl of diffused matter in space. The telescope reveals to us in various parts of the heavens luminous spiral clouds of matter, the spiral nebulæ, which appear to be in rotation about a centre. It is supposed by many astronomers that the sun and its planets were once such a spiral, and that their matter has undergone concentration into its present form. Through majestic æons that concentration went on until in that vast remoteness of the past for which we have given figures, the world and its moon were distinguishable. They were spinning then much faster than they are spinning now; they were at a lesser distance from the sun; they travelled round it very much faster, and they were probably incandescent or molten at the surface. The sun itself was a much greater blaze in the heavens. If we could go back through that infinitude of time and see the earth in this earlier stage of its history, we should behold a scene more like the interior of a blast furnace or the surface of a lava flow before it cools and cakes over than any other contemporary scene. No water would be visible because all the water there was would still be superheated steam in a stormy atmosphere of sulphurous and metallic vapours. Beneath this would swirl and boil an ocean of molten rock substance. Across a sky of fiery clouds the glare of the hurrying sun and moon would sweep swiftly like hot breaths of flame. Slowly by degrees as one million of years followed another, this fiery scene would lose its eruptive incandescence. The vapours in the sky would rain down and become less dense overhead; great slaggy cakes of solidifying rock would appear upon the surface of the molten sea, and sink under it, to be replaced by other floating masses. The sun and moon growing now each more distant and each smaller, would rush with diminishing swiftness across the heavens. The moon now, because of its smaller size, would be already cooled far below incandescence, and would be alternately obstructing and reflecting the sunlight in a series of eclipses and full moons. And so with a tremendous slowness through the vastness of time, the earth would grow more and more like the earth on which we live, until at last an age would come when, in the cooling air, steam would begin to condense into clouds, and the first rain would fall hissing upon the first rocks below. For endless millenia the greater part of the earth's water would still be vaporized in the atmosphere, but there would now be hot streams running over the crystallizing rocks below and pools and lakes into which these streams would be carrying detritus and depositing sediment. At last a condition of things must have been attained in which a man might have stood up on earth and looked about him and lived. If we could have visited the earth at that time we should have stood on great lava-like masses of rock without a trace of soil or touch of living vegetation, under a storm-rent sky. Hot and violent winds, exceeding the fiercest tornado that ever blows, and downpours of rain such as our milder, slower earth to-day knows nothing of, might have assailed us. The water of the downpour would have rushed by us, muddy with the spoils of the rocks, coming together into torrents, cutting deep gorges and canyons as they hurried past to deposit their sediment in the earliest seas. Through the clouds we should have glimpsed a great sun moving visibly across the sky, and in its wake and in the wake of the moon would have come a diurnal tide of earthquake and upheaval. And the moon, which nowadays keeps one constant face to earth, would then have been rotating visibly and showing the side it now hides so inexorably. The earth aged. One million years followed another, and the day lengthened, the sun grew more distant and milder, the moon's pace in the sky slackened; the intensity of rain and storm diminished and the water in the first seas increased and ran together into the ocean garment our planet henceforth wore. But there was no life as yet upon the earth; the seas were lifeless, and the rocks were barren.

Test 6

31

What could be the best title of the passage?

A) The Earth as a heavenly body
B) The Earth in connection with other heavenly bodies
C) The Earth in the solar system
D) The Earth in time.

The best answer is (D).
At the beginning of the passage, the author made it clear that this passage is about "speculation on the part of scientific men upon the age and origin of our earth."

(A), (B), (C); None of these is related to "the age and origin of our earth."

32

According to the passage, the lack of which of the following is the cause of our human ignorance about the age of the Earth?

A) speculation
B) capable scientists
C) proper means of investigation
D) science

The best answer is (D).
"The truth is that the physical and astronomical sciences are still too undeveloped as yet to make anything of the sort more than an illustrative guesswork."

(C); Science can be a proper means of investigation, but there is no proof that science is the only proper means of investigation, so this is a case of TOO BROAD.

33

Which choice in Question 32 can most probably work as a reason that is very closely related to why the author says the earth might be much older than 2,000,000,000 years?

The best answer is (D).
Right after mentioning "an illustrative guesswork", the author said "general tendency", "estimated age", and "now seems probable", so it is very likely that the author continues to make a guess, because science is not good enough to help the author.

34

What does the author mean by "overpowers the imagination" (Line 17)?

A) The concept of speculating on the age of the earth is unimaginable.
B) 2,000,000,000 years is beyond a human's ability to conceptualize.
C) 2,000,000,000 years is an amount too powerful to imagine.
D) The age of the Earth is not something to be imagined.

The best answer is (B).
According to the context, it simply means that two million years is hard to imagine.

35

According to the passage, why did the author say "an illustrative guesswork" (Lines 9-10)?

A) to stress the nature of science
B) to claim that science cannot be depended on
C) to suggest the inherent limitations from which science suffers

Test 6

D) to make sure the reader understands the immaturity of science

The best answer is (D).
Science in this context is described in a negative manner "still too undeveloped"

(A); The fact that "that the physical and astronomical sciences are still too undeveloped as yet to make anything of the sort more than an illustrative guesswork." is not to explain the nature of science in general, but to let the readers know the specific state of some science at a certain period of human history.
(B); Refer to the explanation for (A). (B) cannot mean the specific state of some science at a certain period of human history.
(C); There is no proof that this problem or limitation of science is 'inherent'.

36

Which of the following is probably the reason why the author talks about what the telescope reveals?

A) to show the source of interpretation
B) to provide a source of a possible misinterpretation
C) to introduce a different subject matter
D) to allude to the very beginning of the previously mentioned diffusion

The best answer is (B).
When the author was talking about the telescope, s/he uses expressions like "appear to be in rotation", "supposed", which strongly indicates that something is wrong. The only possible choice in this direction is (B).

37

As used in line 25, "spiral" most nearly means

A) diffusion
B) rotation
C) sphere
D) concentration

The best answer is (B).
Right before mentioning "such a spiral", the author said "which appear to be in rotation about a centre." obviously the only possible concept in this part of the sentence, which can be called "spiral" is "rotation."

38

Which choice gives the best evidence for the answer to the previous question?

A) "The sun and earth and the other planets that circulate round the sun may have been a great swirl of diffused matter in space." (Lines 18-21)
B) "that their matter has undergone concentration into its present form." (Lines 26-27)
C) "luminous spiral clouds of matter, the spiral nebulæ, which appear to be in rotation about a centre." (Lines 22-24)
D) "concentration went on until in that vast remoteness of the past for which we have given figures," (Lines 28-29)

The best answer is (C).
Refer to the explanation for the answer to the previous question.

39

As used in line 50, "incandescence" most nearly means

A) fire
B) temperature
C) bright light
D) emission of light

The best answer is (D).
We need to look for any contextual clue. The author said "because of its smaller size, would be already cooled far below incandescence, and would be alternately obstructing and reflecting the sunlight in a series of eclipses and full moons", so incandescence has something to do with light and probably emission of it ("obstructing and reflecting the sunlight"), but whether or not the light is bright cannot be inferred from the context.

40

According to the passage, the discussion of which will most logically follow?

A) the development of rocks
B) the history of weather on Earth
C) life
D) the continuing cooling process of the Earth

The best answer is (C).
The last sentence is "But there was no life as yet upon the earth; the seas were lifeless, and the rocks were barren." What we need to focus on is "as yet", so it is only natural that the author will talk about how life came along in the earth.

The first and most obvious light in which the sea presents itself from the political and social point of view is that of a great highway; or better, perhaps, of a wide common, over which men may pass in all directions, but on which some well-worn paths show that controlling reasons have led them to choose certain lines of travel rather than others. These lines of travel are called trade routes; and the reasons which have determined them are to be sought in the history of the world. Notwithstanding all the familiar and unfamiliar dangers of the sea, both travel and traffic by water have always been easier and cheaper than by land. The commercial greatness of Holland was due not only to her shipping at sea, but also to the numerous tranquil water-ways which gave such cheap and easy access to her own interior and to that of Germany. This advantage of carriage by water over that by land was yet more marked in a period when roads were few and very bad, wars frequent and society unsettled, as was the case two hundred years ago. Sea traffic then went in peril of robbers, but was nevertheless safer and quicker than that by land. A Dutch writer of that time, estimating the chances of his country in a war with England, notices among other things that the water-ways of England failed to penetrate the country sufficiently; therefore, the roads being bad, goods from one part of the kingdom to the other must go by sea, and be exposed to capture by the way. As regards purely internal trade, this danger has generally disappeared at the present day. In most civilized countries, now, the destruction or disappearance of the coasting trade would only be an inconvenience, although water transit is still the cheaper. Nevertheless, as late as the wars of the French Republic and the First Empire, those who are familiar with the history of the period, and the light naval literature that has grown up around it, know how constant is the mention of convoys stealing from point to point along the French coast, although the sea swarmed with English cruisers and there were good inland roads. Under modern conditions, however, home trade is but a part of the business of a country bordering on the sea. Foreign necessaries or luxuries must be brought to its ports, either in its own or in foreign ships, which will return, bearing in exchange the

Test 6

products of the country, whether they be the fruits
50 of the earth or the works of men's hands; and it is
the wish of every nation that this shipping business
should be done by its own vessels. The ships that
thus sail to and fro must have secure ports to which
to return, and must, as far as possible, be followed
55 by the protection of their country throughout
the voyage. This protection in time of war must
be extended by armed shipping. The necessity
of a navy, in the restricted sense of the word,
springs, therefore, from the existence of a peaceful
60 shipping, and disappears with it, except in the case
of a nation which has aggressive tendencies, and
keeps up a navy merely as a branch of the military
establishment. As the United States has at present
no aggressive purposes, and as its merchant service
65 has disappeared, the dwindling of the armed fleet
and general lack of interest in it are strictly logical
consequences.

41

What would be the best title of the passage?

A) The sea and its military possibilities
B) The importance of the sea in European history
C) The influence of sea power upon history
D) A historic interpretation of sea power in various parts of the world

The best answer is (C).
This passage is about the influence of sea power ("This advantage of carriage by water", "The commercial greatness of Holland was due not only to her shipping at sea, but also to the numerous tranquil water-ways which gave such cheap and easy access to her own interior and to that of Germany.") upon history. ("A Dutch writer of that time, estimating the chances of his country in a war with England, notices among other things that the water-ways of England failed to penetrate the country sufficiently;")

(A); Military possibilities are only one aspect of the author's argument: TOO NARROW
(B); America was also an example: TOO NARROW
(D); Historic means historically famous.

42

According to the passage which of the following can be most directly inferred about maritime trade routes?

A) They were established because they were politically easier to control than other sea routes.
B) They were viewed as the greatest highways of commerce.
C) For some practical reasons they were more frequently taken advantage of than other paths.

Test 6

D) They were the main cause of war.

The best answer is (C).
"Some well-worn paths show that controlling reasons have led them to choose certain lines of travel rather than others."

(A); "Controlling reasons" do not have to be political.
(B); "More frequently" doesn't mean greatest.
(D); "This advantage of carriage by water over that by land was yet more marked in a period when roads were few and very bad, wars frequent and society unsettled, as was the case two hundred years ago." So sea routes could have been a cause of war, but not necessarily the main cause: a problem of magnitude.

43

According to the passage, which of the following can be inferred about the claim made by a Dutch writer?

A) His country had a greater chance of going to war with England than with other countries.

B) England needed more rivers and lakes to avoid war with his country.

C) His country's chances of victory in a war with England might have come from certain aspects of England's geography.

D) His country had to attack England's shipping on the high seas.

The best answer is (C).
"A Dutch writer of that time, estimating the chances of his country in a war with England, notices among other things that the water-ways of England failed to penetrate the country sufficiently;" so the disadvantage for England was its lack of penetrating waterways, which hindered inland shipping and made the transportation of goods more challenging.

(A); England was not compared with other nations.
(B); It is not clear if the number of rivers and lakes is the source of the problem.
(D); The point is that "water-ways of England failed to penetrate the country sufficiently."

44

Which of the following is the most direct evidence for the answer to the previous question?

A) "generally disappeared at the present day." (Line 32)

B) "failed to penetrate the country sufficiently" (Lines 27-28)

C) "nevertheless safer and quicker than that by land." (Lines 23-24)

D) "inconvenience," (Line 35)

The best answer is (B).
Refer to the explanation for the answer to the previous question.

45

Which of the following, if proved, would work as the most direct criticism toward the author's argument?

A) European countries only had peaceful motives for maintaining naval forces which were solely for self-defense.

B) There were so many reasons why countries went to war; needing to control sea routes was just one reason.

C) The U.S. has a history of using its naval forces for more than just the protection of its peaceful shipping.

D) The origin of war can easily be attributed to how ocean highways came into being.

Test 6

The best answer is (C).
The author claims "the United States has at present no aggressive purposes," so if this can be refuted, s/he would be in trouble.

(A); The author never said European countries had militant or violent purposes for maintaining naval forces.
(B); The author never said that the reasons given were the only reason.
(D); The author never expressed an interest in the origin of any war.

46

Which of the following is the most direct evidence for the answer to the previous question?

A) "from the political and social point of view is that of a great highway;" (Lines 2-3)
B) "the United States has at present no aggressive purposes," (Lines 63-64)
C) "disappears with it" (Line 60)
D) "wars frequent and society unsettled" (Lines 20-21)

The best answer is (B).
Refer to the explanation for the answer to the previous question.

47

Which of the following can best be inferred from the claim the author is making about the navy?

A) It was the first form of military endeavor in the history of armed forces.
B) It probably came into existence not as part of a war effort.
C) Historically, most countries used it to protect their peaceful shipping.
D) The U.S. has the largest navy in the world.

The best answer is (B).
Refer to the explanation for the answer to Question 45.

48

According to the passage, which of the following cannot be true?

A) Almost every nation had a navy which was traditionally used for the protection of peaceful shipping.
B) Some sea routes were harder to use than others.
C) At present, in some cases, domestic trade routes are not very important.
D) It was inevitable that the American navy would not expand over the course of the country's history.

The best answer is (A).
"The necessity of a navy, in the restricted sense of the word, springs, therefore, from the existence of a peaceful shipping," but in practice that does not mean every nation: a problem of magnitude.

(B); "Some well-worn paths show that controlling reasons have led them to choose certain lines of travel rather than others."
(C); "Under modern conditions, however, home trade is but a part of the business of a country bordering on the sea."
(D); "as its merchant service has disappeared, the dwindling of the armed fleet and general lack of interest in it are strictly logical consequences."

49

Which of the following is the most direct evidence for the answer to the previous question?

A) Lines 14-18 ("The commercial…Germany.")
B) Lines 57-60 ("The necessity…shipping,")

295

Test 6

C) Lines 53-56 ("The ships...voyage.")

D) Lines 22-24 ("Sea traffic...by land.")

The best answer is (B).
Refer to the explanation for the answer to the previous question.

50

What can be said about land and water transit?

A) One was always cheaper than the other.

B) One was always better than the other.

C) One was always more desired than the other.

D) At a certain point in history one was more available than the other.

The best answer is (D).
At one point in history ("then") sea transit was more available. ("therefore, the roads being bad, goods from one part of the kingdom to the other must go by sea, and be exposed to capture by the way.")

(A), (B), (C); In no part of the passage is there any evidence of the author's use of the word 'always' or any implication of it: a problem of magnitude.

지은이
계관웅
서울대학교 중퇴
미국 오클라호마 주립대학교 생화학과 졸업
렌슬리어폴리테크닉 대학교 화학과 우등졸업
존스홉킨스 대학교 화학과 박사 과정 수료
현 계관웅 어학원 대표
현 엑스퍼트프렙 유학원 대표

이 책을 만드는 데 도움을 주신 분들께 감사드립니다.

원어민 교정자
Robert Allan Webster
캐나다 빅토리아 대학교 언어학과 졸업
한국 유수의 학원에서 28년간 강의

학생 리뷰어
이소담
서울과학고 졸업
서울대학교 생명과학부 재학중

출제에 사용된 지문은 저작권이 만료되었거나 이용이 허가된 글에서 발췌하였습니다.
이 책에 실린 문제와 해설은 저자의 창작물이므로, 무단 전재와 복제를 금합니다.

New SAT Reading Prep

2016 개정 SAT 핵심 대비 문제, 해설, 공략집

초판 1쇄 발행 2016년 6월 10일

지은이 계관웅
발행처 사냥꾼
발행인 계관웅
디자인 이정훈

출판신고 등록번호 제2006-000210호
주소 서울시 서초구 서초중앙로 26, 1818호
대표전화 02-554-9897 **팩시밀리** 02-553-9895
이메일 xpertprep@naver.com

값 29,000원
© 계관웅, 2015-2016. Printed in Seoul, Korea
ISBN 979-11-954910-2-5